JAZZ-ROCK FUSION

the people
the music

julie coryell & laura friedman

Front cover photo: Miles Davis
Back cover photo: Wayne Shorter
Photo on p. 364 by Franca Lavorato
Photo on p. 366 by Carole Zabar
All other photographs © Laura Friedman

Creative Direction by Kristen Schilo, Gato & Maui Productions
Design by Lisa Vaughn, Two of Cups Design Studio, Inc.

ISBN 0-7935-9941-5

Library of Congress Card Number: 00-107185

7777 W. BLUEMOUND RD. P.O. BOX 13819 MILWAUKEE, WI 53213

Visit Hal Leonard Online at
www.halleonard.com

acknowledgments

We would like to thank the following for their contributions to *Jazz-Rock Fusion*: *Downbeat*, *Contemporary Keyboard*, *Guitar Player*, and *Swing Journal* magazines; Michelle Barbieri, Marina Belica, Bette Braxton, Mr. And Mrs. Robert Brecker, Toby Byron, Brian Carr, Marianne Catherine, Jeffrey Cheen, Paul Cheslaw, Carolyn Clarke, Herb Cohen, Michael Cuscuna, Michael Davenport, Joe Dera, Faybeth Diamond, Gregory DiGiovine, Ed Eckstine, Monica Elsas, Jason Emerick, Leonard Feather, David Friedman, Maralin and Jack Friedman, Ken Fritz Management, Miriam Gerry, Amy Gitlin, Ron Greenberg, Nat Hentoff, Tom Iannachone, Wendy Jaeger, Frank Johnson, Chris Jonz, Robert Kenselaar, Bill Krasilovsky, John Lee, Dr. William Lee, Karen Lees, Arthur Levy, Mel Lewis, Gail Margolis, Tim Marquand, Christine Martin, Geri Martino, Pam Masten, John Mehegan, Marty Michael, Jim Mitchell, Dan Morgenstern, Ron Moss, Nighthawk, Marcy Posner, Lester Powell, Marcy Ragovoy, Pat Raines, Lloyd Remick, Carol Ross, Sandy Ross, Stuart Ross, Jim Root, David Rubinson, Laurel Rudd, Elliott Sears, Bill Siddons, Jonathan Siegel, Marcia Silverman, Gail Stein, J. R. Taylor, Helen Tee, Molly Watson, Sally White, David Zabar, and Alan Zavod. Special thanks to Mary Hoeltzel, Dan Pickering, and Eleana Steinberg; and to Chris Kuppig and Martha Kinney for their belief in the project.

Note: The following biographies and discographies are obviously of a transitory nature, for even as this book goes to press, the artists will have made numerous new records, joined new bands, formed groups of their own, and possibly reevaluated and changed their present musical attitudes. At best, we have attempted to provide some background material relative to past accomplishments, and so on, remembering always that change is in fact synonymous, or at least should be, with the art itself.

Our Father, who art a cross between Miles Davis, John Coltrane, and Jimi Hendrix, hallowed be thy name, here in New York, as it was in New Orleans. Give us this day our daily chord changes, and forgive us for playing the wrong changes behind our soloists as we forgive them for playing the wrong changes behind our solos. And lead us not into disco, but deliver us from commercialism. Amen.

Larry Coryell

preface to the
new edition

It's been decades since the publication of this book and as I reflect on that era, I am particularly struck by the word era, for indeed it was. First and foremost, it was a time of great creativity and vitality. There was spirit, joy and hopefulness, a sense of being able to break through and break down barriers, while exploring new frontiers.

Sadly, some of those included in the book are gone though their music surely lives on: Miles Davis, Tony Williams, Jaco Pastorius, Joe Farrell, Richard Tee and Grover Washington, Jr. will not be forgotten. One can only imagine what their continued contributions might have been had they lived. They were all gifted artists with an eye to the future as well as a healthy respect for the past. Even Miles, who was often accused of abandoning his roots, never forgot where he came from. He was quite simply a visionary, an artist who was always true to himself, willing to risk critical approval if it meant compromise on any level. He was such an original, ever challenging and dynamic, not only as an artist but also as a man.

There were critics who contended that the musicians had sold out by combining the elements of rock and jazz to form the musical hybrid which came to be known as fusion, but I do not agree. The intention wasn't to make commercial music, but to express what was felt and experienced intrinsically by those who had the opportunity to do it. The music is classic, it has withstood the test of time. The heyday of the fusion movement is over, but the music inspired a generation of musicians.

Over the years, I have been approached by musicians and fans of the music who expressed gratitude for an opportunity to get inside the heads of the artists whose interviews are in this book. I can happily report that it was my intention to do just that when we began the endeavor, and I am pleased to say that I think we succeeded. It was only possible because of the willingness of the musicians themselves to open up and share themselves and their histories with such generosity.

Laura Friedman's photographs so beautifully captured the spirit and intensity of the period and the music and were a great source of inspiration to me. It was a rewarding project; close bonds were formed that still exist today. I thank all who participated from the bottom of my heart. I will never forget them.

Finally, the current incarnation of this book would not have been possible without the unwavering support, faith and perseverance of Marina Belica. Marina, you are truly remarkable. This book is dedicated to my two gifted sons, Murali and Julian Coryell. You are the two shining lights of my life.

Julie Coryell, *June 1999*

preface

Jazz has been and always will be a changing and enduring art whose roots are firmly planted in the United States. It is sad, when we consider this music to be our only contribution to world arts, that the American people are not more aware and appreciative of this unique art form. During the past, jazz has worn many hats. From time to time it has been called names such as ragtime, Dixieland, swing, bebop, modern, contemporary, and so on. Obviously, people living during these particular eras chose to give the music a name which reflected their tastes, and rightly so. After all, jazz, like other creative art forms, was reflecting the culture at that time. But we must remember that jazz not only mirrored the culture but reflected all that preceded it. Every era has its "heroes" and "workhorses." This book strives to document some of these people in jazz who had a hand in shaping the course of music from the late sixties through the late seventies.

Nothing is permanent, however. Even now, as this book is being published, the stage is being set for the next period. When and how it began, and what it will be called, we won't know until we look back at it. The music which today has come to be known as fusion music had an unusual beginning.

Do people dictate culture or does culture shape people's minds and habits? I ask this question because when this music was in its early stages, the listener accepted it long before other musicians of that time. It is obvious that the birthplace of fusion music was in Chicago. It was during the early sixties that the Lewis Trio (El Dee Young, bass; Red Holt, drums) were unknowingly setting the stage for things to come. Jamal and Harris had long since been using the bass and drums to lay down a chantlike, repetitive figure which gave them the freedom to explore different melodies and harmonic structures at will. They also were not hesitant to use ideas not traditionally associated with jazz. Note the musical content of Jamal's "Poinciana" on Cadet Records, Harris's "Listen Here" on Atlantic Records. These records were the first jazz records to cross over and win best-selling awards.

El Dee, Red, and myself at that time did not consider what we were doing to be terribly new. Without knowing it, we combined into an approach some of the music we had always been exposed to: black church music, rhythm and blues (melodic repetitive rhythms), and jazz. Because of my classical training, in some arrangements we also showed the influence of European harmonies, musical devices, and theories. In 1965, we put out a record called "In Crowd" that clearly drew from the aforementioned styles. From musicians and critics alike, there were shouts of foul play. At that time they said it was sacrilegious to involve any other kinds of music, especially R & B, with jazz. (A point should be made here that rock as we know it today, which definitely has made its influence felt on the jazz field, was an outgrowth of early R & B music.) It had been the practice at that point to stick to traditional jazz literature and/or "standards." It was not until the late sixties when Miles Davis gave his stamp of approval by incorporating some of these ideas into his albums that musicians accepted the fact that rock rhythms and influences other than the traditional ones could be integrated with jazz. Now with Miles's blessing, it was no longer taboo to venture out beyond the traditionally accepted structures, harmonies, and rhythms.

Davis extended the harmonic concepts, employed polyrhythmic patterns, added electronic instruments and devices to his trumpet along with his highly unique and creative ability, and set the pace for what has come to be known as fusion music. Eddie Harris also began using electronic effects on his saxophone in or around 1964. There is no doubt that Miles was aware of what was going on in Chicago before he let on. Listen to his Blue Note recording of his Jamal-influenced arrangement of "Autumn Leaves"; and then on Columbia Records, his recording of Gil Evans's big-band arrangement of Jamal's "New Rhumba." There was also a Davis recording on CBS of an Eddie Harris tune.

I also find it personally rewarding to see a whole era of music reflecting an approach that I have always believed in; namely, that any musical ideas or combinations which are handled with good taste and discretion can be used as a springboard for inspiration and/or improvisation, regardless of the original source. It is also interesting to note the influence that Miles Davis has had on jazz for almost thirty years now. He gave us "Birth of the Cool" on Capitol Records in 1949, which had a great impact on the harmonic and melodic structure of jazz. During the fifties he was personally involved with the careers of such greats as Cannonball Adderley and John Coltrane. It was the Miles Davis bands of the fifties that also showed us the importance of a rhythm section and a new approach to same by putting together the unforgettable combinations of Philly Joe Jones, Paul Chambers, and Red Garland; and later, Wynton Kelly, Paul Chambers, and Jimmy Cobb. It is not at all unusual then to find Miles Davis ever present here in the late seventies. I wonder where jazz would be if there had been no *In a Silent Way* or *Bitches' Brew* albums, and if there had been no Miles Davis groups featuring musicians such as Herbie Hancock, Chick Corea, Joe Zawinul, Tony Williams, John McLaughlin, Ron Carter, Wayne Shorter, Keith Jarrett, and so on, who by the way just happen to be among the forerunners of our current musical trend. It would be interesting to note exactly how many people in this book have at one time or another been directly or indirectly under the influence of Miles Davis.

Julie Coryell and Laura Friedman must be admired and commended for putting together these facts and interviews to give us a feeling and some practical knowledge about what some of the musicians currently on the jazz scene are thinking. I am sure after reading *Jazz-Rock Fusion* you will feel better informed and can enjoy your favorite artists even more knowing them more personally.

Ramsey Lewis
February 1978

introduction

Music is one of the links between man's mortal, earthbound consciousness and his infinite super-consciousness. In this book, we deal with a kind of music that, for lack of a better definition, we will call jazz-inspired improvisatory music. Jazz is one of the few, if not the only, arts that belong to America, and is generally regarded as one of our greatest cultural assets. While the jazz musician has earned the respect of many, he or she has more often than not been denied the more tangible rewards of fame enjoyed by the rock musician. Happily, the last ten years have produced a generation of "jazz-inspired" players who are beginning to reap the bounty they deserve. Some of the credit for this belongs to the media and to technology for making this music more accessible, but in the final analysis, it is the musician himself who is changing the economic power structure.

As in the case of any "revolution," strong leaders are needed to bring about changes. Miles Davis is such a man. Miles succeeded in bringing music rooted in jazz to the attention of rock audiences. *In a Silent Way*, released by Columbia in 1969, and *Bitches' Brew*, released the following year, were landmarks in the history of contemporary music. Davis was one of the first musicians to incorporate the improvisatory skills of the jazz musician into contemporary rock rhythms—utilizing a number of electronic devices to "modernize" the sound further (among them were multiple electronic keyboards and the use of the wah-wah pedal attachment for trumpet). Though some of jazz's more traditional critics viewed the emergence of the "new music" with disdain, its box-office appeal was clearly evident. Davis was able to sell out rock halls such as the now-defunct Fillmores—a sure sign of popular status—while his records sales soared.

Interestingly enough, many of the musicians employed by Miles in the late sixties have become leaders in the contemporary jazz-inspired music of this decade. In fact, a quick glance at some of the personnel on the two aforementioned Davis records reads like an excerpt from a musical Who's Who of the seventies: Herbie Hancock, Chick Corea, John McLaughlin, Joe Zawinul, Tony Williams, Lenny White, Wayne Shorter. All these gentlemen have respectively become leaders in their own right. More than that, they are all innovators—setting new musical standards, and each, in his own way, liberating the music as well as the music business. This book, however, is not concerned with success or failure, but with people—specifically the artist, the musician, and composer.

While we would like to think of music as a pure art form, we must never forget that it is also a business. Nobody is more acutely aware of this fact than the musicians themselves, who are constantly being reminded of it by their record company, their peers, the press (if they read their reviews), and, of course, most importantly, by the consumer. In the end, it is the people who buy the records and fill the concert halls and clubs; they determine who's at the top of the charts, who wins the polls, and so forth. Jazz musicians have only recently begun to display the trappings long associated with rock music, that is, gold and platinum records, personal managers, agents, accountants, and coverage by the media.

Within the last few years, some of our more influential popular publications (such as *Time, Newsweek, People, Us*) have devoted both cover and feature stories to the "new music," and at long last we can see some of the finest jazz musicians on television. In Charlie Parker's time, and in John Coltrane's time, jazz still belonged to the elitists, and musicians really had no choice but to concern themselves with the musical content. Opportunities to do more than that were scarce. Now the musicians have more alternatives; there is the ever-present possibility of commercial success. Some of today's musicians grew up and out of mainstream jazz and are now enjoying a kind of success that wasn't available to them ten or fifteen years ago. The ability to adapt to these changes has proven to be more difficult for some players than for others. Many have undergone major identity crises. Others have made the transition with apparent ease. The change in the music is, of course, also reflected in the business—specifically by the record companies—where new "fusion" divisions are being created for the purpose of seeking out and developing new talent to satisfy the growing market. Once again, the old story of supply and demand threatens the vitality and innovativeness of the scene; what keeps it human is the music—and the musician.

This book is a tribute to those very people who make music. The reader will notice that there is a special section entitled "Composers." Almost every musician in this book must be considered a composer in addition to the other talents for which he or she may be better known. Many of the artists included have also produced their own records or those of other musicians. Also, many of the artists have impressive credentials as arrangers, either of their own compositions or those of others. The biographies that head the interviews list the accomplishments of the musicians in each of these fields, and the discographies at the back of the book give more specific information about the capacities in which a particular artist has contributed to various albums.

We are truly grateful to everyone who has contributed to the making of this book, especially the musicians who spoke with such openness and candor—no facades, no defenses. The beauty of their souls is conveyed as much by what they say as it is by what they play.

Without Laura Friedman, there could be no book. Her photography captures the special vibrance of each person who was interviewed. Music is very visual, and watching a great musician play somehow intensifies the experience; it is all-enveloping.

Finally, although we call this work *Jazz-Rock Fusion*, we wish to emphasize that not everyone included in it plays a "style" of music that can, in fact, be labeled either jazz, rock, or fusion. The title, therefore, is only to identify a period in the history of music and not the music itself.

It is regrettable that we were not able to include the group the Crusaders, who were forerunners in the crossover movement. The Crusaders, originally known as the Jazz Crusaders in the early seventies, dropped the word Jazz from their name, a move which altered not only their image and music but their record sales, where a substantial increase was experienced. Trumpeter Donald Byrd was also a key figure in the musician's fight to change his status. Byrd not only succeeded in that endeavor, but was also an inspiration to one-time band member Herbie Hancock, demonstrating through his own success that new goals were possible.

Because of the ever-changing, growing, and expanding nature of music, this book can do no more than deal with a small portion of it. This volume of collected interviews and photographs represents only a sampling of an entire generation of musicians who have been major contributors to a field of music so vast that its story could never be contained in only one book.

Julie Coryell
New Canaan, Connecticut
March 1978

table of contents

Acknowledgments	3
Preface to the new edition by Julie Coryell	5
Preface by Ramsey Lewis	6
Introduction	8

bass

RON CARTER	16
STANLEY CLARKE	20
ALPHONSO JOHNSON	24
JOHN LEE	28
WILL LEE	32
JACO PASTORIUS	38
MIROSLAV VITOUS	42

brass

RANDY BRECKER	48
MILES DAVIS	54
FREDDIE HUBBARD	64
CHUCK MANGIONE	68

composers

CARLA BLEY	74
MICHAEL GIBBS	80

drums

GERRY BROWN	88
BILLY COBHAM	92
STEVE GADD	96
ALPHONSE MOUZON	100
NARADA MICHAEL WALDEN	104
LENNY WHITE	108
TONY WILLIAMS	114

guitar

JOHN ABERCROMBIE	120
JOE BECK	124
GEORGE BENSON	132
PHILIP CATHERINE	138
LARRY CORYELL	142
AL DiMEOLA	148

STEVE KHAN   152
EARL KLUGH   156
JOHN McLAUGHLIN   160
PAT MARTINO   166
RALPH TOWNER   172

keyboards

BRIAN AUGER   178
CHICK COREA   184
GEORGE DUKE   190
JAN HAMMER   194
HERBIE HANCOCK   200
BOB JAMES   208
KEITH JARRETT   214
PATRICE RUSHEN   222
RICHARD TEE   226
JOE ZAWINUL   230

percussion

AIRTO (MOREIRA)   238
RALPH MacDONALD   242

vibraphone

ROY AYERS   248
GARY BURTON   252
MIKE MAINIERI   256

violin

JEAN-LUC PONTY   264

vocalists

AL JARREAU   272
FLORA PURIM   276

woodwinds

GATO BARBIERI   282
MIKE BRECKER   286
JOE FARRELL   292
JOHN KLEMMER   298
RONNIE LAWS   302
DAVID LIEBMAN   308
TOM SCOTT   314
WAYNE SHORTER   320
GROVER WASHINGTON, JR.   326

Selected Discographies   329
JULIE CORYELL   364
LAURA FRIEDMAN   366
Bibliography   368

for
miles davis

bassbassbassbassbassbassbassbassbassbassbass

bassbassbassbassbassbassbassbassbass**bass**bass

ron

carter

5/4/37

Ferndale, Michigan

bass (acoustic
and electric)

cello

composer

arranger

producer

Ron began playing the cello at age ten, studying privately at fifteen. After his family moved to Detroit, he enrolled in Cass Tech, a high school that offered majors in art or music. Realizing that the opportunities for blacks in the classical field were few and that the caliber of good bass players was low, Ron traded his cello in for a bass and began to practice that instrument eight hours a day. After his six-month crash course on the bass, Ron was awarded a full scholarship to the Eastman School of Music in Rochester, New York, where he obtained his B.A. in music education in 1959. He then went on to the Manhattan School of Music, where in 1962, he was awarded his master's degree. Ron began to work professionally in the early sixties with Chico Hamilton, Cannonball Adderley, Eric Dolphy, and Jaki Byard. In 1963 he joined Miles Davis, with whom he remained until 1968. After Miles, he freelanced—working with Lena Horne, Michael Legrand, New York Jazz Quartet, Stanley Turrentine, Hubert Laws, Lionel Hampton, Joe Henderson. In 1975, he formed his own quartet. Ron has also devoted much time to the field of education; he is the author of *Building a Jazz Bass Line*, vols. I and II. In late 1976 and 1977, he was part of the V.S.O.P. aggregation, reuniting him with Herbie Hancock, Tony Williams, and Wayne Shorter—of the old Miles Davis Quintet—plus Freddie Hubbard.

R: I started playing the cello at ten. The emphasis was classical because those were the only teachers available then.

JC: How would you compare your early studies to the present academic standards?

R: In addition to there being more teachers, there are also more schools that have some kind of jazz department, so things have improved considerably.

JC: Was joining Miles Davis's band a real catalyst in terms of your musical growth?

R: I'm inclined to think that the band was important for all of us to grow in. It is also true that we had decided on our kind of groove before we joined the band. Obviously Miles saw that we had something to offer before we joined, or he wouldn't have asked us. It's clear that he wasn't picking a bunch of total beginners in concept and technique.

JC: You are clearly an exponent of the acoustic bass—why?

R: The sound is so individual. If you have eight acoustic players, you have eight different sounds, eight different tonal qualities. If you have eight electric players, basically the sound is the same. They alter their sound by alternating the kind of amp they use, the kind of pedals they have on it, the kind of electrical devices that are available to them and to the engineering board. But primarily it's the same sound. You take four or five electric piano players, they have the same quality in their instrument. If you don't know the kind of notes they play, you don't hear anything that distinguishes one player from another. What I'm talking about is individual tone quality in the instrument.

JC: Jazz is definitely back; I'm not sure that it ever left. Could you comment on this?

R: The music's too valid to disappear. It self-commands to be heard. It dares to go off the scene for a period of time, whenever the space isn't there, and to come back sounding like it never left. Music has this kind of facility to it. I think the players themselves would become very quickly saturated with what is now available to them. Bebop is not just a style of playing, but a lifestyle. It's jam sessions, where musicians can get together and talk about music.

JC: Is there greater opportunity now for a bass player to become recognized as more than part of the rhythm section?

R: Today there are more bass players who are leaders or making their own records than there were ten years ago, but that depends on the quality of bass playing we are talking about. Yes, bass has come a long way, but I don't attribute it to that bass player who is playing something so different from the other bass players that it commands high-level potential.

JC: Have you found writing books on music as satisfying as playing it?

R: Yes. In many cases, more, because it's only one on one. It's like going solo—where the only thing you have to contend with is an audience, what you come up with, and the scope of yourself. When you write a book on practice, you can't say, "Brother, this is a B-flat." You've got to find some way to communicate this note and how you arrive at it in print.

JC: The recording idiom in contrast to live performing—do you have a preference?

R: No, both have their hazards as well as their creative moments. On a record, I have the advantage of hearing right away what I've done, so if necessary I can fix a note, or better develop a line, or work on a tone quality for a certain phrase. When I hear it played back to me, I can make those adjustments. At a concert, once you've played it, it's gone, so you have to rely on your memory bank; you have to take it home with you and see what you can do at the next concert that will make an improvement in that past level.

stanley clarke

6/30/51

Philadelphia,
Pennsylvania

bass (acoustic and
electric)

vocalist

composer and arranger

producer

Stanley, who names Paul Chambers, Charles Mingus, Scott LaFaro, and Billy Cox (electric bass) as early influences, attended the Philadelphia Musical Academy (The University of the Arts) for four years before playing with rock groups in and around Philadelphia in the late sixties. He spent six months with Horace Silver in 1970, then a year with Joe Henderson, followed by stints with Pharoah Sanders and Stan Getz. Stanley first met Chick Corea while both were playing with Getz. In early 1972 Stanley joined Corea's group, Return to Forever, where he continues to work when he is not playing with his own band, which began touring in 1976. Clarke has arranged for singer Flora Purim and produced guitarist Roy Buchanan and singer Dee Dee Bridgewater. He says of his long relationship with Chick, "The bands that last forever, or at least a lot longer, are the ones in which each individual is allowed to expand. The leader will respect each player's ability enough not to crush or suppress him" (*Downbeat*, March 27, 1975).

S: At about ten, I started playing the accordion. There was a teacher down the street, and it was kind of forced—it wasn't my idea. The next instrument I played was the violin. It was about eight or nine inches long. It was a little, tiny, miniature violin, and I've always had big fingers, so naturally I couldn't get the spacing the violin needed to be played. I canceled on that and moved on to the cello, and believe it or not, I had a small cello, too—too small. About a year after doing all that, there was a bass in the corner of a music room at school I was going to. The bass was tall and I was tall; it was similar to a violin and a cello, which was the direction I was taking anyway, so I started playing the bass. The first music I played was classical music, and that's the basic roots of my music now.

JC: What composers were you especially attracted to?

S: Wagner, who is still my favorite composer today. And I was a great fan of Bach's. The thing I liked about Bach was that it was so sane—very logical. You could almost put Bach's music through a computer and actually come up with a relatively logical mathematical configuration.

JC: Having gone to the Philadelphia Musical Academy (The University of the Arts), how would you evaluate the importance of an academic musical experience?

S: I think music schools are fine. A guy could go to music school and learn music, if that's what he wants. The first two years at school I really learned a lot. After the third and fourth year, I recognized that my purposes were more aligned with performance. I find, for myself, that the two major points any artist who's out in the world needs are technical expertise and the ability to create an emotional impact. If the person has a good heart, for lack of better words, he can let his emotions fly and use his technical expertise in order to bring his feelings across.

JC: You've made a major contribution to the role of bass player in contemporary music. How does it feel to be an innovator?

S: Years ago there was a fixed idea that bass players played background, and bass players have this particular theme—kind of subdued, numb, almost looking numb, and just to make a long story short, I wasn't going for any of that. It's really interesting; I have never really regarded myself as a bass player, I just play the bass. The way I view myself is: number one, I'm me; number two, my name is Stanley; number three, I'm an artist; number four, I'm a musician; and number five, I'm a bass player. It's in order of importance. You notice that the one I put at the top is that I'm me, and I could do anything. So, just having that sort of viewpoint about art, when I went out to play, I would play the way I played, and the way I heard things. I was very aware when I was doing it that I was running into fixed ideas. I was barred from many gigs because of playing too much, playing too little, playing too weird, for just being myself. That was fine because that was a learning experience for me. One of my biggest pleasures in life is whenever a bass player comes out with an album, I sort of feel responsible for it, and I get joy from it—it's like sanity. It's letting a guy self-determinedly do what he wants.

JC: What are the implications of the word "commercial" when it is applied to music?

S: Commercialism extends from the word commerce, and commerce has to do with exchange. If a record comes out, and it's put on a disc, and has a cover on it, and goes into the store, and a guy buys it, it's intercommerce, right? Now, having that as a definition means that any record that sells is commercial. John Coltrane's music could be considered commercial music. When I hear people talk about commercialism versus artistic something, it sort of makes me think that there is possibly some sort of weird computation behind that. I picked up the flow from lots of people where they say, "Well, if your music sounds very, let's say eccentric, it's not commercial. And if it sounds very clear-cut and very accessible, and has a very high level of communication, it's not art." And to me, that's weird, because when I look at myself, my purpose for getting on the stage and playing music is to communicate. Now, where commercialism comes in—I sell records, and so my music is commercial. Also, my music has a lot of artistic integrity to it, because I'm still happy and I'm not walking around hiding from people. You do things right, but there might have been a time in your life when you've done something and you weren't quite satisfied with it, and that's called compromise. Each person has his or her own code of honor—it's like you won't compromise with your own integrity. If you know something is right, you say it's right.

alphonso johnson

2/2/51

Philadelphia,
Pennsylvania

bass (electric and
acoustic)

guitar

electric stick

composer and arranger

producer

Alphonso first backed the vocal group, the Majestics, 1967-1968. The following year he joined the fusion band Catalyst and played with it through 1971, when he joined Woody Herman. Al then played with Chuck Mangione before becoming a member of Weather Report in 1974, with whom he remained until 1975. In 1976 he became a member of the Cobham/Duke Band, which disbanded in 1977; he then began to record under his own name as a leader. In 1977 he toured with the CBS All Stars—Tom Scott, Steve Khan, Billy Cobham, and Mark Soskin.

A: The first instrument that I actually played was the voice. It started during my junior-high school days when I used to sing in the neighborhoods and on the street corners and finally I got into the All-City Choir. I sang with the Philadelphia Junior High School Boys Choir.

JC: What was your initial experience of mainstream music?

A: My earliest exposure that I can recall to jazz are things like, maybe hanging out on the street corners and here comes this guy in a car wheeling by with his girlfriend, he's got 96.5 on, which was a very popular jazz station in Philadelphia, and he's got that on the radio and then we would hear it. So to us, that was cool, that was jazz music, and that was the type of exposure I got. But, basically my jazz influences began when I was working with a group called Catalyst in Philadelphia and they were into very free music. What I mean by "free" was that we would allow each player enough self-expression within the normal boundaries of music. In other words, we didn't play the same way every night. You know, it was that kind of group. I could take harmonic solos if I wanted to rather than take the normal "get the audience's attention" rock solo type of thing. It was pretty loose.

JC: Do you believe in the concept of multimedia?

A: Yes, I've done concerts and productions where dancers and orchestras were involved. I think it's got a very, very strong future and it's just opening up. Look at what's happened to the concert scene. All the groups are getting involved in the visual aspects as well as the music.

JC: What are your feelings regarding the music business at large?

A: It's very rough and it's really geared not toward music but toward making money. It's pretty much a reflection on today's society. It's hard to be an innovator, a composer, a musician, an artist, and at the same time be an accountant, an attorney, and a manager. I spent the last three weeks not practicing, basically because, between spending time with my family and just taking care of business with the record company and my accountant and my lawyers, it's so time consuming to do it correctly. I believe that the most important advice that I give a lot of musicians who ask, "How do you get into the music business or how do you get into a group?" would be to tell them to take their time. There is no hurry. Most of the mistakes that I have seen musicians make are rushing into a situation, rushing to get a manager, rushing to get a record contract, and then later on finding out that is not what they wanted.

JC: Do you get speed with two-finger technique or with your thumb?

A: I don't concentrate on speed as much as I concentrate on definition. If there's a line that has to be executed very fast, it depends on where it falls on the instrument. There are some things that are easier to play with the thumbs and some things that are easier to play with two fingers. Some things are quicker to play without even using your right hand very much, just more of the left hand hammering. So, it really depends on what it is.

JC: Any comments on the apparent trend of the new exponents of the electric bass who seem to be playing in the higher register more than the previous generation?

A: I've sort of prided myself as to the reason why my style differs from most players is because I do still maintain the identity of keeping the bottom to the band as well as crossing the line and playing melodies and solos. So, when I'm playing bass, I merely think of myself as another member of the orchestra and when it comes time for me to play up high, it's probably more likely because the bottom is being covered by another instrument, as far as orchestration is concerned.

JC: When you compose, what instrument do you compose on and what influences have you drawn from?

A: The way I used to do it, I would get a vibration spiritually and I would grab the guitar, sit at the piano, or sit at the bass and expand upon it, develop that idea. Now pretty much I'm writing for a specific reason. I'm writing for someone, I'm writing for a record, I'm writing for specific things. So I can write pretty much for that area, feeling wise musically, harmonically, and melodically. But still, I just wait for the vibe to happen. I don't really sit down and say, Okay, I'm going to write a song. I'll be walking on the street and a melody will hit me and I'll just let it develop by itself. It usually just sort of flows through me; I'm just a tool.

JC: Would you say that music is the central force in your life?

A: I don't believe that anything is absolute, and for me I would think if music was all I was involved in, I would be a very small person as far as my life was concerned. Wayne Shorter said something to me when I first met him. He asked me to show him the palm of my left hand and then after about ten seconds he said, "Music is going to be a very small but important part of your life." That's something I've always remembered.

john
lee

6/28/52

Boston, Massachusetts

bass (electric and
acoustic)

composer and arranger

producer

John grew up in Connecticut and Long Island, moving to Philadelphia at age seventeen. He attended the Philadelphia Musical Academy (The Universtiy of the Arts) from 1970 to 1972. In 1971 he played with Carlos Garnett; and, in 1972, with Joe Henderson, Pharoah Sanders, and Max Roach. In late 1972 he moved to Holland and he and his friend, drummer Gerry Brown, became members of Dutch flutist Chris Hinze's group. He remained in Europe until 1974, playing with Joachim Kuhn, Philip Catherine, and Charlie Mariano. In 1974 he returned to America, where he played with Lonnie Liston Smith before becoming a member of Larry Coryell's the Eleventh House. He stayed with Eleventh House until its breakup in 1976, when he became a member of the newly formed Coryell/Mouzon Band. In 1977 John left Coryell/Mouzon to co-lead a band with Gerry Brown. He has produced and/or arranged for flutist Art Webb, reedman Carlos Garnett, and violinist Zbigniew Seifert.

J: My father was a bass player early in his life before becoming a minister. He was a big fan of Duke Ellington, Count Basie, and Miles Davis. He had a lot of jazz records, so I was constantly exposed to these beautiful sounds. My mother, on the other hand, was into classical music. Music was all around me as far back as I can remember. And of course, since my father was a minister, there was a heavy gospel influence in my early years.

I started listening to jazz before I ever heard Motown or rock. In the fourth grade I began classical studies on the acoustic bass. I had a wonderful teacher, Mrs. Carolyn Lush, with whom I studied for the next seven years. Two years later I started to play in different school and All-County orchestras and bands. Also during this year I began a seven-year affair with the trombone. I had a strong desire to be in the school marching band, but string bass just didn't make it in a marching band. So trombone became my second instrument. When I was in the seventh grade I was asked to join the school jazz band (on bass). That was great fun.

I got my first electric bass during the summer before eleventh grade. Shortly after, I started to play with other kids who were into hard rock and soul.

After I graduated from high school, I went to the Philadelphia Musical Academy for two years, where I had the opportunity to play with some really great musicians who have subsequently emerged as some of the best players in contemporary music.

During my second year I got my first big road gig with Max Roach. Playing with Max was unbelievable. We played in trio and quartet with no piano so it was really wide open for bass.

JC: When did you hook up with drummer Gerry Brown?

J: It was kind of a destiny trip, I think.

In 1969, one year before graduating from high school, my father was transferred from Amityville, Long Island, to a church in Philadelphia. The first week in school I was asked to audition for the jazz band. Up to this point in my life, school jazz band meant "stock," big-band arrangements, so I thought I would probably have to read some charts and play a blues. Well, I was in for a surprise! The teacher, Bill Munich (Overbrook High) was on piano, there was a tenor player, and Gerry Brown was on drums. After introductions, I was leisurely asked, "Do you know 'A Love Supreme'?" The question went over my head. I thought to myself, He couldn't mean John Coltrane's "A Love Supreme," could he? "You mean by Trane?" I asked. Gerry Brown then said, "Yeah." This really blew my mind. I never imagined playing this with anyone other than my record player, no less auditioning for the school jazz band. "Sure," I replied. My first real musical experience in Philadelphia was very symbolic of what was to come. The music scene was wide open. I played all kinds of jazz gigs, bop to avant-garde, played in a rock band, did club dates, and boogied at some dances.

We continued to play together through college. In the summer of 1972, we joined Dutch flutist Chris Hinze's group and moved to Holland where we remained until 1974. With Chris we experienced recording and performing in many different musical settings. With orchestras, choirs, big bands, and small groups from quartets to octets. The group did festivals, concerts, and jazz clubs all over Europe. We even did a three-week concert tour of Israel. Through our travels we met a lot of great musicians, some of whom we also played and recorded with, most notably Philip Catherine, Joachim Kuhn, Zbigniew Seifert, Jasper Van'T Hof, and Charlie Mariano. Charlie lived in the same city we lived in, The Hague. Living and touring in Europe was a great experience that enabled us both to expand as musicians and as human beings.

JC: As a player of both the electric and the acoustic bass, how would you compare the two?

J: I love the acoustic bass, especially the tonal quality, but I have more or less confined my playing of it to home, because the demand for it in a professional musical context is almost nonexistent.

JC: What kind of music will you and Gerry Brown be making within the context of your own group?

J: We really want the music to be very accessible and really turn people on—not just from the mind, but a total feeling—mind, body, and soul.

will
lee

9/8/50

San Antonio, Texas

electric bass

vocalist

composer

Will grew up in Texas and Florida, where his family moved at age twelve. He attended the University of Miami from 1969 to 1971 as a French horn major. He was a cofounder of an early fusion band Goldrush, a Miami-based group for which he wrote music as well as sang lead vocals, and played bass. Moving to New York in the early seventies, Will became a member of the group Dreams, with whom he recorded replacing bassist Chuck Rainey. During the seventies, Will became a highly sought after studio player, handling music of all styles and genres with ease. He has played with many artists both live and on record, among them Paul Simon, Bette Midler, Barry Manilow, Carly Simon, Patti Austin, and Boz Scaggs. In 1974 he appeared with Horace Silver for six months. He has also played with the Bill Watrous big band, David Sanborn, Joe Beck, Steve Marcus, Herbie Mann, and Steve Khan. From 1976 to 1977, Will was a member of the Brecker Brothers Band, with whom he toured and recorded. An original member of TV's *Saturday Night Live* house band, he has made frequent appearances on national television.

W: I was about three years old. I had pajamas on with built-in textured feet. My parents were having a party and there was an unmistakable Miles Davis mute sound playing on their phonograph most of the night. It could only have been Miles. That's the first record I remember hearing. My father's a great bebop piano player. He's also dean of the University of

Miami School of Music where he is responsible for the jazz program. He does not teach; he makes radical changes in music education. He's had buildings built for practicing, recording, and performing (the actual "playing" of music). It's great down there.

JC: When did you first explore music in terms of playing it?

W: It really took the Beatles being on *The Ed Sullivan Show*. I loved them and their music. The camera would focus on what each musician was doing; they showed Ringo playing the drums. I was a drummer at the time and that showed me some technique on the instrument. I can remember begging for drums when I was five or six.

JC: When did you perceive the bass as your ultimate instrument?

W: When I was a kid of thirteen, I was in a band and we couldn't find a bass player, so I switched to the bass.

JC: Did you teach yourself how to play it?

W: Yes, just by listening to records and copying a riff, or a touch, or a direction of movement with the notes. Nobody had to say anything. I never had any formal training on the bass. I played trumpet for a lot of years and that gave me a lot of reading chops. That's just a pure coincidence.

JC: How about your singing? Did that start to develop when you were young?

W: Yeah, without even thinking about it. When somebody had to sing songs with the band, I couldn't see any reason why it shouldn't be me. I used to play drums and sing all the time.

JC: Do you imagine that, say as far back as thirteen, it occurred to you to pursue a professional career in music?

W: In music, yes, but not on the bass. I went through a whole year of college majoring in French horn, until I finally realized that the music I enjoyed playing on Fender bass every night in clubs and bars could be applied in college.

JC: The choice to move to New York City—that was a fairly deliberate choice. When did that occur to you? And why?

W: In 1971, the beginning of May. The New York group Dreams* needed a bass player.

---

* An early fusion band consisting of, among others, John Abercrombie, the Brecker Brothers, Billy Cobham, Don Grolnick, Barry Rogers, and Lee. They had tried everybody that they had hopes for in town, and the only choice left was to send out beyond New York. I happened to get into a jam session in Miami with someone who was a friend of the Dreams' horn players [Barry Rogers and the Breckers], which led to my joining it.

JC: What was the attraction to that particular music?

W: I guess it was because I was in the middle of a rock 'n' roll career at night and bebop-type training during the day at school. Somehow it made complete sense as the perfect fusion. I never even tried to play along with the first Dreams record, which was made before I joined the band. I came to New York without preparation. I was able to sing the lyrics and play the bass without having to think about it. I was so involved with jazz and so involved with rock, the two just met each other when Dreams appeared.

JC: What led you into the studio? Was it the direct result of working with musicians like the Brecker Brothers who were already established studio players at that time?

W: Yes, although I never dreamed it would happen to me. It was my ultimate goal. It seemed so desirable to be able to walk into a room and hear different cats every couple of hours playing totally different types of things all the time and never having to hear it again. It's like a game—pretending you are in this kind of band or that kind several times a day.

JC: So what you like about the studio is the diversity. Can you always establish an instant rapport with the other musicians at a record date?

W: It depends on the player—if you're playing with Billy Cobham or Steve Gadd on drums, you don't have to think about it. It's like you're floating downhill backwards on your back, downstream.

JC: Now that we have entered the "era of the bass player," don't you feel compelled to establish an identity outside of the studio?

W: It's like deciding not to have children until you grow out of your childhood. Musically, I feel like I am a child. I could easily throw out a record, but I have to find something that is unique and meaningful to me and the culture itself.

JC: What do you think about our present musical culture?

W: Right now there is so much happening, you have to follow it and lead it at the same time. You can't fight it. There are always going to be areas in which to be creative, even if you allow yourself to play only one note on a song. I guess that is what music boils down to—space. If you get past the basic groove itself, if you get past everything, even chord changes, if you get down to one note, chances are that one "realized" note might be played by any one of a number of players, which enables that one note to change the feel of the music by each individual player. So technically that one note really has to be successful, that one note has to be identifiable—it has to be your note, your sound. In music you can never be perfect. The more you learn, the further you get away from the end of the stretch that you can see at the time. As you are playing, you are learning and growing. You get smaller and smaller with the ever-growing spectrum. Every time you reach a peak, you see how much further you have to go. In other words, the more you get into the music, the more critical your ear becomes, and no instrument is perfectly in tune with itself, especially the bass. The better you are, the more you realize how imperfect the instrument is, which can drive you nuts!

JC: If you had to ignore certain things and focus on others, what would they be?

W: If I had a choice, I'd focus on every positive thing about playing. Once you have realized that dreaded syndrome that no instrument or musician is perfect—using these as your tools, the next step is to look for new sounds. That's my idea of perfection. That could make me happy—to keep arriving at new sounds. They can lead to other ones, so I would be happy just knowing how to play three notes at the right time over and over again in a song.

JC: Do you equate happiness with perfection?

W: Yes.

J: What is your opinion of contemporary music?

W: It's like seeing the sun's rays coming over the horizon before you see the sun itself. There is something very exciting that is about to happen in music, something so heavenly and appealing, like the mythological Greek sirens—something irresistible. It's going to be appealing to musicians as well as non-musicians. Right now rhythm and lyrics are the two things that allow a musician to enjoy the same song, as well as a guy who's banging out dents in a car body for a living, because they can both understand music at that level. There is something happening; I feel something new is coming on, and it's not rhythm anymore. It's grown past that. The music is going to be visual. The sounds will be so colorful that they will paint a picture, and musicians, as well as listeners and non-listeners, will be able to enjoy it.

jaco pastorius

12/1/51

Norristown, Pennsylvania

electric bass

composer and arranger

producer

Jaco grew up in Fort Lauderdale, Florida, where his father, a drummer and singer, provided an early musical influence. Before settling on the bass, Jaco played drums, piano, saxophone, and guitar. On bass, he worked with many of the concert headliners who came through Florida: Wayne Cochran and the C.C. Riders, the Temptations, the Supremes—just to name a few. In addition to his musical skills, Jaco, a painter, decided against a career in art because it was "too tangible" and not "spontaneous." While still in Florida, he wrote big-band charts for the University of Miami, where he also taught for a semester. He also wrote for Ira Sullivan's Baker's Dozen, and for Peter Graves's big band. While playing in the house band at Fort Lauderdale's Bachelors III (1975), Jaco encountered Bobby Colomby, the drummer in Blood, Sweat and Tears, who later became the producer of his first record as a leader. Jaco began to receive wider recognition when he became a member of Weather Report in 1976, and later, when he recorded with Joni Mitchell.

J: Growing up in Florida, nobody said, "You have to play jazz, you've got to play R & B." I just listened and whatever I liked, I liked. I listened to everyone from Elvis to Miles Davis.

JC: What were the advantages of growing up in that environment?

J: Florida is great because there are no musical prejudices. My family moved there when I was seven. I heard steel drum bands, Cuban bands, James Brown, Sinatra, the Beatles—and I heard most of it on the radio.

JC: You seem to put a lot of emphasis on Florida.

J: I do. Where I come from, nobody cares what style of music you play. Everybody down there just lives.

JC: Besides music, were you especially concerned with anything else in your adolescence?

J: Yes, sports. I was, and still am, a complete sports fanatic. This is why I play the bass, because I got really beat up in one of those red-neck football rumbles when I was thirteen. My hand was almost severed from my left arm. I was playing the drums in a local band at the time. It was a good band and I was a good drummer, but I wasn't strong enough to lay down a heavy backbeat. Within two years, I had to give up the drums. There was a real good drummer in town who took my place. A week later the bass player quit the band. So, the other guys called me up and said, "Jaco, you think you can play bass?" I said, "Yeah, sure." I never played bass in my life. I had exactly four hundred dollars in the bank from paper route earnings, and I went out and bought a brand new Fender jazz bass. I was working the next day, and I've never been out of work since.

JC: What bands did you play in?

J: Mostly soul bands. I played just about every soul tune written in the sixties. At the same time, I used to sub for this bass player who had National Guard duty twice a week. The music was a kind of pop/jazz, jazz standards that were being played as pop music, so I learned all those tunes.

JC: How did you incorporate that into your music?

J: I incorporated it in one way—playing music and making money for it.

JC: Is that what really got you into music—poverty?

J: Yes…"Pragmatism City." I started playing the bass because it was so easy, and then I had to go and make it hard for myself. When I was nineteen my daughter was born, and I gave up music. I thought nobody wanted to hear what I was up to because my approach was so different. My whole focus has always been on living—one hundred percent—being a man, being a husband, and being a father. I've got two kids who I love more than anything in the whole world, and there was no way that I was leaving Florida until I established some sort of relationship with them.

JC: You weren't playing at all while you were learning the "art of fatherhood"?

P: I was playing my ass off the whole time. I stayed in Florida, stayed a daddy, but I wasn't making a very good living. Most everyone in Miami thought I was crazy, because I was playing the bass as a lead instrument. It was ironic, because I already had an underground reputation; I was sort of a rumor nationally—through my playing with Wayne Cochran and the C. C. Riders. I had played one-nighters in lots of different cities, but I was never recorded.

JC: How many years did you actually spend practicing the bass?

J: I really only practiced for one year, 1971-72, which is when I left Wayne. This is when I met Ira Sullivan* who, jazz wise, was probably one of my biggest influences. It was the first time I ever got to incorporate my concept into a jazz format. I also met bass trombonist and big-band leader, Peter Graves, and I started writing for big bands.

JC: How did you acquire so much knowledge of the bass with only a year's practice behind you?

J: All you've got to do is keep your ears open. Most of my musical knowledge comes from playing experience.

JC: What bass players, if any, have you been influenced by?

J: I've been influenced by bass players, but not much. Some of the players I used to dig when I was coming up were Bernard Odum, who played with James Brown, Jerry Jemmot, Ron Carter, Bill Rich, and Gary Peacock. My greatest inspiration has always been singers—they have the ability to get personal. When I play the bass, most people can usually tell that it's me, because of that kind of personal thing I try to get in my tone.

JC: What about competition?

J: I have no competition, because I'm not competing.

JC: How would you describe your music?

J: Punk jazz.

* Trumpet, flugelhorn, saxophone, flute, percussion, and composer. One of the important Chicago modernists of the late forties who moved to Florida in the early sixties, where he played clubs and concerts and became an educator of some importance—teaching in elementary schools, junior colleges, and churches.

miroslav vitous

12/6/47
Prague, Czechoslovakia
bass (acoustic and
electric)
guitar
keyboards
composer and arranger
producer

Miroslav began playing the violin at age six, the piano at fourteen, and finally the bass. He attended the Prague Conservatory where he played in a trio which also featured his brother Alan on drums and Jan Hammer on piano. He also played with a Dixieland band while still in Czechoslovakia. At an international music contest in Vienna, he won first prize—a scholarship to the Berklee College of Music in Boston. He came to the United States in 1966, but only remained at Berklee for a short time. In 1967 he came to New York where he quickly involved himself in the music scene, playing with many different artists—Walter Booker, Art Farmer, Freddie Hubbard, the Bobby Brookmeyer–Clark Terry Quintet among them. He worked briefly with Miles Davis before becoming a member of the Herbie Mann group, with whom he remained for two years. In 1970 Miroslav toured with Stan Getz. In late 1971, he was co-founder and member of Weather Report, with Joe Zawinul, Wayne Shorter, and Alphonse Mouzon. In 1973 he left Weather Report and embarked upon a career as a leader. In 1977 he replaced John Lee in the Coryell/Mouzon Band, remaining with that group for a few months before resuming the role of leader again in 1978.

M: My father is a musician and he has always encouraged me in my career. He discovered that I had almost perfect pitch when I was quite small, and felt that I had great talent. I started studying the violin when I was six, but I gave it up about three years later because I wanted to study the piano. Finally, when I was thirteen or fourteen years old, I fell in love with the bass. I had had private lessons in violin and piano, but I studied the bass at the Prague Conservatory. My teacher was František Posta, a fantastic man.

JC: As both an electric and acoustic player, do you feel equally articulate on both instruments?

M: I think that the electric bass, compared to the acoustic bass, is flat—completely flat. It doesn't have the overtones and it doesn't have the freedom. It's like half of the instrument, because on the acoustic bass I can go all the way up near the bridge and play almost soprano saxophone range—with the bow I can do that, especially lately since I've been getting back into practicing. In fact now, I'm playing about eighty percent acoustic and twenty percent electric bass.

JC: You went through a real transition in your music wherein you became a guitar player both in live performances and on records. Are you still using the guitar?

M: No, I'm not playing the guitar right now. I'm going to use it with the polyphonic synthesizer for some lines, but not as a solo guitar because I can play as much on acoustic bass. I think, after Weather Report, something happened to me and I had to expand myself. I learned a lot of keyboard work and I was beginning to study guitar just because I had to get away from the bass. When I picked up the bass again, I found out that my playing was better than before and that everything I had learned on the guitar came out on the bass. I was amazed because I had thought I'd have to learn the bass all over again, but my mind must have translated all the guitar to the bass or else I was playing the guitar like a bass player. Who knows!

JC: What do you think about contemporary music now?

M: I think it is lacking in warmth and juice. It seems to me it's getting a little bit flat because of the commercial influences.

JC: What is your approach to composition?

M: I compose on every instrument—on guitar, bass, piano, synthesizer…I learned the harmony and counterpoint elements in Czechoslovakia. I think that all composition basically comes from counterpoint, from three voices. But, as far as I can tell, my knowledge of composition is a natural thing. All of a sudden I start hearing music in my head and I just put together the pieces based on my understanding of the form. It's nothing that can be taught. One thing I always try to stay away from is over-learning. For example, you can go to Juilliard and have great marks and then compose a piece which turns out to be half-Beethoven and half-Stravinsky—the originality is absent. That's why I'm not for studying too much, though it helps to a certain point…one has to be loose about it, free.

brassbrassbrassbrassbrassbrassbrassbrassbrassbr

brassbrassbrassbrassbrassbrassbrass**brass**brass

randy
brecker

11/27/45

Philadelphia,

Pennsylvania

trumpet and flugelhorn

piano

drums

composer and arranger

producer

While still in high school, Randy began taking local gigs in Philadelphia, "mostly R & B." He enrolled at the University of Indiana for three years, 1963-1965, where he played in a big band as well as a small group. He also studied privately with David Baker. The Indiana big band won the competition at the Notre Dame Jazz Festival, which took him and the rest of the band on a State Department tour of Europe and the Near East. He never returned to school, staying in Europe for three months. He then came to New York and played at small clubs and college proms. In 1966 he played and recorded with Blood, Sweat and Tears; and in 1967 with Horace Silver. Randy also played with the Duke Pearson and Clark Terry big bands, with Stevie Wonder for six months, and with Art Blakey. In 1970, he helped create the early fusion band Dreams, with his brother Michael, Billy Cobham, and Barry Rogers; the group recorded two records for Columbia. Randy joined Larry Coryell's the Eleventh House in 1973, touring with Larry in both the United States and Europe. During that time, he also made various appearances with Deodato and Johnny and Edgar Winter. At the end of 1973, he and Mike became members of Billy Cobham's band, which again took the Breckers across the country and throughout Europe, where some live recording was done. Since 1975, Randy and Mike have made their own group, the Brecker Brothers.

Since the late 1960s, Randy has recorded with the Rolling Stones, Charles Mingus, Larry Coryell, Ringo Starr, Bruce Springsteen, Laura Nyro, the Average White Band, James Taylor, Elton John—to name a few. More recently, Randy has appeared with pianist Hall Galper's Quintet, a group which also includes Michael Brecker.

R: I started playing trumpet at eight. I guess my parents planted the seed, but reluctantly. They really liked the fact that we played but they didn't want us to do it for real, because they never thought we could make any money. I studied privately in Philly and went to Indiana University. At Indiana, I played jazz in a big band, and a small group, and went to the Near East on a tour. I stayed in Europe for a while, and then came to New York. I've stayed in New York ever since.

JC: When did you first start getting into the electric sound?

R: With Dreams* and John Abercrombie, when wah-wah pedals were first coming into prominence. John had one, so I tried it out and liked it.

JC: What musical directions are you now contemplating?

R: I don't know; I was always involved in all different kinds of music. I haven't tried to put limits on it. That's what I really like. At first I didn't enjoy rock and roll, but eventually, as it got better, I got into it. I just figured there wasn't any sense in limiting yourself or anything. Now it's all happened; it's all come together. All the young guys you can't really classify—they can play everything. I belong to a generation of musicians who grew up with jazz, and then when rock took over, we had to learn everything again. These guys just learned both together, so there's no separation. The good ones just feel both, and they don't have a stigma about being commercial.

JC: What do you think the future of jazz is?

R: It's hard to define what "jazz" is today. Electronic music has really kind of taken over in a way. Most of the new things come as a result of new instruments being invented. Harmonically, improvisation is about as advanced as it could ever be, so in the last few years it's been new textures and new sounds, and incorporating a lot of different elements, like Indian music, classical music, and R & B.

JC: How does making money fit into the scheme of things?

R: It's important, although it's not the only factor. To devote amazing time and energy to something of my own makes it definitely a factor, because I can't see doing it for free. But whatever success I've had has allowed me to do gigs where I don't have to worry about the fact that I'm only making

---

*Early fusion band of the late sixties.

thirty dollars a night or something, because it's not my only source of income, which is nice. So I can really do it and enjoy it.

JC: What is the mental process you go through when you write? Do you lock yourself in a room?

R: It goes in stages. I go a couple of months where I'll do it for hours every day, and then I won't do it at all. Every tune is different. Sometimes I'll write a whole tune real fast, and other times it will take months to put it together.

JC: Of all the music you listen to right now, what do you relate to the most?

R: I'm really sick of everything, to tell you the truth. A few years ago, when the first fusion music came out, that was interesting. But now there's so much of it, it's like everybody's trying to find something. I still listen most to bebop from "Bird" to Coltrane and Miles, and then R & B and some R & R. You know, there are certain formulas to follow if you want to make a hit, which I'm trying to learn.

JC: Do you believe that the only way you can have a hit is to follow that formula, or do you believe you can be esoteric?

R: You can be lucky but, if you want to be safe, you should follow the formula and try to extend it. On one of our records, I wrote one real commercial tune, and that was by far the hardest one to write somehow. Although it sounds like it probably was the easiest, it was the hardest, because the simpler it gets, the harder it is to make it sound at least a little believable or different.

JC: Do you feel more comfortable playing with people you've played with for a long time, as opposed to spontaneous musical encounters?

R: Well, both. It's nice to make a change, because a lot of spontaneous things happen on first meetings. It's hard to surprise anyone you've played with for a long time, because they know you; they know what you're going to be doing, and everyone starts feeling weird because they know each other so well that nothing sounds new. But maybe that's better because then you really have to try to come up with something new…Plus, a lot of things that the band will do, because they know each other, will sound spontaneous to a listener.

JC: How do you feel about critics?

R: I don't think they play that much importance, luckily—not like movie critics. They don't feel the experience of being a musician. If you're trying to make a commercial record, you have to keep in mind that there are good ones and bad ones. So, when a critic is reviewing a commercial record, he should view it from that standpoint, instead of saying it sucks just because of, say, lack of playing, because that wasn't the point of the record anyway.

JC: What about peer pressure and the competitive spirit—do you find it productive or counter-productive?

R: It's good. That's what's so groovy about New York—just to be around a lot of great players—it's always good to feel like shit, because if you thought you were real great, you probably wouldn't really do anything to improve yourself.

JC: What do you think of yourself in terms of your own musicality—are you satisfied?

R: I'm never satisfied; I just try to keep getting better.

JC: Do you feel that musicians have enough control over their own lives, or that they're sort of victims?

R: They're definitely victims and it's pretty hopeless, in a business sense. Just the way it's set up, because lawyers and businessmen set it up.

JC: Have you personally felt exploited?

R: Yes, definitely, because of the way the system is set up. I mean, you have to have amazing record sales to make any money—far and beyond whatever I thought you would have to sell. It's not only records, it's just the general situation of economy, I guess, and the cost of everything. So, it's not even necessarily the record companies; it's just not feasible to go out on the road anymore unless you sell four hundred thousand records; that is, if you have a band with more than two people in it…

JC: Then, the only solution, as you see it, is to sell a lot of records?

R: Yeah, but that's if you really want to go out and work with a large electric band with equipment, and so forth—and get involved with a manager and agent. If you don't, then you can make a jazz record if you want to work around the New York area and various jazz toilets around the country. Conceivably, I could actually do that now, because if I wanted to just remain in the studios and play around occasionally, I could, which actually, at this point, doesn't seem like a bad idea. But basically I'm an ambitious person. I'd like to have a band, make a lot of money, and I don't like going out on the road and making three hundred dollars a week and paying your hotel bill and taxes out of it. Whenever I've been out on the road, I've actually ended up with nothing at the end, or owing money, although I made more money with Horace Silver, for instance, than I've ever made with the Brecker Brothers, at this point.

JC: If Charlie Parker were alive today, what do you think he'd be saying?

R: He'd probably be playing his ass off. He was a real open guy. I think he'd be digging all of it.

miles
davis

5/26/26

Alton, Illinois

trumpet

flugelhorn

keyboards

composer and arranger

Miles, the son of Miles Dewey Davis II, a successful dentist and dental surgeon, and a mother who played piano and violin, moved with his family to St. Louis when he was one. Miles's father was a landowner as was his father before him. His grandmother taught organ. His sister played piano, and his brother, a dancer, played trumpet and piano. Miles's background was middle class; the Davises moved to an all-white neighborhood while Miles was still in grade school. He received his first horn when he was thirteen. His first teacher was Elwood Buchanan, a patient of his father. He taught Miles to play with no vibrato. He also helped him get his first gigs in St. Louis. There, Miles met Clark Terry, an early inspiration, when he was fourteen. By the time he was sixteen, he was playing in Eddie Randall's band the Blue Devils. He began to gain recognition in St. Louis and was asked by Sonny Stitt to join Tiny Bradshaw's band, but couldn't because his mother insisted he finish high school. In 1944, Charlie Parker and Dizzy Gillespie came to St. Louis with the Billy Eckstine Band. Miles sat in for a few weeks, replacing the third trumpet player who was sick. After that, he left for New York City. He enrolled at Juilliard, but stayed for only a semester and a half. He found Charlie Parker during his first week in New York and the two became roommates. He also encountered Thelonius Monk who wrote out tunes for him, as well as Dizzy Gillespie who advised him to study piano. He followed Bird around, writing down on matchbook covers what he heard Bird play at night and playing it himself at Juilliard the next day. About Parker, Miles has said "Bird used to play forty different styles—he was never content to remain the same" (Nat Hentoff, *Jazz Is*, p. 143).

Another influence was trumpeter Freddie Webster, Miles's best friend. In 1945 Miles played on Charlie Parker's first record as a leader. In 1946 he toured with the Benny Carter Band. That same year he met Charles Mingus, with whom he recorded. In late 1946, Fats Navarro quit the Billy Eckstine Band, and Miles replaced him. After that came a brief stint with Illinois Jacquet. He then returned to Bird. In 1948 he left Charlie Parker and joined Oscar Pettiford and the following summer, he began to collaborate with Gerry Mulligan and Gil Evans. The music that was created between 1949 and 1950 with Mulligan and Evans was subsequently labeled "cool jazz." In 1949, he became heavily involved with heroin. A four-year battle with that drug followed, and in 1954, Miles, who cured himself of his habit, was on the verge of major recognition. In 1955, he made a historic appearance at Newport—some called it a "comeback." He also recorded as a sideman with Mingus, and later with Jackie McLean. In late 1955, he signed with Columbia Records. About that time, he also played the flugelhorn for the first time in public. A quintet was then formed with Red Garland on piano, Philly Joe Jones on drums, Paul Chambers on bass, and John Coltrane on saxophone. Coltrane said of his tenure with Miles, "Miles' music gave me plenty of freedom. I could play three chords at once, but if I wanted to, I could play melodically" (Leonard Feather, *From Satchmo to Miles*, p. 237). That band broke up in 1957; new bands were formed and records were made with changing personnel, which included, for brief periods of time, Cannonball Adderley, Bill Evans, Sonny Stitt, and J. J. Johnson. After four years, a permanent band was created with Hank Mobley on tenor sax, Wynton Kelly on piano, Jimmy Cobb on drums, and Paul Chambers playing bass. In 1963 George Coleman replaced Hank Mobley, and Ron Carter replaced Chambers. Tony Williams and Herbie Hancock succeeded Cobb and Kelly. In 1964 Wayne Shorter replace George Coleman, and the legendary "quintet" was born; a record, *ESP* was recorded—a title which most accurately conveyed the kind of telepathic communication demonstrated by the members of that band. In 1967 Coltrane died. In 1968 the quintet disbanded. *Miles in the Sky*, recorded in 1968, featured the not-yet-famous George Benson on one track, and Herbie Hancock for the first time on electric piano. In June of 1968, Chick Corea replaced Hancock and Dave Holland, Ron Carter, on the record *Filles de Kilimanjaro*. In 1969 *In a Silent*

> Music is the song I love,
> And nothing comes between,
> Melodies are à la carte,
> But they reach my selfish heart.
>
> —*Miles Davis*
> February 1978

Way was released; the record featured Joe Zawinul and John McLaughlin among others. The following year, *Bitches' Brew* came out, with Bennie Maupin, Larry Young, Harvey Brooks, Lenny White, Jack DeJohnette, and Don Alias in the group. That album was to catapult Miles's career to new commercial heights, and confuse, dismay, and delight his critics. Still to come were the live recordings at the Fillmore East, and other bands which featured Keith Jarrett, Steve Grossman, Michael Henderson, Billy Cobham, Gary Bartz, Airto Moreira, Hermeto Pascoal, Carlos Garnett, Khalil Balakrishna, Collin Walcott, Badal Roy, Billy Hart, M'Tume, Reggie Lucas, Cedric Lawson, Dave Liebman, Al Foster, and others. Miles once told critic Leonard Feather, "Everybody I get is special. All the guys I've used have changed the whole style of music today" (*From Satchmo to Miles*, p. 246). He also told Feather, "I don't want to go back into the past. What's important is what's happening now, the new music and the music of the future" (*From Satchmo to Miles*, p. 250).

The first music I heard was on the radio. I could tell if it was black or white by just listening to it the first time I heard it. Once, my father was fixing a music instructor's teeth, who said, "Send Miles around. I go to the grade school every Wednesday; buy him a trumpet." My mother said, "Why don't you play the violin!" I said, "If I take a violin out on the streets, I'll have more knockouts than I have now." My sister Dorothy studied music for ten years—she says her mother wanted to keep her off the streets. My brother Vernon went to the Roosevelt Conservatory in Chicago for three years. He went to Howard University too. He played trumpet and piano and he's a dancer. Now he dances with Katherine Dunham. He's also been with the IRS for over twenty years.

My mother bought two records—Duke Ellington and Art Tatum. She hit on the right thing, didn't she? The public completely ignored Duke; he was a great man. I'd put him and Stravinsky in the same category. He was trying to teach everybody something...I used to buy a lot of books on theory. Also, people would show me different things—like Mabel Higgins, who showed me some things on piano—a great woman; she was fat but great. I spent a lot of time learning this shit—reading a lot of books, canceling on a lot of people I thought I liked.

So, I started to play; I picked it up quick, of course. Most of the cats were larger than me; they used to call me "Little Davis." I used to make a lot of noise, but my instructor liked me 'cause I liked the way he played. He used to say, "Little Davis, come here." I'd say, "What you want?" He'd whisper, " 'Do nothing 'til you hear from me; pay no attention to what's said …"* Every time he'd get drunk, that's what he'd sing—that song. My second teacher, Gustat, also made mouthpieces. I've had a Gustat mouthpiece since I was thirteen; someone told me to have it copied. As soon as I did, Jim Rose, my road manager, lost it. Gustat could run chromatic scales in two octaves, seventeen times in one breath. Vachiano, my teacher in New York, would say, "Play 'Tea for Two.'" The Motherfucker wouldn't teach me. I'd say, "Man, I'm

---

* A Duke Ellington composition.

paying you—teach me something!" Levi, a trumpet player—one of Gustat's best students—he'd play all those pretty notes. Boy, we used to have fun…God damn! …maybe 'cause we were at home.

When I was eleven, my mother said, "Spank Miles"; and my father would say, "For what?" She'd say, "He's crazy"; he'd say, "Remember that." When I was fifteen, I was making a hundred and twenty-five dollars a week. I was driving my father's car and I had ten suits. I got them from the pawnshop. I'd get them down to twenty dollars a suit—Brooks Brothers, and so on.

They were sicking me on the greatest trumpet players in the country and I didn't know it. I had this friend, Bruz. I'd say, "Man, you really sound bad," and Bruz would laugh. He was one of the baddest of the bad. He would play very few notes—a man of few, but choice statements—musically, I mean. I learned a lot of shit from him.

School started at nine a.m. I had to hear "Harlem Renaissance" before school. I was awake until five in the morning, then in class at nine, talking about Shakespeare. Miss Johnson, my teacher, was too hip— she saw me with a girl and said, "That bitch ain't nothing." I made all A's, and I got out of school and said, "Fuck it!" I didn't make my own graduation. My father didn't care; he just said, "Anything you're gonna do, do it well." My father went to Northwestern College for Dentistry, Lincoln University in Pennsylvania, and Arkansas Baptist College—three degrees. He finished when he was twenty-four. My uncle went to Harvard and studied in Berlin. He was the editor of *Color* magazine. He used to tell me everything. My mother said, "Oh, God, Ferd and you together!" (He had a suite downtown.) I said, 'We're the only ones in the family with any brains"—Ferd, me, and my father. He talked to me about Caesar and Hannibal. I asked him why he was working with Rockefeller. He said, "Because he's going to win." He was a brilliant guy. They made me feel dumb. My grandfather made a hundred dollars a day during the Depression. When his kids got old, he gave them land. My uncle Frank was his bodyguard. My father told them to always count their money.

There was a schoolteacher in St. Louis who was a hell of a trumpet player. They needed someone in Springfield, Illinois, who could read and he told them about me. That's where I made my first hundred dollars. Sometimes we'd play for strippers then a guy would come in and tell jokes.

When Clark Terry and I were friends, in order to get inspiration, he would play with me. He could play real fast. People would hear that we were playing and the place would be full. I wasn't drinking or anything then…Clark was with the school orchestra. I had short white pants and he had a brown zoot suit. He'd say, "You play trumpet?" I'd say, "Yeah." But all the time he was talking, I could tell he was a trumpet player because of his embouchure, his lip.

My best friend was a man named Duke Brooks. We used to have great days. He was a real genius; he played piano like Bud Powell although he never saw or heard him.

The trumpet players in St. Louis said, "Hey, Little Davis, you can't get any jobs because you play too modern." I said, "So what!" Me and my boys said, "Fuck it!" So we got our own band. The union would pass out jobs, but not to us, not to me. I didn't care 'cause I was carrying my horn around, playing and jamming. Me and Clark—we'd be playing in a club for fifteen minutes and it would be packed. We'd go to jam sessions with guys who had just come off the boat from New Orleans… We'd play from six in the evening till six the next day—all night—and I loved every minute of it. Fat Fichon was a fat cat who played piano; Stanley Williams was just a little lighter than me, with straight black hair. They could swing like a motherfucker—those funky meters, the way that they play today. I said, "Oh, shit, that's how bad I want to be." But I learned from everyone. There were some guys—you'd just look at them putting their horn to their mouth, and you knew they couldn't play shit. I used to watch the way different guys carried their horns, and the way they'd lip their horns. I could tell what they were trying to play and what embouchure fit.

…The boat would stop in St. Louis and Clark would call me up and say, "Let's go to a session." I had to get the okay from my father. So, we'd go to a session; we'd jam all night. Guys would drink whiskey, change drums. Drummers would do all kinds of tricks with their sticks; trumpet players doing different shit—playing high notes, changing keys. They didn't care what you wanted to play—"Let's play!" They dared me to call Eddie Randall [trumpet player], because he had the only band in town; it was called the Blue Devils. You know how I take dares—I called him and he said, "Come on over."

Clyde Higgins, Mabel's husband who was in our band and played like Bird, could read anything, but Jimmy Lunceford wouldn't hire him 'cause he was too black. They only wanted to hire handsome cats. All of the guys came up from New Orleans…Fats Navarro was in a band with Andy Kirk and Howard McGhee that played in town. He started that whole style from New Orleans. Fats is a Creole; nobody ever mentions him. He's one of the greatest trumpet players I ever heard; he could also play saxophone like Coltrane. He didn't imitate anybody—he had his own style, he created it. He and I used to play together and we'd sound alike; but when we played separately, we didn't sound alike. I used to show him some things. He couldn't play a ballad. He would always play the same thing, so I loosened him up. I told him what it was he was trying to play and couldn't. I showed him; I said, "It's this chord right here. You don't have to play the same thing every time you play this part; play something different right here—invert the chord." That's the way I used to talk to him. He used to call me "Millie." He'd say, "Millie, why can't I play something different on 'I Can't Get Started'?" I said, "Because you don't know what you're doing. You know on the end of the part that turns around—the first eight bars, you have to go back." He didn't know how to do that, so I showed him what it was. "All you have to do is run these two chords differently and you can go back." He said, "Oh." Then he said, "Thanks." …Fats and I would jam all night. It's nice to do something you like.

…Nobody was playing anything like I did, except for Dizzy and Charlie Parker and Max Roach.

I went to see Ella [Fitzgerald] sing. They had a makeshift bandstand. All the kids would come and ask me to play. I played "I Want You; I Need You." All the players that came to town could get in with their union cards. Alonzo Pettiford [Oscar's brother] was one of the best trumpet players I've ever heard; he could play real fast. But my main man used to play sax and trumpet—his name was Charlie Young. All those guys came from Kansas City and Oklahoma; they were playing Eastern music. Ann Young, Billie Holiday's niece, said, "Let me take you to New York and buy you a new horn." But I was making a hundred twenty-five dollars a week and buying slick suits in pawnshops, and I had just bought a horn, and I wasn't fucking.

…Clark used to play so fast 'cause he played out of a clarinet book, and I used to play out of a piano book and a French book on clarinet. I'd play a whole page in one breath. He'd play everything down the scale. Sometimes, just to tease him, I'd play just what he'd play. We had a ball; I tried to get him to come to New York, but I couldn't. He came three years later.

When I came to New York, I went to Juilliard. I didn't believe it; they showed me some things I already knew when I was fourteen about theory and all that shit. There was an entrance exam. I played a song called "Youth Dauntless"—I don't know what that means, but it was very fast. My best friend Henry was taking the exam, too. He said, "If I don't get in, my mother will kill me!" I said, "What are you gonna play?" He said, "Clyde McCoy's 'Sugar Blues.'" We both got in but he just couldn't play—he turned out to be a good writer; he was pretty cool! He just looked wrong playing the trumpet. I never have to warm up; I just make certain sounds with my mouth and I can play trumpet—right now. In St. Louis I used to spit rice to school every day and back, or spit half a pea—it makes you used to playing the trumpet. If you do a sport, or music, or anything—if it isn't smooth, it's wrong. Everything you do is supposed to be professional. If you don't know, go to a pro and ask him to please teach you to be like him. I went to Gustat and played one note. He said I was the worst trumpet player he ever heard in his life. I said, "That why I'm here—I'm the pupil, you're the teacher." He'd go up and down the scale—he could do it seventeen times…when Dizzy got fucked up in the mouth, I told him to go to Gustat. He sent him to a doctor who gave him a shot from inside of his mouth. I used to tell Dizzy, "Play in the low register 'cause your low register is out of tune." See, he and I could talk; nobody else could tell him. Dizzy's like a relative.

…I did Juilliard summer school in one night—Mozart's *Requiem* in E-flat; I took it apart musically, with Hindemith's *Kleine Kammermusik* for an introduction. I went back to St. Louis and told my father that there was a new type of music we were playing. There was this guy name Yardbird Parker… My father said, "Okay—just do it good. If you need a friend, call me." So I went back to New York. I was allowed to quit Juilliard 'cause they stretch everything out there, and I did improvisation, and I had imagination. They were my best times—in St. Louis and the first part of my being in New York on 52nd Street. Billie Holiday was playing there; Art Tatum, Charlie Parker; Dizzy was there; Coleman Hawkins, Ben Webster, Kenny Clark. Bird used to listed to Art Tatum play with Slam Stewart, John Collins, and a trumpet player named Victor Culson. He'd come out saying he never heard anything like it. Art Tatum was the first genius I ever heard in my life—a motherfucker!…Coleman Hawkins told me never to play with someone older than me, and I never have. With older players, there's no force, no drive. With younger players it's not that you know it all, or I know it all—it's I'm trying to learn it all.

…There was this dancer, Baby Lawrence, and this other motherfucker, Groundhog, whose name was Walter, and they would jam uptown at Minton's. Baby Lawrence would call me in to hum an introduction I wrote for his show at Birdland, and Baby would dance to it. You'd hear like paradiddles—Baby Lawrence used to cut off everything on the fourth beat. I liked Groundhog. He was a drug addict and was able to disguise his habit 'cause he looked tall, cool and handsome.

…The beginning and the end is everything. You've got to start and stop gracefully. I've heard some ragged endings…you can't force someone to do what they don't want to do. If I don't feel like playing, I don't play—not until I feel like it. I could make the cats in my band play by just looking at them. I'd look at them and not say anything. They'd wait and watch. Finally, I'd say, "Motherfucker, will you get down!"

People steal everything. First they steal your money, then they start with your life and characteristics, and then your jokes, and then your dreams—they steal everything. I've never stolen anything from anyone. I've looked at a lot of people, though, and their approach to different things.

I know what the power of silence is. When I used to play in clubs, everybody was loud; there was a lot of noise. So I would take my mute off the microphone, and I would play something so soft that you could hardly hear it…and you talk about listening. Roy Eldridge did that; he's one of my favorites. I was never insecure. Coltrane was never insecure. Herbie [Hancock] used to say, "Sometimes, Miles, I feel like I shouldn't play anything." So I said, "Then don't play; just sit there and look funny."

The only thing I'm interested in is the music and the musicians. I don't acknowledge applause 'cause I'm giving *them* something. They're not giving me anything with their applause. Can I write *that* down?

Bartok makes me sick—he sounds like a Martin Luther King speech: falderal—black bullshit! Chopin always disguises the tonic, like you would if you had on a padded bra. When I listen to Chopin, it's like reincarnation; I know everything that's going to be played before it's played. Stockhausen—I love him. Gil [Evans] says, "Stockhausen sounds like you."

Flattery will get you somewhere; it won't get you everywhere. If you want something done, there's no flattery around for that.

Women—tell them what they want to hear; whatever you think they want to hear, tell it to them.

My temper—I try to control it. It takes a lot to make me mad…They were always calling me a black motherfucker. Man, I got tired of that shit. I was sitting at a bar once in this club called the Lighthouse in Hermosa Beach in California, and it was Max's [Roach] birthday. When I go into a place, being black, I always look around for the escape routes. So, it's Max's birthday, and he's about to play. This cat at the bar says, "Max says you have to pay the bill." I said, "Shit, Max, it's your birthday, you pay the bill." The bartender said, "I'm gonna kick your ass 'cause you're a black motherfucker." It's a funny thing, 'cause I had a knife on me, in my pocket; I had just taken it away from Max, who I was living with. So Max says, "I'll leave this with you," and goes on the bandstand. The bartender says, "When I get off, I'm gonna kick your ass." So I said, "If you're gonna kick my ass, you don't have to wait until you get off—you might as well get off right now!"

…All those guys—Dizzy and all of them—taught themselves.

Some people are afraid to be famous. They're famous, but they're afraid. That's where drugs come in. Now if they didn't make drugs, drugs wouldn't be out there. There are a lot of housewives who sit home waiting for their man all day. They have to have a drug, or a mailman, or both, or they turn tricks. See, they shouldn't pick on musicians.

…Bessie Smith—she got her head cut off…Billie Holiday—she was the nicest woman in the world, you know. All she wanted to do was sing. They picked on her and picked on her to get money out of her. You do drugs 'cause you like to, not 'cause it's a lifestyle…They picked on Billie so much. She said, "Miles, come and see me in Long Island." She was in love with one of my kids and his curly hair—he used to ride my bicycle and watch the horses at Aqueduct. She said, "Miles, if they'd *only* leave me alone; they could have the house—everything." You know the way singers shake their asses now. Billie didn't have to do that. Her mouth was so sensuous; she was pretty and she would say certain words and her mouth would quiver, and she always had this white gardenia and long gloves.

Charlie Parker's father was a tap dancer. That's why he wrote like that.

There's no such thing as bebop. It's a white man's word to sell black music. Nobody started a style; it just happened. It happened when I was thirteen. Everyone who came from Oklahoma, Kansas City, New Orleans, and St. Louis played like that.

My bands—I don't have any favorites.

Concerning critics—ugh. I don't even know the name of one critic.

Which comes first the song or the joke? Or, as it may be, the joker.

"MUSIC IS AN ADDICTION"
MILES DAVIS, FEBRUARY 1978

Much has been written about Miles Davis. The press has not always treated him kindly. Its lack of perception concerning the man and the artist is at times keenly apparent. Still, it is not easy to understand the nature, persona, essence of a genius, which Miles Davis unquestionably is. Never mind the mystique; it is part of the beauty of the man.

I got to know Miles in early 1978. I had already almost completed *Jazz-Rock Fusion*...I had seen and heard him before, several times. First, when I was in junior high school, my best friend Susan, a musician, played his records for me. Later, we would go and see him play in New York City where I grew up. I saw him again in Harlem when I was nineteen; Chick Corea was in that band, as was Dave Holland, Wayne Shorter, and Tony Williams. In early seventy-seven, I met him for the first time. The following year, my very good friend, writer Eleana Steinberg, was instrumental in bringing Miles and me together. Miles trusted Eleana, and so he talked to me. He came out to Connecticut where Eleana and I live, and the three of us talked. I already knew about his cars, his love for boxing, his exquisite taste in clothes, his popularity with women, his two marriages, his children, and a much-alluded-to secluded lifestyle. Never mind what I'd read, heard, or imagined. Now I know—Miles is a teacher. He always has been; with every act, every gesture, he is able to communicate, without words, without music. He can cook like the best gourmet; he's seen and remembers all the great movies—he has, in fact, a photographic memory. He is a remarkably aware and shrewd businessman. He likes Al Green, James Brown, Stockhausen, Chopin, Stravinsky, Duke Ellington, Jimmy Webb, and Richard Pryor. He is an extraordinarily kind and compassionate man who once climbed fifteen flights of stairs to rescue me when I was trapped in an elevator in a deserted building at 2:00 a.m. in New York City. He is very patient, very amusing when he wants to be; he can make me laugh. He is serious when he needs to be, and can also make me cry. Most of all, he is a lot of fun to be with.

He has an aunt who knows all about mysticism. Miles himself constantly reveals an almost supernatural, uncanny ability to read the thoughts, hopes, wishes, and fears of those around him. He is a great innovator who has changed the face of contemporary music, and he is much, much more.

The preceding transcript was acquired and edited over a period of three weeks, with a great deal of assistance from Eleana Steinberg, to whom I shall always be indebted, and who is one of the truest and most inspiring friends I've ever had. There are, of course, many references to Miles in the book, for he has given birth to a generation of players who still speak of him with reverence, admiration, respect, and love. I can say this of Miles Davis: he has changed my life more than once. Every time I'm with him I learn something. He can always make me smile by just looking at me.

Julie Coryell

freddie hubbard

4/7/38

Indianapolis, Indiana

flugelhorn and trumpet

piano

composer

producer

Freddie, who was the youngest of six children in a musical family, began playing the tonette in junior high school, before moving on the E horn, trombone, tuba, French horn, and finally trumpet. He attended Jordan College of Music in Indianapolis after being awarded a French horn scholarship. Freddie had his own groups while still in Indianapolis, playing with other local musicians, among them the Montgomery brothers (including Wes and Monk). He moved to New York in 1960 and put together a group featuring Wayne Shorter and Philly Joe Jones. He began to receive wider recognition in the early sixties when he played with Art Blakey. Since the mid-sixties, he has been recording as a leader and touring extensively in the United States, Europe, and Japan. In 1972 he received a Grammy for the record *First Light*. In 1977 he recorded and toured with Herbie Hancock, Wayne Shorter, Tony Williams, and Ron Carter in the group V.S.O.P.

F: I started playing the tonette when I was real young, then switched to the E-flat mellophone; finally in junior high school, I picked up the trumpet. Before you really get into trumpet, you should know something about the other brass instruments, so you can develop pitch and get the feel and sound and resilience of a brass instrument. I even played the tuba and sousaphone. Also, I used to play piano at the different youth centers. I won all the contests. They'd have contests in the neighborhood at the park when I was about nine or ten. There was music in the house all day. I had a sister who played classical piano and sang spirituals. My mother played the piano by ear and I had a brother who played the bass and tenor. So the music was hot and heavy. You'd hear somebody singing, somebody playing the piano, and always a record playing. My sister also played the trumpet, and I think that's what got me into the competitive thing because she always had a better sound than me, a legit sound.

Indianapolis was a great city—it had so much music. This was the early fifties. When I was about seventeen, we had a strictly jazz band. We would take all the tunes off records, transcribe them, and set up and practice, and we formed a group.

As soon as I got into jazz and heard people like Bud Powell, it was such a challenge. Most of the other stuff I could just sit down and read, but now I was trying to figure out where they were getting those ideas from. So I sent off for some Chet Baker books; they had Chet's solos written out. I read the solos along with his solo on the record, and I said, "Oh, so that's how they're doing it." At that time, people like Charlie Parker and Miles Davis were kind of heavy for me, but I would sit down at the piano and pick out the chords, because my brother was a piano player and I'd watch him. He taught me a lot, but there was a guy in Indianapolis back in the late fifties who came to town, Dizz Hummel. Nobody knew where he came from, but he taught me how to phrase and how to play "Confirmation." So you see, I had a lot of help.

JC: How did you originally get to New York?

F: I came to New York when I was twenty. I had made up my mind at an early age that I was going to play. At first I said I'd go to college and get a degree and teach school, but right away I dug that it wasn't going to work. It was boring to me. It wasn't a challenge at all—especially in Indianapolis. So I was in a hurry to get to New York. This cat told me he was going there, and I had a place to stay, so I split. I packed up all my things, jumped in the car, and we drove to New York.

JC: How did you initially make contact with other musicians?

F: When I started living in New York, I just went out with my horn in the street. People would tell me about jam sessions and I would go. They had a clique—all the cats who were recording for Blue Note—so they didn't want anybody to sit in. But the fourth week I just ran up there, I didn't care who was playing. I just took my horn out and blasted in. I made sure I knew the tune—I think it was "I Love You." So I jumped up—I didn't even care what key it was in—nothing. I must have played for an hour. Then I opened my eyes; I looked up and saw Donald Byrd. Certain situations, though, I wouldn't get involved in. If the cats were playing something I couldn't play, I wouldn't just get up there. Before I'd jump in with Coltrane, I would go over to his house and say, "Hey, man, what are you doing? Teach me some of this before we get hung up." He'd say, "Oh, you want to learn?" and he'd play a little something.

JC: What was Trane like?

F: Well, I used to go over and practice with him. He was cool, he was quiet. But I could tell he was going through some changes. He wasn't ever satisfied with anything he played. This man would practice so much that he'd go on to sleep with the horn and then wake up and practice some more.

JC: Freddie, how do you play in tune? One of the biggest problems trumpet players seem to have is staying in tune.

F: I almost have perfect pitch. I can almost hear any note and tell you what it is. That's a gift—a natural gift. But, playing out of tune happens when your chops are getting tired. You have to learn how to pace yourself, because if you don't, you're not going to last. However, if you've got a small group, you play the head for the first solo and people still expect you to outburn the tenor player. You know, you've got to kind of have an idea, otherwise you would blow yourself out and I've done it. The most important thing is breathing; but if your chops are cool, you're breathing. If I see my chops are not going to work, I just won't play, because if you force it, you tear down tissues, and it's going to take longer to heal anyway. So, if you're tired to the point where you're going to mess it up more, then you quit.

JC: Do you think there's ever going to be another revolution similar to the one Dizzy and Bird were involved in where all of a sudden the music sounded like it was coming from the moon?

F: Well, the impact music had then is not going to happen again, because there are so many different styles. They came out with one thing and they kind of unified all the jazz musicians at that time. Whereas now you've got guys who are in the big bands in the studio, and they're all good. I was in the midst of it. I was hanging out with the cats in the Village. I was a hippie when you weren't supposed to be a hippie—before the name was even invented.

JC: Is there much competition between trumpet players in terms of technique and dexterity?

F: I always practice with saxophone players. I find when you get around trumpet players, you get into competitive playing—who can play the loudest and the highest. After you develop your own style, you don't want to get into that, because you find out that you can't. I couldn't play "The Flight of the Bumblebee" like Doc Severinsen. I couldn't play as tricky as Dizzy. I couldn't play as pretty as Miles. So, I tried to find something for myself out of all of them, and then take it from there.

JC: Can you remain a jazz purist and make money?

F: Trane's music was on the radio. He made big money. Miles makes big money. All the jazz cats I know who are making it are making big money, or trying. You have to put limits on it, though, as far as going for the money. It's still basically up to the artists.

THE
BOTTOM LINE
Cabaret
CURRENTLY APPEARING
CHUCK MANGIONE
NOV COMING
2-3 CHUCK MANGIONE
-5 CHRIS HILLMAN/DAN
6-7 NONA
10-13 YUSEF

chuck mangione

11/29/40

Rochester, New York

flugelhorn and trumpet

piano

composer and arranger

producer

conductor

Chuck grew up in Rochester, where he sought out many of the great musicians who passed through town, among them, Dizzy Gillespie, whom he regards as his "musical father." Chuck and his brother, pianist Gap, formed a quintet known as the Jazz Brothers, which lasted from 1958 until 1964. Chuck received his B.A. in 1963 from the Eastman School of Music. After graduation, he taught music for a year in Rochester. In 1965, he moved to New York and joined Art Blakey and the Jazz Messengers with whom he remained for two and a half years. In 1968 he returned to Rochester and began writing for a Cleveland-based rock group, the Outsiders. While in Rochester, he also taught at the Hochstein School of Music, setting up All-City and All-County high school jazz ensembles and improvisational courses. Later, he joined the faculty at Eastman and directed the Eastman Jazz Ensemble. In 1969 he formed a quartet in which he played piano as well as flugelhorn. Later that year he put on a concert called "Kaleidoscope," and was subsequently asked to guest-conduct at the Rochester Philharmonic in a concert of Mangione music. In 1974, Chuck formed his own record company, Sagoma, which he has since dissolved. He has also published a choral series of his own compositions designed for high school choruses. Chuck has conducted and performed with the University of Pittsburgh Marching Band, and is the recipient of a Grammy.

C: My first introduction to music that I can remember was from

Gap, my older brother and the first musician in the family, when he started taking piano and accordion lessons. I kind of followed in his footsteps, taking my first piano lessons when I was eight. Then, at age ten, I took a music aptitude test in school and scored well, and I took up a band instrument. When I saw the movie, *Young Man with a Horn*, the story of Bix Beiderbecke, that really made an impression on me. We grew up in an era when big bands were the music of the time—we weren't freaks for getting into jazz. Every kid in high school had a big band, instead of a rock band, and the music on the radio was very much instrumental rather than vocal. At the high school hangouts, I remember that the records on the jukebox were Count Basie and Chet Baker. Rochester (where I grew up) was a very healthy environment for musical growth, because there were two jazz clubs that brought people in on a weekly basis, six nights a week—like Dizzy Gillespie, Max Roach, and Clifford Brown, Horace Silver, Oscar Peterson, or Sarah Vaughan. If I had to name some music that was really influential to me—just going to the Eastman School of Music (where I went) and sitting in the middle of a Brahms symphony would change one's life, I'm sure. And hearing Clifford Brown with strings, "Lady in Satin," a Billie Holiday record, and, of course, all the things with Gil Evans—especially his work with Miles Davis—all of that was a strong influence on my love of and admiration for large ensembles. In the meantime, there were all the small quintet-type of bands—Horace Silver, Art Blakey, Cannonball Adderley, Max Roach, and Clifford Brown, and all the Miles groups—good ensemble playing where the improvisation was happening over the songs with harmonic movement, rather than stagnant, repetitive, band-type situations. I think that is very much reflected in my music today.

JC: How would you characterize the kind of contribution Miles Davis has made to contemporary music?

C: Miles, more than any other musician, has represented a growth and change of music. He has always been a leader and one who is constantly in the state of change. I love him like I love Dizzy, and there is a very great difference between the two. Dizzy created a music style called bebop and it will live forever. It doesn't have to change; it's unique and doesn't have to go out of style

JC: Do you consider the growing preoccupation with electronics in music a positive trend?

C: From a technical point of view I don't like anything that is so complex that I need a dictionary to understand it. I'm the kind of guy who is not mechanically oriented. If my record player doesn't work, I kick it. But, I think anything in the hands of a creative person is a valid musical instrument. I will say that I do not like music that assaults you with volume or that hurts you physically. But I love the electric piano, I use a wah-wah pedal with my horn, and I use a Fender bass in my group. I play an acoustic instrument—it's very obvious that the flugelhorn is that—but I like all the unique possibilities electronics allow us.

JC: How would you describe the musical climate now?

C: We're at a very good place. I think that through education in the schools, young people are much more aware of music that involves improvisation; they are much more aware of quality. When you think about all the changes that have come about since Bill Haley and the Comets through the Beatles, and the return of the brass instruments—thank goodness, with people like Blood, Sweat and Tears and Chicago—you can definitely see that new goals are being established for young players.

composers

carla bley

5/11/38

Oakland, California

composer and arranger

producer

piano

organ

saxophone

vocalist

Carla Bley, one of the most prolific composers of contemporary music, is also one of the few artists in the business who has managed to establish almost complete control over her music. Along with her husband Michael Mantler, she helped created the Jazz Composer's Orchestra and the Jazz Composer's Orchestra Association (JCOA), a nonprofit foundation to support the orchestra and to commission and record new works. She and Mantler have their own record company (Watt Works, Inc.), publishing companies, and recording studio (Grog III). Carla also helped to develop the New Music Distribution Service (NMDS) for all independently produced albums of new music, and edited the JCOA, NMDS newspaper, *Corrective News Distribution*. She has written music for Gary Burton and bassist Charlie Haden, among others. She is the composer of *Escalator over the Hill*, an opera ("chronotransduction") done in collaboration with lyricist Paul Haines. Carla has been the recipient of a Guggenheim Fellowship and has also been awarded several grants for composition from the Creative Artists Program Service, the National Endowment for the Arts, and the Ford Foundation. In 1976 she toured Europe with the Jack Bruce Band, which also featured guitarist Mick Taylor. In 1977 and 1978 she led her own ten-piece band, performing both in the U.S. and abroad.

C: I started playing piano when I was three. My father is a piano teacher and I heard everybody else working all my life and it came quite naturally. My first performance was at church,

I played "Three Blind Mice" with my little fist on the black keys. Dum, dum, dum. Dum, dum, dum. That was the beginning. All my early playing was restricted to church until I was fourteen. I played like for Youth for Christ. I played ten variations of "Onward, Christian Soldiers"; I also sang in the choir. I was the only one who could sing the harmony parts. By the time I was ten I was singing the harmony parts in the *Messiah*. I had a little tin cup and I sang "This Little Light of Mine" and whatever the audience wanted to hear and they gave me coins.

JC: Did you clean up?

C: I don't remember; my father and mother took all the money.

JC: So how did your academic background prosper after that?

C: I quit school as soon as I was fifteen years old and went to a trade school where they taught me to be a dishwasher. It was before it was the style to drop out and I was the only one who had dropped out except for the children who couldn't read or write. So, I was instantly put into dishwasher camp, and for about four years I tried to decide what to do with my ruined life because I didn't consider music as something you could make a living from and I still don't. But I thought I should learn what to be in life, what part of society needed me. So, I thought—washing dishes or being a secretary (but I couldn't spell)—and finally much, much later I found that I could play music and make that kind of an exchange with society. I should have known when I was a very small child, but I think when I was in high school, just before I quit, they gave vocation tests to find out what you were suited for and, of course, music was never anywhere on there.

JC: What other kind of music aside from church music were you exposed to?

C: Beethoven, by my father, and then I got interested in what they call sepia. That was, I guess, rhythm and blues or black music. I was born in Oakland, California, and they had a station that was really beautiful and had music that sort of resembled church music harmonically so I felt quite at home with it. I listened to the radio all the time and that was those groups that had a name, like, the Golden Chords or the Purple Chalices.

JC: Did you play with other musicians when you were growing up or did you always consider yourself a composer?

C: I'm not a player, I'm a composer. I'll compose a piece on the spot with all the mistakes right in there. I feel as if I can't think of anything quickly. I have to consider it and then I have to edit it and when I come up with something it is quite carefully thought out.

JC: Have you ever felt that being a woman and an artist has caused any conflict, and have you ever experienced any kind of discrimination based on a sexist kind of thing?

C: No more than I discovered that my parents were ripping me off by taking the cup after I had collected the coins. I don't think that way. I mean, people could take advantage of me and perhaps I am taken advantage of as a woman, but I don't know anything about it. But in my own circle, I'm certainly not.

JC: What about motherhood? It takes a lot of time to compose music and it also takes a lot of time to raise a child. How do you resolve this?

C: I never had that problem. My daughter understood from the beginning that I wrote music, and she stayed out of my way and still does.

JC: As a composer of operas are you writing specifically for singers?

C: Well, I write them for amateurish voices. I don't like trained voices; I use trained voices only as a joke. I write for musicians who sing. I don't like a person who starts out as a singer because then you are born with a voice that wobbles in the right places or something and so you spend your life making music but that is not necessarily going together, is it? To have a voice and make music could be two totally different things. So, I'd rather start with the music.

JC: As an artist do you feel that you have received the kind of support you feel you deserve from the industry?

C: No, we have our own everything. We have our own recording studio, or own record company, and our own distribution service. Everything that we wanted that we couldn't get, instead of going through life without it, we just managed to get ourselves. I am cynical about the business for a person like me. I didn't fit into what they needed at the time so it was either stop or do it myself, and I'm not alone. There are a hundred and one companies that we distribute now—all musicians who found themselves pretty much in the same place I was.

JC: So do you think that is the solution, for musicians to gain control by learning to do these things themselves?

C: I think it is important to keep as much control over what you own as you can. If you have to at some point in your life give away a part of something, then I can't criticize you, but if you don't have to and can hold on to all of your music, all of your publishing, all of your records, then it is best and that is what I do.

JC: And not to be manipulated?

C: Oh, no, I would love to be manipulated, but nobody wants to manipulate me so I have been saved—absolutely pure.

JC: Do you listen to records now?

C: No, I prefer silence. Either silence or the sound of me trying to write a piece. Those are my two favorite sounds, and I listen to my finished records once and then never again. I like silence.

JC: Do you have some kind of daily schedule that you work with?

C: Yes, nine to five and a break for lunch. I'm not being flippant; I really like to work like a bricklayer works.

JC: Do you have any interests outside of music?

C: Well, I skated on the pond all day today. We built a fire on the pond and we cleared it with shovels. Other than that, I like the outdoors, I like my garden, I like to build houses, I like to sweep the snow into piles, I like having a little say over what's around me—it makes me happy.

michael gibbs

9/25/37
Salisbury,
Southern Rhodesia
composer and arranger
producer
trombone
piano

Michael began private studies on the piano at age seven and continued them for ten years. At seventeen, he began to study trombone. He attended Berklee School of Music in Boston from 1959 through 1963 and majored in composition. He also received a scholarship to the School of Jazz in Lenox, Massachusetts. He attended the Tanglewood (Massachusetts) summer school in 1963 on a scholarship while studying privately with Gunther Schuller. In the early sixties he played trombone with Herb Pomeroy. While living in England in 1965, he played with John Dankworth and Cleo Laine. He formed his own big band for a BBC concert before returning to the United States in 1968 as composer-in-residence at Berklee. Gibbs has composed and/or arranged for many artists in the field of contemporary music, among them, Gary Burton, John McLaughlin, Narada Michael Walden, Joni Mitchell, and Lenny White.

M: I began my involvement with music when I was seven years old by learning to play piano. This was at the encouragement of my mother who also played the piano, and I learned to play piano and learned music theory.

About the age of thirteen, I became interested in the pop music of the day and changed teachers. The teacher I had for pop music encouraged me, introduced me to jazz. Some of the music he played me was Dave Brubeck, Gerry Mulligan, Shorty Rogers, which I found very exciting. At his encouragement I started playing with other musicians and playing in little bands at school and this led me to discover other instruments for myself and eventually to take up the trombone which I did at seventeen. During this time I was also motivated by music I heard on the radio. There was a jazz program where I heard some particular pieces of music that really inspired me and one of the first was the Bunk Johnson Band; a few pieces in particular were "When the Saints" which when I heard, I thought I would never, ever tire of, and "Dark Town Strutters Ball." I learned the trombone parts off by heart and also on the Voice of America, Willis Conover's program, the Billie Holiday songs he played, in particular a piece called "Don't Explain," which meant a real lot to me. My teacher also taught me to write music and I started writing little arrangements. All this time music was still a hobby; it was something I did in addition to school. At school I was doing well at chemistry and decided to have a career in science and went to the University of Pietermaritzburg in South Africa to study science. I failed my second year in science, and I got very involved with all the jazz musicians in the town and decided then to go into music. I was nineteen at this stage.

I got a job to save the money to come to America. This was 1955—the year Charlie Parker died—and I got to hear him because a lot of his music was being played on the radio when he died. I read about him in magazines, and also in these magazines, discovered Berklee College of Music, so I decided to come here. I came to America in 1959 and began my four years of studies at Berklee for a degree in music.

I came to Berklee wanting to be a jazz trombone player, but I was kind of an introvert, and playing the trombone seemed to be a real extrovert activity, so I opted for composition as a major instead. During my years at Berklee, I also got scholarships to the Lenox School of Jazz which was run by the Modern Jazz Quartet, and where I met Gunther Schuller, with whom I later studied composition, and J. J. Johnson, with whom I studied trombone, which was really nice for me. During this period, some of the music I felt most influenced by was that of Gil Evans—especially the albums he made with Miles Davis in the later fifties and early sixties. They are still a source of reference for me and a source of listening pleasure.

While I was a Berklee, I discovered for myself the composers—American composer Charles Ives, whose music to this day I am still discovering, finding pieces of his that I hadn't heard of before and getting to know the ones I have heard. Also, the French composer Olivier Messiaen; it was Messiaen's harmonic sense that interested me. There was a direct relationship for me with jazz music, especially Duke Ellington. With Ives I think it was that his music is *so* powerful and very challenging to the ear and I like this a lot. I still draw on both of these composers today for inspiration. Also, Miles Davis; all of Miles Davis's bands have been a source of inspiration for me.

I left Berklee in 1963, and after a brief stay at home, I went to England. I worked for a while as a trombone player with Graham Collier and then for a long while, six years or so, with John

Dankworth and Cleo Laine, and these opportunities gave me a good start in my career. I started playing trombone in the studios for a living, and I got to know a lot of people and started writing for John which got me a lot of publicity as a writer. About 1968, the BBC asked me to form an orchestra and give a concert. And the concert was such a success that I kept the band going, got a record contract, started making records, started doing concerts and dates at Ronnie Scott's Club, traveled to Europe with the band, and started writing for singers and pop albums in the studios. Gradually I was asked to play a little less and to write a little more. So I made a gradual transition from player to writer.

JC: Do you prefer composing and arranging for small groups or an orchestra?

M: I don't know. Composing and arranging is composing and arranging whether it be for small group or an orchestra. The things I did for Gary Burton were composition. What he wanted in the days that I was writing for him was something to play with his quartet, so I didn't arrange for the quartet, I would write a tune, a lead sheet, and a musical idea, and he would realize it for the group. When I've done things for an orchestra, there have been two processes: I would write a tune, it would be something like I did for Gary, a lead sheet, an idea, and then orchestrate it. It was two different things. The relationship to composing and arranging was interrelated, but they also are different procedures for me. I like both very much.

Writing for an orchestra is concerned a lot with colors and palettes or scope to create colors in sound. For me, usually, this is after a composition's been conceived. I need to understand the composition, whether it's mine or someone else's, and then look for ways to realize this in sound; and if it's for an orchestra, I have all these aural colors at my disposal to realize the composition as I understand it. I haven't written any compositions for a long time now. I find since I am teaching and talking so much about music and analyzing it, that I'm not composing very much. I am, on the other hand, arranging a lot these days. I'd like to get back to composing. The ideas I get nowadays are different; the goals I would try and achieve are different.

JC: Do you believe in the concept of the self-taught musician?

M: I don't think of school and learning to be a be-all and end-all, and I do think musicians can be self-taught. On the other hand, I like teaching at Berklee a lot, and I do recommend it, but it really depends on the individual. Some individuals have such strong natural talent that I think school could be harmful, but a lot of people can only find themselves in a more concentrated academic situation. Berklee, for example, is a technical school where one could come and get a lot of contemporary skills, and it's up to the individual then to go out and use them and find his or her own voice and also it's a good situation to mix, interrelate with other musicians, which can be very stimulating, and get to know something of the music world beyond school.

JC: How do you feel about contemporary music?

M: I hear this word "fusion" a lot, and although *fusion* between musics and cultures is going on, I think to label a particular music "fusion music" is to limit the music. There's a lot of jazz-rock fusion at the moment, and as long as that music is labeled that way, it always remains two musics and the fusions don't have room to take place. I know that the influences I am most aware of are jazz, a lot of contemporary non-jazz music, some classical music, some rock music; but what I put out I don't see as a mixture of all these, I don't. It's one kind of music to me, and I wouldn't want to label it jazz, rock, classical, contemporary, or fusion music. I've been to concerts that have been mixtures of jazz bands and symphony orchestras, and they never seem to work because they are advertised that way and the elements are separated all the time. If they aren't separated, if the music is presented as the music of one composer, that seems to stand more of a chance. There is a fusion going on every time somebody writes music, all the things that have influenced that writing. It's not just a fusion between jazz and classical, or jazz and rock; there are all sorts of elements going in, all sorts of inspiration and influences which come out in the composer as one thing.

msdrumsdrumsdrumsdrumsdrumsdrumsdrums

msdrumsdrumdrumsdrumsdrums**drums**drur

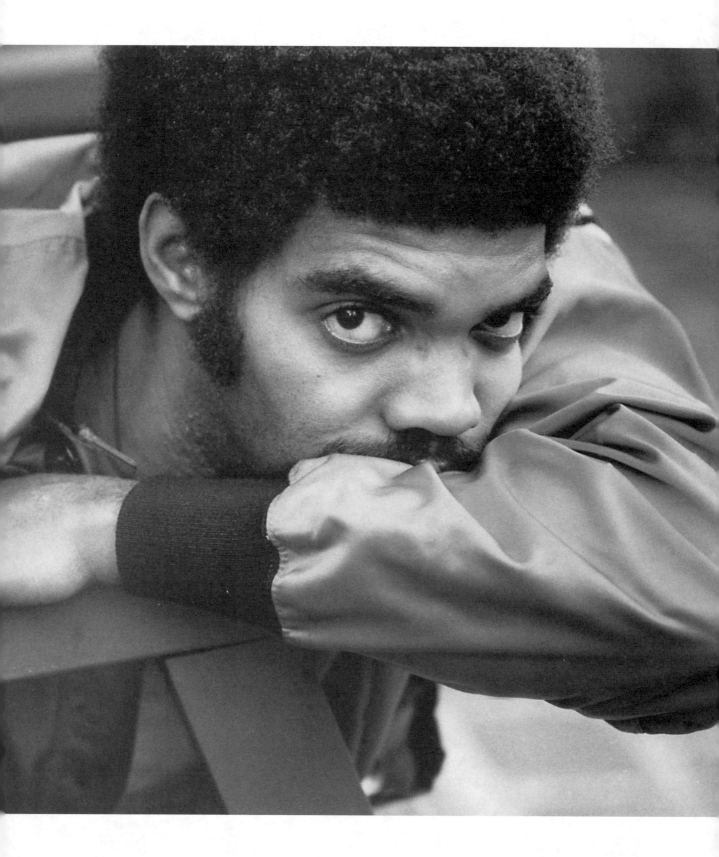

gerry
brown

11/9/51

Philadelphia,

Pennsylvania

drums

percussion

composer

producer

After spending two years at the Philadelphia Musical Academy (The University of the Arts), Gerry began to play professionally with Carlos Garnett in 1971. In 1972 he moved to Holland where he and his friend, bassist John Lee, became members of Dutch flutist, Chris Hinze's band. He remained in Europe till 1974, when he returned to America and joined violinist Michal Urbaniak, 1974-1975. In 1975 he replaced Alphonse Mouzon in Larry Coryell's Eleventh House, with whom he played until the end of 1976. He left to join Stanley Clarke's group, and then played with Chick Corea, 1976-1977. He returned to work with Clarke's own group again in the summer of 1977. In 1978 he and John Lee formed the John Lee/Gerry Brown Band.

G: I started playing the tin can. I used to take old coffee cans and cookie cans and play them. I'd pull them out and watch the *Arthur Godfrey Show*.

JC: Were your parents musical?

G: No, but they realized I was, and they took me to this place in West Philadelphia and hooked me up with a teacher. I started playing when I was just five.

JC: So you learned theory and the basic fundamentals of music at that age?

G: Just drums and the rudiments. The rest I learned in the programs in the Philadelphia school system, All-City Elementary Orchestra and Band, and Junior Orchestra. I was playing mostly classical music: Barber and Bartok, all the heavies. I didn't explore bebop until I was around fourteen, when I started checking out one of my brothers who is not musically inclined but he's got a good ear. Also, when I was in junior high school, they had this junior high school jazz band that was pretty hip. We started doing some R & B, bebop, and club gigs in Philadelphia. Then I started attending the Settlement School of Music in Philadelphia. About that time I met Stanley Clarke through the Philadelphia music programs and we started playing together.

JC: Did you and Stanley play together in school?

G: We only played together when we would meet of the All-City concerts and if there were some gigs that we knew about and could play them, we would.

JC: What kind of music were you listening to then, besides the music you played in school?

G: I was listening to Cozy Cole, Art Blakey, Philly Joe Jones, Roy Haynes, Mickey Rodker, people like that, and I was listening to Motown. Philadelphia has been, in a way, like New York. It had definitely become accepted as a place from which a lot of musicians have learned how to express themselves. In other words, it's been an inspiration. There seems to be something happening in New York and Philadelphia. They have hip radio stations there. Good jazz stations. Musically there are a lot of cats in Philadelphia, too. This high school I went to, although it was a normal high school, was very heavy into music.

JC: And after high school?

G: I graduated from high school and then I went to Philadelphia Musical Academy, and I was there for about two years. It was an all music school and music was even interjected into the other subjects, somehow, to keep our interests. If we had a short prose class, we'd get into different writings and literature and how these writings affected the composers of that time—different hookups. The jazz program at the school was really happening. The caliber was really high and the education was well-rounded and thorough.

JC: What do you specifically listen for in other people's music, as well as any musical situation you might participate in?

G: I listen for the quality in the music—what point, if any, they are trying to put across. Tuning or intonation between band members; I listen for the time, to see if people are rushing or falling behind. Mainly, I'm concerned with whether everyone's listening to one another and not playing by themselves or with themselves, but playing, you know. That's a wholesome feeling; I guess the word for it is "cohesiveness."

JC: What elements go into creating and maintaining a band where the communication is free-flowing—both on and off the bandstand?

G: I think, first of all, there's got to be a lot of love, there's got to be a lot of luck, and there should be some form of monetary help or financing. The air should be clear among the musicians about what is going on. Everyone takes responsibility on the bandstand. Off the bandstand, everyone should be on their own, but there should be that type of tight feeling happening all the time—that comes down to love. There has got to be a certain amount of luck in keeping the band together, and timing has a lot to do with it. There should be considerable support from the record company. The biggest thing about holding a band together is the money. People do have to worry, unfortunately, about keeping roofs over their heads. This society isn't made up in such a way that everything is just handed to you. We are a very competitive, free-form society, so you have to take that into consideration with the music you are playing. Of course, the main thing is that the music be unique. It should express the feelings of the persons creating it. Then, it will be communicated to the audience and record buyers.

JC: Within the last couple of years, you have played in a number of different bands (among them Stanley Clarke, Larry Coryell, Chick Corea, and now your own band with John Lee). How have the transitions you've experienced as you've moved on to new situations affected your playing, your attitude toward music and the business, and your essential understanding of people?

G: Well, I should say that my playing has just gotten better and better, and I'm happy with the direction that it's going now, and the direction I'm moving in. I'm never satisfied, and I don't think I ever will be satisfied with what I'm doing at the time. Directionally, it's fine, but I think that when I'm satisfied, I should give up playing.

billy cobham

5/16/44

Panama

drums and percussion

composer and arranger

producer

Billy played with the Jazz Samaritans, Grover Washington, Jr., Billy Taylor Trio, and New York Jazz Sextet through the mid-sixties before joining Horace Silver in 1968. He recorded for films and did jingles as well, and also played with Stanley Turrentine and Kenny Burrell. Billy was a cofounder of the early fusion band Dreams in 1969-1970, during which time he also recorded with Miles Davis. In 1971, he became a member of the Mahavishnu Orchestra. He formed his own band in 1974. In 1976 he co-led a band with George Duke (Cobham/Duke). Billy toured with the CBS All Stars in 1977, along with Tom Scott, Alphonso Johnson, Mark Soskin, and Steve Khan. He has devoted considerable time to teaching—giving clinics and seminars at various musical schools and universities.

B: I grew up in Panama and I can remember my cousins pounding on what turned out to be steel drums; this was in 1946. It turned out that's how the family made their money. They made drums and timbals, among other things. I just remember music. Panama is a Spanish-speaking country, basically, it's a combination of the English and the Spanish coming in and colonizing what was part of Columbia at one time. What I remember is carnival which happens once a year in February, and they really do a number. I don't remember so much about that but I do remember the marching music a lot. I think it has a lot to do with why I'm really into marching music and parades. I was about eight when we moved to the East Coast. My father used to play piano in a club in Westbury, Long Island, and I would sit in and play drums. I had a ball.

JC: So, essentially, would you say from your early childhood you knew this was what you were going to do in your life?

B: I knew when I lived in Brooklyn. I had to be around eight years old, 1950, somewhere in there. I knew that's what I was going to be. They used to ask you in school, "What do you want to be when you grow up?" and some kid would get up and say, "I'd like to be a doctor." Another kid would say a lawyer. I remember saying, "I don't know for sure, I think I'd like to be a musician," and the teacher would frown and say, "No, aside from that, what would you like to be?" and then I would really say, "I'm not sure," because then I didn't know where she was coming from, what she was looking for. In analyzing that for myself coming out of school and saying, "Well, what the hell does she mean by that—'aside from that'?" it started to make my interest in school wane, and only when I would hear some music would I really perk up and get into things. So, therefore, school was a hard time for me on an academic level.

JC: Who taught you to play drums?

B: I am essentially self-taught. I attempted to take lessons on many occasions with many different people and they all turned me off because they dictated how they wanted me to play, as opposed to how I teach and lecture my students. What I do is to suggest what I think might work for them and I always look upon them as being individuals and not as a blanket situation where what I say works for everybody, no matter how they play, whether it's with their feet or their hands or with their heads. Most teachers have definite rules. You hold the sticks, thus. You don't hold it any other way and if you do, I'll slap your hands. I used to say, "Well, hey, man, what happens if I do it the other way and it sounds good, sounds exactly the same?" and they'd say, "Well, then you're a freak." So I ended up being a freak.

JC: Do you feel that the system has improved?

B: It's gotten more inspired. The teachers in musical education are getting pressured because a lot of the pros are being sought after by their students. They say, "I want to play like him. You teach me." The schools are having to take a look at that situation. So what's happening is that the pros are starting to come into the schools.

JC: What about the caliber of today's music students?

B: Serious. Kids are really starting to play. They're opening up and they're asking very intelligent questions and their ears are so open and it's not just to rock and roll. They're going the other way, too, and they're playing swing. What's going to come out as a result is this hybrid music of all of it together. I'm really happy about that.

JC: How do you feel about the competitive approach to music, the concept of people trying to outplay one another?

B: If the situation presents itself, I'm always going to play as if I want the job, as if I want to work again and every time I play, it's going to come off like there's somebody out there that wants your gig and it's me, so you either play or get played out. When I come to play I say to myself, this is a chance to play and show what I can do, not overplay, but play exactly what the contractor or conductor wants me to play and maybe a little more, if I can fit it in. But definitely, give him what he wants.

JC: You were part of the *Bitches' Brew** experience. What did it mean to you?

B: The spirit that prevailed was a unifying one. The unifying spirit was Miles. He brought together a lot of musicians from different parts of the world and then would scream at them in a soft whisper, 'I want you to do this! No, don't play, play this, don't play," that kind of thing, and out of it came this concoction, this brew. I mean, it was like he was stirring a big, black pot of notes and it stands as the foundation of a lot of what's going on right now. For me, it was an education, a school of higher learning.

JC: As an original member of the Mahavishnu Orchestra, was that a positive experience?

B: That was a great education. When we started, I still didn't really understand what John McLaughlin was trying to do and also the music was very taxing on me because I didn't know how to approach it. So I used to put all my energies into it and I'd come away huffing and puffing and really, it would frighten me. I'd come off the stage and my heart would be beating so fast because of the energy. I didn't think that I could physically play at that level of intensity and get over and still keep myself together. Then, all of a sudden, I began to learn how to pace myself. It was either that or die. I started to think about it, "Hey, man, all you've got to do is just breathe and don't try to make it all happen in the first tune; take some of that energy and save it for the next tune." Music is built on hills and dales and valleys. You've got to have that intense thing, but you also have that little bit, where you just lay back and let it happen on its own. You don't have to drive it with a whip all the time.

---

* *Bitches' Brew*, Miles Davis, Columbia Records.

steve gadd

4/9/45

Rochester, New York

drums and percussion

Steve grew up in Rochester, where he and his brother tap-danced at a small club, and where he played with local musicians and bands that passed through. He studied privately with Bill and Stanley Street; later with John Beck. He attended the Manhattan School of Music for two years, then transferred to the Eastman School of Music in Rochester. After finishing school, he played in Rochester with Chuck Mangione. In 1960, he went into the Army for three years. He came to New York in 1971 and quickly became one of the most sought after studio musicians in town. Steve, a musician who "doesn't believe in labels," has recorded with artists of all styles and genres, among them Paul Simon, Carly Simon, Phoebe Snow, Steely Dan, Ashford and Simpson, Aretha Franklin, Judy Collins, Bette Midler, James Brown, Joe Cocker, Nancy Wilson, Bob James, and Chick Corea. Until the late seventies, he remained almost exclusively a session player, appearing briefly with Chick Corea, Mike Mainieri, Herbie Mann, and several others. In 1976 he became a member of the group Stuff with Gordon Edwards, Richard Tee, Eric Gale, Cornell Dupree, and Chris Parker, while continuing his heavy schedule of studio work.

S: When I was a kid of about three years old, my parents, my brother, my uncle, and I lived with my grandparents in one big house. My uncle, who was a drummer, noticed that whenever I was listening to music, I'd pick up a knife, or whatever I could to make some music, and I'd play along with the music. So he gave me a pair of his old drumsticks, and he showed me how to hold them. I used to play with records all day on this old round piece of wood that I had. I chose to listen to marches, John Philip Sousa's mostly. The family would play records, and my uncle and I would play together for hours. Then my father and brother would pick up sticks and play along with us. It wasn't pushed or planned, we just did it for fun. There were no preconceived intentions as to what was going to happen.

Rochester, where I grew up, was a great place for music. The Ridgecrest Inn would have sessions on Sunday afternoons. My whole family would go down, and artists like Dizzy Gillespie, Stan Getz, and Carmen McRae would let kids like me sit in with them. It was great. During that same period I got heavily involved in a drum corps. It had a great drum section and I got into rudimental drumming. I realized there were so many ways to play drums. For example, playing snare drums in an orchestra, which I studied when I went to college and when I took lessons, is one way of doing it, and then there's a very rudimental approach which drum corps are really involved in. So I was playing a lot of different ways. I'd be playing in drum corps using some gigantic sticks and then after drum corps rehearsal my dad and I would go down to the club where they had organ groups and I'd sit in, playing totally different, with smaller sticks. They were getting into heavy backbeat, which influenced me. Then I took lessons to try to learn reading and orchestral approaches like phrasing in order to get a very musical blending way of playing.

JC: Did you go to music school?

S: I went to the Manhattan School of Music for two years and then transferred to the Eastman School of Music and began taking lessons with John Beck with whom I had studied before. There were more playing ensembles happening at Eastman and a great wind ensemble. I really got into playing in a percussion section and occasionally had a chance to play in one of the orchestras. I was becoming a real good concert snare drummer as well as a good cymbal player which is a real difficult instrument to play. Mallets, xylophone, bells, and tympani were always harder for me to get into.

JC: After college you played with Chick Corea. What was that like?

S: Chick came to Rochester and formed a band, Chuck Mangione, Chick, Joe Romano, Frank Polaro and me. We were working six nights a week. We got into the same kind of stuff that Miles was doing and the influence came from Chick. He was real innovative. Working with Chick was inspiring and confusing; it was different. I remember going to the club one night—we'd worked about three weeks and there was some tension. Joe Romano was a real strict bebop player, like real Charlie Parker. Chuckie had been playing with Chick and was really aware of the musical power he had, Frank Polaro was a helluva bass player, and then there was me. I could play with all my might all night without getting tired but there was something that just wasn't happening; there wasn't a real blend. The tenor player was feeling uncomfortable at the way Chick was playing behind him, Chick was feeling real locked in to the way I was playing, because I was playing a very rhythm-oriented thing, and Chuckie was aware of all the shit happening and just let it go by.

One afternoon Chick said let's go down to the club and play. I said great. He ended up playing some drums for a while and I watched him. I said, holy shit, not because he was a great technician, but just the musical approach—he got so much more music out of the instrument. At that time my original set was a big bass drum, and I had ordered a new, smaller set. Chick had to go into New York for the weekend and while he was there the new set came, and, man, I'm telling you, when he came back the band was steaming. I forgot the backbeat, eliminated playing the high hat on two and four. There's a thin line between real free-form music and music that's loose where one isn't really heavily influenced. There's a thin line between when it happens and when it's bullshit.

JC: How would you compare your various band experiences with your present career as a studio musician?

S: I think it's been very musically rewarding for me to work in the studio. I'm not by any means saying I don't want to play live because I think that's just as valid. I really think that rapport with an audience is very important. Maintaining both is really the answer, whether it's recording during the day and going over to a club at night or doing some concerts on the weekends.

JC: Reflecting, then, on your role as an artist, what is your general concept of your own contribution?

S: I don't consider myself an artist. I go out there and I try to play what's right for the music. It seems to be a much more open approach and it would seem to allow me to be able to expand as the music of the time expands. I think people who get hung up in their own artistry often get into a certain style they feel is them and that if they do anything different the public won't be able to identify their artistry, which is kind of limiting. I don't think that way. I have a good time playing. I try to play the best I can. I know I can play the drums and I want to play the best that I can possibly play. I want to play better a year from now than I'm playing now, not because my artistry is at stake, but just because I like it.

alfonse
mouzon

11/21/48

Charleston,

South Carolina

drums and percussion

keyboards

vocalist

composer and arranger

producer

Alphonse attended Bonds-Wilson High School in Charleston where he played in the band under the direction of Lonnie Hamilton, with whom he also took private lessons. In 1966 he moved to New York where he studied medicine, working in a hospital, and played with the Ross Carnegie Orchestra on weekends. He attended City College of New York and played in the orchestra of the Broadway show, *Promises, Promises*. He then freelanced with Roy Ayers, Gene McDaniels, and Roberta Flack. In 1970 he went on the road with Ayers for a year. In 1971 he became a member of Weather Report, with whom he remained for a year. He joined McCoy Tyner in 1972, staying with him until 1973, when he left to join Larry Coryell's Eleventh House. Alphonse stayed with Coryell until 1975, when he left to record as a leader and perform under his own name. In 1976 he and Coryell were reunited in the Coryell/Mouzon band with John Lee and Philip Catherine. Coryell/Mouzon disbanded in 1977, and Alphonse began touring America and Europe with his own band.

A: I started playing drums at age five. I made them out of boxes and cans. I used to play for pennies and nickels on the street in front of my house. I also used to tap-dance until I sprained an ankle. There was a lot of music being played around my house, but no one was musical there except me. I listened to a lot of R & B on the radio and a few jazz records that my family owned. When I turned twelve and was in junior high school, my mother promised me a side drum if I passed my exams and went on to the next grade. So I worked hard and passed. I got a side drum and I joined the school band. I started reading and in the eighth grade, I came in third in the All-State Competition, and in ninth grade I won the award. When I was in tenth, eleventh, and twelfth grades, I came out number one, three years straight; Senior All-State with a perfect score. I got scholarships from all the colleges, but they weren't full scholarships, and the money wasn't enough because my family was very poor. So I couldn't go to college.

JC: Playing with McCoy Tyner really catapulted you to notoriety. What did playing with McCoy do for you?

A: Playing with McCoy Tyner from 1972 through 1973 was the heaviest music thing in my whole career. It was a natural high. We'd play for hours, one song—just taking it in multidirections. It was a spiritual relationship. We just went right onstage and did it—just played. It wasn't a planned set; we started playing and it just happened. Being with him as a musician and as a person was overwhelming. The musical experience was one that I had never experienced before.

JC: Right now, if there were no pressures on you in the world, and you were independently wealthy, what kind of music would you be playing?

A: I'd be playing a combination of all. I like different things.

JC: What is great music to you?

A: Great music is just good music—whatever it is.

JC: What makes it good?

A: The musicians make it good. The composition, the way it is played. How the musicians and the listeners feel afterwards. It's like what makes ice cream good—the taste. You know it's good because you like it; you get off on it.

JC: Do you think sex and music are in any way related?

A: They are related—as far as emotion and sensitivity are concerned

JC: And how do you feel about the avant-garde school of music?

A: I love it. But it is accepted more in Europe than here.

JC: How do you feel about critics?

A: Most of the critics are frustrated musicians, and they are envious of other musicians who are creating and doing things they wish they could do. The only way to attack them or put them down is to criticize them. There are some fair critics who are honest in judgment, and there are some idiots. That's just the way it is. There are good guys and bad guys. You can't let them control you—you've got to do what you feel.

JC: What do you think the main purpose of music is, as an art form?

A: Music is supposed to bring happiness into your life. Just like a painting—it's supposed to make you smile.

JC: Are you very competitive?

A: I've always been positive—always trying hard. I want to be the number one drummer in the world. My goal is to be the best.

narada
michael walden

4/23/52

Kalamazoo, Michigan

drums and percussion

keyboards

vocalist

composer and arranger

producer

Narada, the oldest of six children, began taking music lessons at age ten in rural Plainwell, Michigan. He grew up listening to music that included hard rock groups like The Who and R & B groups like the Temptations and the Miracles. Narada's earliest group was the Ambassadors, a duo of drums and organ that used material by Jimmy McGriff, Jack McDuff, and Jimmy Smith; Narada was ten, the organist, twelve. Other early bands included Distance in the Far, for which he provided the music as well as arrangements, and the Electric Flag-styled Promise. In 1970 he attended Western Michigan University for a summer semester as a music major. In 1972 he became a member of a free, progressive rock trio, the New McGuire Sisters, led by former Edgar Winter guitarist, Sandy Torano. Finally, in 1973, he became a member of the Mahavishnu Orchestra, making his first major appearance. The orchestra had recently disbanded and was in the process of being re-formed. Within a month of the inception of the new band, Narada went to London to record *Apocalypse*, conducted by Michael Tilson Thomas with orchestrations by Michael Gibbs. The large orchestra assembled for this session toured for several months, coheadlining with Jeff Beck.

After this tour, Beck invited Narada to London for sessions with producer George Martin that resulted in the recording *Wired* for which Narada composed four songs. His most recent compositions can be heard on the newest releases of Carlos

Santana and the Pointer Sisters. Mahavishnu disbanded in 1975, and Narada began work on his first recording for Atlantic, a project that continued until 1976. In April of 1976 Narada joined the late guitarist Tommy Bolin's group, touring with them until Bolin's death. Narada then composed and played on a Roy Buchanan album and produced trumpeter Don Cherry's recording in December 1976. Narada did his second album for Atlantic in 1977. That same year he put together his own band which toured extensively throughout the U.S.

N: There wasn't a time in my life— in this life anyway—when I wasn't involved in music. Ever since I was little—three, four, and five years old—I always knew that I wanted to be a drummer and in music. I used to watch records spin for hours and beat on pots and pans, or on the crib; and for Christmas I'd always ask for toy drums and things like that. I've always had a very strong pull toward being creative.

JC: You also play piano.

N: Yeah, I love to compose. I think that composition is my first love and drumming is just a part of the creative expression. I love to write music, especially melodies that everyone can just sing along with.

JC: When did you become a lyricist?

N: Back when I was sixteen. I had a very deep love for songwriters like James Taylor and Joni Mitchell. They are able to take words and express their feelings, their emotions, so it's a beautiful art. To me, that's the genius of a performer or an artist—to be able to express what you're feeling. We all feel things, but to be able to share what you feel with someone else, to be able to say what love is or how it feels, how anything feels, is the genius of an artist.

JC: I understand Jimi Hendrix was an early inspiration.

N: Yes. When I was in high school I was just flipping over that guy. He gave me such a feeling of freedom and strength. I felt that if I could play with him I could gain so much. I planned to graduate in 1970 and then go and shine his shoes or iron his clothes or do anything just to work with him, but unfortunately, that was the year he passed away. I felt very, very sad, but then I became aware of John McLaughlin, who, at that time, was starting to come on strong, and he also was very powerful and genius-like. So I kind of directed my attention toward him, and I don't know, God's grace kind of allowed me to play with him.

JC: Tony Williams once said, "It's hard for a drummer to make it in the music business." How do you feel about that comment?

N: I can only say that—and I don't want to talk about drummers now—unless you're really evolving and always transcending yourself—and we can apply this to drummers—it's easy to kind of go back into the past. That's why, in my life, I'm not trying to be the world's greatest drummer. No, drumming is just part of my life. And I think that as long as I keep that attitude and put music first in my life—the music and melody and harmony—and make drumming a part of it—as long as I can keep that attitude, then things will always be expanding.

JC: What drummers have made a really strong impression on you?

N: I remember that when I was about four, five, or six years old, my father brought an album home—a collection of drummers. It was an album of all the greatests, like Max Roach and all these different people doing what made them famous. I used to listen, and I think that that was my first impression of great drummers playing all different styles. I loved Louis Hayes when I was real young. He was eighteen then, and did an album with Horace Silver called *Pieces of Silver*. He did a drum solo, and I tell you it was so exciting. Those were my early influences as far as drums are concerned. Then I went on to love Mitch Mitchell of the Jimi Hendrix group because he had that freedom and strength, and yet he had that rock thing. I don't know, I love everything that's good in drummers.

JC: Have you ever felt any kind of external pressure to make commercially oriented music?

N: If there is any pressure, it's from me, because I feel in my life that my mission, you could say, is to play for people. If I'm given the talent to be a musician, if I'm given the talent to sing something or to play something, then let me do it for people, let me say something people wish they could say, let me play something people wish they could play. Because to me, there's no joy in being selfish. Many musicians are like that and I'm not putting it down, but it's not my way. My way is to make thousands smile. I want to express to all musicians not to be afraid to be soulful, not to be afraid to be who and what you are, because that's the magic, that's the beauty, and that's what people want to hear.

lenny white

12/19/49

Jamaica, New York

drums and percussion

keyboards

composer and arranger

producer

Lenny, who has had no formal education in music, studied art at the New York Institute of Technology. He started playing professionally with the Jazz Samaritans in 1967, and in 1968 he spent a year with Jackie McLean. In 1969 he recorded with Miles Davis on the *Bitches' Brew* sessions. He joined Joe Henderson in 1970. During the mid-seventies, Lenny recorded and played with several musicians, among them Freddie Hubbard, Stan Getz, and Luis Gasca. In 1973 he became a member of Return to Forever, one of the most popular groups to emerge out of the seventies. He remained with that band until 1976. Lenny has recorded as a leader and toured with his own band since the late seventies. In addition to his musical talents, he is an accomplished painter and photographer.

L: Music was always around my house. My father didn't play an instrument but he played jazz records, like Lester Young, Count Basie, and Duke Ellington. I remember growing up on that music and when I became older I had my own discretion in music and realized what I liked. Then I started to get into the Drifters and the groups of the early sixties. I didn't like jazz music. My next transitional period, I got out of the teenager scene and I started to listen to jazz music again but I wasn't playing it. I didn't start playing until I was about fourteen when I went to a specialized art school. I was playing while I was in school, but I went to school for art. I don't even know what provoked me to play drums. I just picked up some drumsticks and started playing.

JC: How did your professional career begin, how did you break in?

L: At the beginning I played with this group called the Jazz Samaritans in the late sixties. There was a thing in the old West, you know, the fastest gun. Everybody would go seek him out. So, if you were an up-and-coming cat, people would seek you out. Everybody was into playing and being the loudest and the fastest and I met some people. I played a lot of sessions where people would get together over at somebody's house and we'd play and the word would get out. Somebody would say, "Hey, man, he's a good drummer," and it got back to Jackie Mclean who had never heard me play. He hired me and I played with him for about a year and a half while I was still going to school. Then I did an album with Miles Davis, *Bitches' Brew*. He had never heard me play, either. I had gone to see Miles a lot and Jack DeJohnette came to see me play. There was this thing that was happening where Tony Williams first played with Jackie McLean, then he went to Miles. So everybody said that I was the next cat. I was playing this gig out in Queens, with Rashied Ali. A friend of Miles's, who happened to be there, said, "Has Miles ever heard you play?" I said I didn't know and he said he was going to tell Miles about me. So one day I was doing my homework and I got a call and it was the same guy. He said Miles wanted me to come over to his house to do a rehearsal for a session. So I went over to his house and we rehearsed for about an hour and for the next three days we played. That was in 1969 when we made the record.

JC: Tell me about the experience of working with other percussionists on *Bitches' Brew*.

L: It was a unique experience because of the fact that there were four percussion players playing at once. In Latin music, everybody has a role and it adds to the rhythmic sound, but this was different because it was a blending of the jazz harmonies with the rhythmic structure, insofar as the drums and those rhythmic instruments, of rock. We all used our instruments. We used the small bass drums, eighteen-inch bass drums, and little tom-toms and everything. It wasn't like today where we use the bigger drums. The colors were more or less the same as the jazz colors, but there was a different approach to playing that music and it was really free. Miles would say play and he'd play something and then he'd say stop. Then he'd say, now, Bennie Maupin, you play something and we'd be playing and he'd say, stop. There weren't any real roles. There was a sketch and everybody would play to the sketch for a minute or however long the sketch was, eight or twelve bars. There would be a tonal center and the rest was left up to everybody else. He got all these people who were great improvisers and put them together. We all played and there was just a blend; it was like a palette of a lot of different colors. Everybody was adding a lot of things. For that time it was really different. To this day, it still is.

JC: As one of the original members of Return to Forever, how do you feel in retrospect about that experience? How did it affect your music and your concepts in general?

L: Musically it was a challenge because it was totally different from anything I had done before. As far as my personality is concerned, I was adamant and hotheaded, belligerent and cocky all that time and I was at constant odds with Chick Corea. It took me awhile to learn how to adapt. I learned as much about life and about relating to people playing with Return to Forever as I did about music. But I've learned more about nonmusical things, which is really a groove because it helps you in the world, to deal with people, because you have to do that. You don't play music to plants. You play it to people and with people. In retrospect, I've found out that a lot of what I had to say was valid. A lot of those things shaped and changed the music.

JC: Were you aware of any peer pressure within the group?

L: Oh, yes, definitely, but it was healthy for the group. There was lots of competition. Every night a cat would play a solo and they'd say, "Oh, yeah," to the point that the audience was waiting for someone to come along to really dazzle them. That's what was happening. I totally got my playing together with Return to Forever.

JC: Can the artist control his life creatively and economically?

L: Well, you see what you have is this—you have music and you have the music business. You actually have a business that was formed and based on an art form and what's happened is that the business has engulfed the art so that the art is no longer the main focal point. The art is subservient to the business. You're thought of as a commodity, like a number, and how many units you can sell. If you're a bad business risk, nobody will take a chance with you. I mean they're into making money. That is the name of the game. It's really gotten bad and it's going to get worse. That's part of the reason why you have the jazz-rock-fusion music, whatever you want to call it. It's not a matter of guys selling out; that's not it at all. I guess people say the music has evolved. But, you know, music is a reflection of the times, and what's happened is you can't go and play acoustic piano, acoustic bass, and acoustic drums comfortably. Those kinds of bands are still happening, but they're not at the forefront anymore. Now there's this new kind of music that's been developed where you improvise more, like the traditional jazz music, but you use different instruments. You use instruments that appeal to a large audience. Attitudes have changed. You have a second transition. You adapt. Some of the traditional jazz leaders have adapted to this new music and they're still up on top, while some of them haven't, or refuse to. They found it hard to work, to achieve any sort of momentum with this new stuff. It has a lot to do with the fact that certain people control the airways and what goes over them. It has a lot to do with what people buy.

JC: Who, in your opinion, really makes or breaks an artist?

L: The people who play the records on the radio, the program directors who say I want to play this or I want to play that and they choose the albums that the disc jockeys play. They control the airways. I mean, in actuality, what you should do is you should make a record that the program directors would like. If they like it, then you've got it made. People will buy anything they hear, if they hear it long enough.

JC: Is modern music technology an aid or a hindrance to creativity?

L: Both. You have kids who come along and play three chords and they become millionaires. That's not really a creative thing but it works. On the other hand, technology has really advanced to the point where you can get great-sounding records and you can do a lot of things with instruments. Technology has progressed and when it progresses there's a point where new musics can be formed. But what happens in relation to the world when technology advances is humanity goes down, because everybody is dependent upon technological things and not depending upon themselves and their own emotions. Mr. Technology walks ahead, so humanity has got to take a step backwards, they don't progress at the same rate. That never happens, you know. It didn't happen in Rome and it ain't happening now either.

tony williams

12/12/45
Chicago, Illinois
drums
composer

Tony, who grew up in Brooklyn, played his first set of drums on a stage with his father, saxophonist Tillmon Williams. He grew up listening to all kinds of music: Bill Haley and the Comets, Chuck Berry, Elvis Presley, Max Roach, Count Basie, Miles Davis, and classical music; later the Beatles, Jimi Hendrix, and Cream. While still in his teens, Tony played with saxophonist Sam Rivers, and took drum lessons with drummer/teacher Alan Dawson, a major influence in his life ("especially in terms of precision and melodicism"). Max Roach, Art Blakey, Louis Hayes, and later Roy Haynes and Elvin Jones were also strong influences. Tony was a member of the Boston Improvisational Ensemble, "a chamber group of avant-garde European musicians who played a mixture of classical music and jazz, but not in an obvious or clumsy way" (*Swing Journal*, 1977). During this time, he became very interested in classical music, especially the twentieth-century composers. When he was sixteen, he moved to New York and joined saxophonist Jackie McLean's band, and appeared in a play, *The Connection*. In 1963, at the age of seventeen, he became a member of the Miles Davis band.

Tony left Miles in 1969 to form one of the earliest fusion bands Lifetime, with John McLaughlin, the late Larry Young, and later, ex-Cream bassist and composer, Jack Bruce. When McLaughlin left to form the Mahavishnu Orchestra in 1971, the original Lifetime was dissolved. Since that time, Tony has formed several groups and taught privately. In 1975 Lifetime was re-formed with the following personnel: Alan Holdsworth, Alan Pasqua, and Tony Newton; it lasted until 1976. In late 1976 and 1977, Tony toured with the V.S.O.P. Quintet. He has been studying orchestration "for myself, because it's something I want to get good at."

T: I started playing the drums when I was in the third or fourth grade in school. They had what they called a rhythm-and-drum class for kids. So that's really the first time I had some drumsticks. But my father would play saxophone in his band and he would take me with him on his jobs. So when I was nine I started playing with his band. This was around 1954. We played mostly dance music and the music that was on the radio. It was good. I remember after I'd get through playing a couple of numbers, all the people in the place would really like it, a little kid playing the drums. So they would give me money, and at the end of some of the nights I'd have more money than the guys in the band. I'd get thirty-five dollars in one night, and the guys in the band were working for fifteen or twenty dollars. So it was ironic.

JC: Did the older musicians accept you?

T: I could sense that some of the musicians might have been resentful. It was never an overt thing. It was all that under-the-table kind of resentment that you pick up as a kid.

JC: Did your father teach you to play?

T: No, I taught myself.

JC: Did you ever want to do anything besides music?

T: Yes, I liked to draw and sketch things—pencil drawings and I'd paint watercolors.

JC: Do you still do that?

T: No, not as much as I'd like to, although I've got the equipment and all the tools.

JC: Do you feel that you had a normal childhood?

T: For a long time I thought it wasn't, but I'm starting to really get in touch with the fact that it really was, because I led two kinds of lives. When I went with my father, everyone around was much older and I was a kid, but then I had my friends who I went to school with. So it was two kinds of lives. But I have a lot of childhood memories that let me know that I really did have a lot of childhood. I mean, I could say that I've been a child up until I was about twenty-seven.

JC: Who influenced you musically?

T: First, I think the drummer who influenced me the most was Max Roach. The first music I fell in love with was the music that Miles Davis wrote. I just heard other things in that music and liked it;

also the music of Tchaikovsky, Beethoven, and Wagner. Sam Rivers, the saxophone player, was the first guy I worked with who actually asked me to work with him, outside of my father's framework or his friends. Sam was a big influence on me, because he was the first guy I played with who was really interested in just bearing down on the music. Before that it was mostly guys who had families, and they were all weekend musicians, but this was full time. I met Sam when I was fourteen or fifteen—very formative years for me. I think I should include Alan Dawson, too, because he was a big influence on me just the way he played. Max and Alan were about the two biggest influences on drums. I studied with Alan in Boston. Boston was, and still is, a very academic-type town. There are so many colleges and universities there. I was just right in it and I could see a whole lot of people and a lot of music that would come into town. I got to see all the best musicians and meet them.

JC: How did your years with Miles affect and shape your concepts as they were realized in the original Tony Williams Lifetime?

T: When I put the original Lifetime together, it was really an attempt to play music that was completely different from the music I had made with Miles—it was a definite reaction to what I had been playing.

JC: If you were lost on a desert island and you were left three albums to listen to—what would they be?

T: One would be *Milestones*. I think that's the best of any of them. And then I would have to take…I don't know—if I had that one, I wouldn't need anything else. Paul Chambers, Philly Joe Jones, Red Garland, Trane, and Cannonball—that's a smoking record. If you want to know what jazz is, listen to that album. It embodies the spirit of everyone who plays jazz. But if I had to pick others, I'd probably say Jimi Hendrix's *Electric Ladyland*, Edward Elgar's *Enigma Variations* for orchestra (1899), and anything of Stravinsky's.

JC: Do you believe the artist is a law unto himself?

T: That's a characteristic trait of some artists. I do believe that applies to the artist to some extent. You have to be sensitive to yourself and a lot of things that you need. You have to be sensitive to all those things that you need in order to produce.

JC: Having played so many different kinds of music in various contexts, that is, with Miles, the first and second Lifetime bands, and V.S.O.P., how does that reflect upon your present music and lifestyle? Do you have any comments?

T: I feel like I'm making a new beginning—I'm forming a new band. I've gone through many changes in the past few years—good and bad—and they've all contributed to what and where I am now. I'm able to see more good in things. I seem to be able to live now the way I always thought I could.

guitarguitarguitarguitarguitarguitar**guitar** guita

john
abercrombie

12/16/44

Port Chester, New York

guitar

bass

composer

John attended the Berklee School of Music in Boston from 1962 to 1967. From the late sixties through the seventies, John worked with Johnny "Hammond" Smith, Chico Hamilton, Jeremy Steig, Gil Evans, Gato Barbieri, and with the early fusion band, Dreams, 1967-1968. In 1974 he joined Billy Cobham's band where he remained until 1975, when he left to play with drummer Jack DeJohnette.

J: I started playing the guitar at the age of thirteen, in my home-town of Greenwich, Connecticut, taking lessons with a local teacher and playing the popular music of the fifties. I would guess that my early influences would be similar to those of other musicians [guitarists] my age. People like Chuck Berry, the Ventures, Elvis Presley, and others were like heroes to me, whom I listened to and tried to emulate.

It seems to me that the motivation for playing music was far from aesthetic at the time. Playing music was, however, something that I could do that would separate me from, and at the same time involve me with, people of my own age group. Most of the people that I went to school with, whether they were scholars, athletes, or hoodlums, all had one common bond, and that was the popular music of the day. So, essentially, becoming a rock musician was an early attempt at gaining attention and communicating with my peers, while at the same time giving me an identity that would make me recognizable and individual.

Some Dave Brubeck and Barney Kessel records, along with a not-too-clear picture of my life, led me to Berklee School of Music in 1962. I remained at Berklee from 1962 to 1967 (mostly to avoid being drafted), and for at least three of those years studied with an excellent guitarist by the name of Jack Petersen, who was not only a fine musician, but an inspiring teacher as well.

Besides the school curriculum and private lessons, I received much encouragement and knowledge from fellow students and local musicians around Boston with whom I worked, jammed, and spent time learning about music and life. During that period I listened to many musicians, both on records and live. I think the musicians that made the biggest impression on me at the time were Bill Evans, Jim Hall, Miles Davis, and John Coltrane. To me they represented, and still do, a certain quality and integrity that transcends the physical part of playing the instrument itself, and enters an area that is much more intellectually and emotionally satisfying.

Two guitarists that were very important in shaping a new direction for jazz guitarists were Gabor Szabo and Larry Coryell. They brought to jazz music other influences, like rock 'n' roll, country, and folk, that gave the music a more impressionistic quality. It made me realize that there are many ways to play music and it is up to each individual to channel his or her own personal experiences and influences into a way of playing that will suit their needs and reflect their ideas and feelings.

Upon graduating from Berklee in 1967, I traveled with organist Johnny "Hammond" Smith, playing a very straight-ahead kind of jazz, blues, and so forth. It was an invaluable experience because it gave me not only a good foundation in jazz, but the confidence and desire to continue playing, to improve upon what I already knew, and to keep myself open to the changes that were bound to come.

JC: When did you first become involved in so-called "jazz-rock" music?

J: My first real involvement with jazz-rock music came shortly afterwards in 1968-1969 when I was asked to join a newly formed band called Dreams which included, at that time, Randy and Michael Brecker, Billy Cobham, and Barry Rogers. It was my first experience playing a sophisticated type of rock in which I found myself, with my knowledge of jazz phrasing and use of electronics, attempting to fuse the two into some kind of sensible-sounding music. Even though it wasn't commercially successful, I think that Dreams was one of the really important bands playing this kind of music.

In 1970 I moved to New York to work with Chico Hamilton's band. The band consisted of myself, Chico, Marc Cohen (sax), and Glen Moore (bass). With Chico I developed in many areas which included straight-ahead jazz, jazz-rock, as well as some free-form playing. I also started writing more music during this period which was something I had stayed away from in the past.

After spending about one and a half years with Chico, I was a permanent New Yorker (until working with Chico I had lived mostly in Boston) and working with anyone who gave me the opportunity to do so. I worked and recorded with Jeremy Steig, Gil Evans, Dave Liebman, Gato Barbieri, Jan Hammer,

Barry Miles, Ralph Towner, Jack DeJohnette, Miroslav Vitous, Enrico Rava, Michal Urbaniak.

In about 1973 I joined Billy Cobham's band which I worked and recorded with for about a year. The band was sort of a throwback to the earlier Dreams, but with more emphasis on playing than vocals and such. The band was a great experience for me; I developed more technique and also started to earn a better living playing music.

It would be foolish not to mention at this time the tremendous influence of John McLaughlin and the Mahavishnu Orchestra on the music of this period. The new concepts that this band pioneered, like Coltrane and Miles, set the standard by which all other bands to follow were judged.

About the same time that I was with Billy Cobham's band I was also doing some gigs with Jack DeJohnette. When the time came to make a decision, I left Billy's band to work with Jack full time. Of all the people I've played with, I would have to say that Jack is, without question, the most creative and continually challenging.

While working with DeJohnette, I met Manfred Eicher from ECM Records who expressed an interest in recording me. We corresponded for about a year in regards to this and in June of 1974 I recorded my own album for ECM, *Timeless*, with DeJohnette and Jan Hammer. As a result of my affiliation with ECM I began to record quite regularly with other people on the label: Dave Liebman, Enrico Rava, Collin Walcott, Jack DeJohnette, Ralph Towner, and Dave Holland.

JC: What advantages has working with a record company like ECM afforded you?

J: Being with ECM is an ideal situation for me because Manfred Eicher and I agree almost all of the time on the music that should be presented on a record. I never feel pressured to sign long-term contracts that involve a lot of legal issues. Being with ECM virtually eliminates all pressure from commercial success versus my ideals in music. I'm becoming financially successful since recording for them, and my own personal success is determined by how I feel about myself as a person and a musician.

JC: What kind of music are you especially attracted to now?

J: I find that in my listening nowadays quieter electric and acoustic music is by far more pleasant and inter-esting to me. I still enjoy playing loud electric guitar, mostly because of the increased sustain that's achieved, allowing for greater playing ease. On an acoustic instrument, however, you must work harder to draw the sound from the instrument which causes you to become more involved with actually playing it. I want to continue playing both, and I believe that with enough practice and playing, they can learn from one another to the point where there is really very little difference between them. I have developed, over the years, a growing dislike of certain electronic instruments, namely, synthesizers, string ensem-bles, electric pianos, and other such artificial-sounding devices. I must admit, however, that I am/have been one of the worst gadget people of all time, but I am taking steps to eradicate this problem.

joe beck

7/29/45

Philadelphia,
Pennsylvania

guitar

keyboards

composer and arranger

producer

Joe came to New York in 1963 and worked with various bands, among them Paul Winter, Charles Lloyd, Gary McFarland, and Chico Hamilton. In 1968 he joined Jeremy Steig's group, the Satyrs, about which he says: "I was never really into rock till I was with Jeremy's group, and we went on a tour with Eric Clapton and Cream in 1968" (*Guitar Player* magazine, September 1977).

Joe was an active studio musician in the late sixties, and wrote over a hundred jingles for both television and radio. He left the music business in 1971 to become a dairy farmer, but he returned in 1973 to resume his former activities in the studio, as well as performing and recording under his own name. He has composed the sound tracks both for feature films and documentaries, and has also produced and arranged for many artists, among them Frank Sinatra, Esther Phillips, Gloria Gaynor, and Larry Coryell.

J: The first guitar music I heard was a Segovia record on the radio. My mother taught piano and was aware of my musical ability because I played the banjo when I was very small. I wanted to play the guitar, but had only seen it and never heard it. After I heard Segovia on the radio, my mother bought the record for me. It was compulsory in our family that you take piano for a year from my mother, which was part of our upbringing. I was the only one out of four kids that she declared "hopeless—you're never going to be able to play the piano, ever." I ended up playing guitar instead. As it turned out, twenty years later I did learn to play the piano, partly out of spite.

JC: Who taught you to play the guitar?

J: I just learned by myself.

JC: Do you teach guitar?

J: I did when I was in high school because I needed money, but I don't ever claim to have been a teacher. I tried a few times, and it's hopeless. It's difficult for me to relate to a beginner, but if it's somebody that can already play, it's all right. But for me to teach somebody how to start to play is hard because I don't remember how I started. I didn't develop any style of my own; I listened to other guitar players when I was just a kid, and then I began listening to horn players—like Cannonball [Adderley]. They have a particular way of expressing a note. They can play a note and make it get louder after they play it, which a guitar, when I was learning to play, couldn't do. There were no volume pedals and stuff like that, and I always tried to phrase like them, but never got close.

JC: When did you begin your professional career?

J: In eighth grade I started to play bass with my brother. We had a trio.

JC: Did you feel like you were having a normal adolescence?

J: Not at all.

JC: Could you say why it wasn't normal?

J: Because I was playing in gin mills all the time since I was fourteen.

JC: How does a fourteen-year-old kid relate to that kind of experience?

J: I jumped right in. The first time I saw a stripper was in the Catskills. It was a total surprise. I didn't know what was happening. She was billed as a dancer, but everybody knew she was a stripper except me. It blew my mind.

JC: What happened to school?

J: It was sort of split between music and school. I got stuck in an advanced science program when Sputnik happened, so I had all kinds of school training in math and science as well.

JC: Did you ever consider that as an alternate lifestyle?

J: I never considered anything else. I never for a moment thought about music as a living. I was going to be a research chemist or something of that nature.

JC: Did that really turn you on?

J: Yeah, it still does. I think I should have done it, but when I got out of high school, I had this amazing tragedy with my girlfriend of ten years. She got married. I guess it was an excuse not to go to college. I started to play the guitar in New York six nights a week.

JC: How did you break into the studio scene?

J: I was the only guy in my age group that could play at the time in New York. At that time it was about the only way you could make any money. It just happened that there was a bunch of guys doing jingles who were starting out at the same time that I was. It was a very special time, and I don't think it could ever occur for a kid again. I just happened to be in the right place at the right time. There are so many guitar players now in this town that are great—it's incredible.

JC: Guitaristically speaking, who was your biggest influence?

J: The biggest influence on the guitar to me was George Van Eps. He completely destroyed me. To this day, I think he's the most eloquent guitar player.

JC: How did you develop your skills as an arranger?

J: That was purely coincidence again. A guy approached me in a bar and asked me to do a demo for a jingle. I said okay because he said he had a budget of two hundred and fifty dollars, and I figured I'd play all the parts myself and take the two hundred fifty and split, which I did; but they bought it for thousands of dollars. I ended up doing hundreds and hundreds of commercials for every conceivable instrumentation, and they paid me very well to learn how to arrange. It was another situation that hardly anybody on earth would get a chance to experience.

JC: Once you got into arranging by accident, did you start checking out arrangers?

J: I always liked to listen to arrangements, and chords were the things I listened to the most.

JC: How do you feel about the whole avant-garde school?

J: It's always put me to sleep.

JC: What elements keep you awake?

J: A groove—that's the first one, and the melody's the second.

JC: What do you think about contemporary music in relation to that statement?

J: I'm hoping that some of us can contribute to making those two things be the major ingredients of contemporary music. It's approaching it now.

JC: You have said that if you had to skip any one era in music, in terms of becoming a musician, the one you could do without would be bebop. Can you elaborate?

J: Bebop is like a competitive thing. When you get three horn players up there or three guitar players up there trying to play better than each other or show that they know more hot licks, that's got nothing to do with music. If you practice it, you can play it, and once you've done it—what's the point? I just mean that it's rather absurd to call it music when you're trying to cut somebody on the bandstand. I think trying to keep up to the level of your peers is a must, but I don't think the bandstand is the place to do it.

JC: You left the music business to become a farmer. What was behind this drastic change in direction?

J: I wasn't getting any better which was really boring, and I just didn't seem to be able to pull anything out of that. So I quit, and got a lot better on the farm without playing at all. I didn't even have a guitar or a piano up there, and the hi-fi broke down within the first three months we were there. I lived that way for three years. Every couple of months I came to town and did a jingle or something, but that was the extent of it.

I heard a lot of things in my head, though, and when I came back to playing the guitar, they were all still there. So it really worked—something happened up there. I've always been told and always believed that there's no way to practice except by muscular teaching, and it's not true. If you think about a thing clearly enough, it translates into muscular discipline sooner or later.

JC: In other words, you can send a message from the brain to the body.

J: Directly to your music without having to translate it through some repetition of it. I know that I came back able to play things I couldn't play when I left. That's all. It sure didn't come from practicing; it came from milking cows.

JC: You said you weren't enjoying your playing.

J: That was about the busiest point I had been at in the studios, and it didn't leave me very much time to play music that was of my own choosing.

JC: Would you say that being in the studio was, in some way, counterproductive?

J: Absolutely. I always have said it. If you get totally immersed in that, you might just as well give up music and sell Popsicles in the park. It's just as creative, and I always admired guys that had the ability to do it and turn down the money thing of it, and went on and played and became really good players.

JC: What about your whole knowledge of integrating music which you now utilize as an arranger?

J: Well now, as an arranger—that's different. Being able to write was definitely contributive because I was working for many great arrangers. I would steal whatever I could hear from them and try to figure out how to do it. It sounds like something original, but I think that the last original thing I played was in the forties.

JC: You've said that one of the fundamental differences between a "rock guitarist" and a "jazz guitarist" is volume. How do you feel about playing loud?

J: I love to play loud, but it changes what you play. It changes what I play in that one note has a completely different value than it does at a low level; it becomes a sphere that you're throwing around—a lead one at that.

JC: You've implied that anyone who plays fast has to resort to repetition. Why is this so?

J: To execute really fast, you have to have played it before. I don't care who it is, there is no way you can play superfast without practicing. You can play little variations on something that you've already practiced and change it slightly. This is the only way you can get by with it, but to be totally free and play it at ridiculous tempos is impossible. I don't think I ever heard anybody do it.

JC: There seems to be a real ambivalence that creative people suffer from—making money versus their art. It seems to be a very seductive thing. What's the answer?

J: Just stop the seduction. In the end, the music is probably better if you don't succumb.

JC: Generally speaking, can you define the present caliber of today's musician?

J: It gets higher every day. There is more exposure and more people are doing it. The guitar itself has gained a wider acceptance. I think it is much more true of the guitar than other instruments. I don't see nearly as many hot alto players coming out as I did ten years ago. Now it's rhythm sections, drummers, bass players, and the guitar players. The biggest jump has been in bass players, because now it's an audible instrument, and there are many bass players out there that are really incredible musicians. It used to be that bass players were the guys who wanted to play trumpet and couldn't, wanted to be piano players and couldn't, or guitar players and couldn't. They settled for the bass, because they could still play in the band, and nobody would notice if they made any mistakes. There is more opportunity to make money with music now than there used to be. There are some long bucks for some bands that are pretty sad.

JC: How do you feel about the electric revolution and the advent of the synthesizer over the last few years?

J: I think that it has widened the available spaces you can put music into. Acoustic music is limited to only specific notes at specific times. If you play the right notes at the right times, you get a C-chord, whereas if you get five keyboards all hooked up to different sounds and sound effects and volumes, it opens up another horizon or a number of them. That hasn't done anything but make music more complex and more worth checking into. I get a little bored with complexity for the sake of it. That is my main complaint with a lot of the fusion bands that you hear. They feel duty-bound to show their ability to play weird chords and strange melodies in an incompatible context. It's absurd; you don't have to prove anything. The only people you're going to prove it to are people who have already done it anyway, and people who haven't done it really don't care or don't understand it, so you're missing them with half of your ammunition. You might was well aim it all where it hits them and make them happy. That's more fun for me at least.

george
benson

3/22/43

Pittsburgh,

Pennsylvania

guitar

vocalist

composer and arranger

After three years with organist Jack McDuff in the early 1960s, George formed his own group and toured with it from 1965 on. In 1976, after a long association with producer/executive Creed Taylor—first at A&M, then at CTI—Benson had a major hit on Warner Brothers with his LP *Breezin*, the first record by a "jazz musician" to go platinum, occupying the number one slot in pop, rhythm and blues, and jazz charts simultaneously. He also began to incorporate songs with lyrics and scatting vocals with his new approach to music. An early success in this area was his version of the Leon Russell composition "Masquerade." George, who has designed two guitars for a company called Eyes and Ears, continues to be a very active musician, touring worldwide and appearing frequently on television.

G: I remember the first records I ever heard in my life were by Charlie Christian and the Benny Goodman Band, which was my introduction to guitar. Very shortly afterwards, my stepfather, who was the first to introduce me to the guitar itself, got his guitar out of the pawnshop and hooked it up, and I heard the sound that has stayed with me ever since— the sound of the electric guitar. I remember sitting with my ear pressed against the speaker of the amplifier all night long until I fell asleep, but that sound has been with me from that day to this. I was seven years old when I had that first experience with the guitar. But when I was five or six years old, I remember winning a singing contest at a street dance. From that point in my career, I was always at the demand of someone who would urge me to sing him a song. I was known as Little Georgie Benson, the kid from Gilmore Alley who had a set of pipes. I felt as if I was at the demand of the public. Somebody would always pull out a quarter or fifty cents, or offer me some sort of bribe to sing them a song. If it was a pretty girl, I'd sing it anyway. She didn't have to have money.

But it wasn't until years later that I began discovering the differences in music, because the public is always separating things. They put jazz in this category, they put rhythm and blues in a certain category. Now these were things I wasn't aware of until I was in my late teens. The thing that convinced me about this category situation was Charlie Parker, because he was definitely a cut above everyone else. After hearing my first record by Charlie Parker, a record called "Just Friends," I was convinced that I had finally heard a musician who had learned how to make his instrument speak louder than any voice could. He delivered a message that even the human voice couldn't put over any better, or even as well. So I embarked on a journey of trying to make my instrument do what he did with his instrument. It was a new experience for me because I had never tried to play to that degree. I only used the guitar to back up my singing prior to that point. I had done stints with singing groups and organ groups who were involved in what I later found out was rhythm and blues and some popular music.

Jazz music had no widespread popularity like most of the music I had been involved with. It was popular on some level; it was popular among black people or, if it was a pop song, it had widespread popularity across most of the country. But jazz music had a very limited audience. We had to search for our audience. We couldn't play our music just anywhere and get an audience. That forced me to leave Pittsburgh, Pennsylvania, which was my home, and go out on the road.

My first experience was with a group called the Jack McDuff quartet, which was an organ group. At that time, the organ was the most popular combination, especially for black musicians. It was easy to find work, and Jack McDuff was certainly very popular at that time, so I got a built-in audience by working with him. I was put in a light that I had never seen before. You had to always be on your toes, because everything you did was carefully examined by critics or people who knew what jazz was all about, and were anxious to see if you had anything to offer. So it forced me to do what I had never done, and that was to practice my instrument. Before that time, I was considered a natural, a person who had good ears who could play relatively anything heard that was within reason, that didn't require any real scrutinizing or any real technique. Jack McDuff was a good challenge for me, because he made me play the guitar. He told me to "either play it or put it down." I thought that was a fair way of putting it. Even though it was harsh, it made me think about the guitar more seriously than I had ever thought about it before.

JC: How do you feel about the role of sideman versus the role of leader?

G: My role as a sideman with Jack McDuff taught me a lot of things. It taught me how to relate to the other musicians. It taught me how to fire up very quickly in a short space of time, because Jack McDuff was not necessarily featuring me all night long. He was featuring other musicians, and he was featuring himself a lot. And so I had only certain segments where I was allowed to "show my head" so to speak, and during that short period of time I had to "speak my piece." It taught me how to cram things and how to be exciting in a very short space of time. That experience made me very valuable to record people, because everybody was trying to make that three-minutes record that could get airplay, and very few jazz musicians could strike up a solo in a limited time that would be interesting. Jazz musicians have always been allowed to build their solos. It might not happen for twenty-four choruses. On the twenty-fifth chorus he might hit something really interesting, and it might become a classic solo. But unfortunately, radio stations didn't allow us that luxury. So in the record industry, a solo artist who could play an interesting guitar solo in a short space of time was a valuable man, and I think that was the thing that led to my record potential. People who heard me on records in the record business considered me a valuable asset as a sideman on records. Even though I wasn't qualified in a lot of senses as a musician to play alongside jazz greats, there was a spot for me on records because I could play fiery, semi-funky solos that would add interest to most of the people I played with.

JC: Did you ever feel exploited, for example, in your days as a sideman when you had less control?

G: Of course. Of course we're exploited. Any man who has ever had an association with a producer has been a man who has been thought of in different lights. He's been thought of as an artist, I'm sure, by the producer. If the producer has any style about him at all, he's always wanted to be associated with someone whom he thought important as an artist. But on the other hand, he's a man who has a commitment to his peers, the people in the industry, or the record companies who he is responsible to. And they are trying to turn this artist into a person who is also valuable as a commercial entity. So, yes. But I was looking for that exploitation, someone who could do it with style, someone who had the ability to take the things I had to offer as a musician and turn them into a listenable, or an audible, or a palatable thing for the public, without taking away from me as an artist. I realize that that has been a job, or a feat, that few men have conquered. But that was the desired effect as far as I'm concerned, and a lot of other people that I know in the industry search for the same thing.

JC: Do you think that music is a reflection of the times and the culture?

G: In most cases, yes, but not in all cases. Some types of music are just designed for the effect that they have on people, no matter what period you're from. Some music is designed to reflect, and some music, without even being designed, automatically reflects. Music has different areas, as everything else does. There always will be music, there always has been music—some form of music that we can recall in history, we've heard about it all of our lives. So, I'm a man who looks for tomorrow's music too. It's not even invented yet, but we can search for it and we can shape it. We can also work in reverse.

We can also shape the environment; not only does the environment shape the music, but we as artists are shaping the environment by creating music, by bringing about music from a different point of view that has never been conceived of before. People like John Coltrane helped to shape the thinking and the design of tomorrow's music. And that has effect on the listeners, who may not be able to relate to the intellect of the music, but it does have some effect on them, and causes them to think in certain ways and causes their attitudes to change toward certain things. So, yes. In some other way or inadvertently, it does affect the listeners. It isn't a one-dimensional thing. I think that's the thing that we must remember about music. It has all kinds of dimensions and we shouldn't think of it as one entity, or a one-sided item, or a one-sided art. There are many facets to music, some things that we have discovered and some that we have not.

We have to be willing to admit that we don't know it all about music. Most people who understand music think about the theory of music, and we have to realize what theory is. There are a lot of things being tested, not everything that is being played is considered "classic," or even relates to what is known as the classics. So, if we remember that about music, I think the relationship between artist and listener will become a much more easy-going, or much more "welded together," or harmonious situation.

miles davis

carla bley

herbie hancock

freddie hubbard

billy cobham

al dimeola

jan hammer

john mclaughlin

lenny white

george duke

chuck mangione

jean-luc ponty

alphonse mouzon

stanley clarke

miroslav vitous

george benson

alphonso johnson

gerry brown

larry coryell

john lee

gato barbieri

steve khan

mike manieri & mike brecker

philip catherine

randy brecker

dave liebman

airto (moreira)

chick corea

steve gadd

joe zawinul

flora purim

jaco pastorius

philip catherine

10/27/42

London, England

guitar

composer and arranger

Philip was born during World War II to a British mother and a Belgian father. He moved to Belgium at age three, lived in Germany from four to six, then returned to Belgium, where he still resides. From 1954 to 1962 he attended school and studied Greek and Latin. Philip received his degree from the University in 1969 after studying philosophy and economics. He began playing professionally during the late fifties with American organist Lou Bennett. During the seventies, he appeared with Jean-Luc Ponty for about two years. In 1972 he spent two months at the Berklee School of Music in Boston. He returned to Europe, and in 1973 formed the group Pork Pie with Charlie Mariano. Since the mid-seventies, he has had various groups of his own. He has also performed as a soloist, and with Larry Coryell in a guitar duo, and for a brief time in 1976 with the Coryell/Mouzon Band. He has appeared in concert with Stephane Grappelli, Klaus Doldinger, and the European groups Passport and Focus, touring for several months with the latter.

P: I bought my first guitar at the age of fourteen and had a few lessons with a teacher who showed me the basic guitar chords and their symbols, and also recommended that I listen to Django Reinhardt. I then started to learn how to do variations or improvisations on chord changes. At the age of sixteen, I was playing in some local clubs with professional "older" musicians.

JC: As a player of the electric guitar who has more recently been playing the acoustic guitar in a solo context and along with Larry Coryell, how do you feel about the instrument?

P: I see it as a choice—it can be a very good one, by the way. But still, it remains a choice based on musical taste, or even on practical reasons. I feel myself quite open on this subject.

JC: How do you compose?

P: My main guide is feeling and intuition. The techniques I use are often based on a combination of modes, tonality, melody, and rhythm patterns—the usual things. But I try in every tune to have an identity which makes it sound personal. Improvisation is very important to composing, and the use of a tape recorder is helpful.

JC: How do you feel about technology and the use of electronics as far as music is concerned?

P: Some of the electronic devices, because of fast progress, become quickly obsolete and are very expensive and heavy (sometimes). A young musician starting out hears great musicians using these devices and thinks he has to possess them to be able to get "that sound." That is something which disturbs me. But still, I myself use some of them which are particularly effective in playing solo concerts.

JC: Is your music a complete reflection of you, or have you ever felt obliged to play a certain way because of pressure from others?

P: A musician tries hard to play and write music he likes himself—very deeply hoping that others will share his joy. His knowledge of music has to be rich enough for him to go on growing, and he must be organized enough to give his music every chance of being heard. Music must not try to be commercial and make concessions to itself. If it gets commercial as a result, it's fine. There is some kind of confusion between popular music and commercial music. What happens is that the public—not being composed of people who specialize in music—will remember, and like better, the music which has a groove or a nice melody. Mozart, Beethoven, the Beatles, Stevie Wonder are all popular but not commercial, I think.

larry coryell

4/2/43

Galveston, Texas

guitar

piano

vocalist

composer and arranger

producer

After attending the University of Washington where he majored in journalism and studied music privately with Jerry Gray, Larry came to New York in 1965 and studied classical guitar with Leonid Bolotine. In 1966 he played with drummer Chico Hamilton and was one of the founders and the musical director of the early fusion band, the Free Spirits. He joined Gary Burton in 1967 and remained with him for a year and a half. In late 1968 he played with Herbie Mann for three months, then left to form his own band. In late 1969 he toured the United States and Europe with ex-Cream bassist Jack Bruce, drummer Mitch Mitchell of the Jimi Hendrix Experience, and Mike Mandel. Larry has had his own groups since 1969, among them the Eleventh House, 1973-1976, and Coryell/Mouzon, 1977. During the late seventies, he has toured the United States and Europe both as a soloist and in duo context with guitarists Philip Catherine and Steve Khan. A part-time teacher of the guitar since the mid-seventies, Larry now writes a monthly column for *Guitar Player* magazine.

L: I think the first time I could identify music as such was when I was a very small boy, driving somewhere with my mother, and we were harmonizing together to a Christmas carol. My mother was very musical; she played a lot of piano.

JC: When did you start to hear music that became more meaningful to you and when did you start applying it?

L: When I moved to the state of Washington at the age of seven. That's when I first heard country music—most notably guitar, and Chet Atkins. I was very impressed by the way he played the guitar, because it was so orchestral—all the parts. I learned to play the ukulele when I was twelve. Also, my parents made me take piano lessons, which I took for a while, and then I rebelled against it because I was more athletically inclined. At that time, piano lessons still smacked of that horrible "Little Lord Fauntleroy" stigma where, you know, I felt kind of silly— I would rather have been playing football.

JC: So country music was a formative influence at that time?

L: Right. And that was a rural area in the state where this was happening. The other guitar players my age also liked to play country music called "finger style." And you usually had to wear a thumb pick instead of a regular pick that I use. It was a hybrid of styles—a little country, a little classical, very little jazz—although some "jazz" chords were utilized.

JC: When did you really start to play with other musicians?

L: When I was about sixteen—at the same time I was taking guitar lessons. I belonged to a group in high school with a piano player, a bass player, and a drummer.

JC: How did playing with other people affect your thinking then?

L: I discovered something. It was amazing that you had to play totally differently when you played with other people than when you were playing by yourself. When you play by yourself, there is just nothing to play to except your own imagination. With other people, the way they would respond to your playing would radically alter the content of the music.

JC: You went on to college and you majored in journalism. Why not music?

L: I really felt I wasn't talented enough.

JC: When did you finally believe that you were?

L: When somebody told me that I wasn't talented. It was my roommate—we were talking about Dave Brubeck, and he said, "Well, man, of course you'll never be able to work like that and be like him." That's what got me started to seriously become a professional—when that guy said he didn't think I had it.

JC: You were challenged.

L: I immediately took up the gauntlet, like a typical Aries. I went to war on the idea that I didn't have enough respect for my ability.

JC: How did you get yourself together?

L: Here's how I did that—I just stopped doing my scholastic studies and studied nothing but music—day and night. I just hung around with the best musicians I knew of in that particular town, and went to every jam session. I just never slept—I wrote music, studied it, and played it constantly. I listened to a lot of jazz, then bebop, and can remember hearing "Donna Lee" by Charlie Parker. I'll never forget the first time I heard a trumpet player and a saxophone player playing "Donna Lee" in unison. After I got off the floor, I said, "That's for me—I've got to learn how to play that!" That's when Coltrane was doing his best stuff—right after he left Miles. I would listen to the music and it would lose me—like "Chasin' the Trane"—that particular blues. At age eighteen, I just wasn't mature enough to understand it, but yet it had a special mysterious sound. Even though I didn't comprehend it, I knew it was important.

JC: Did moving to New York affect your music?

L: New York represented two things: the old jazz tradition, because all the great players were there, and something new, because Bob Dylan and the Beatles were just happening then, and I felt that New York was kind of going to have something to offer in the way of non-jazz music as well. I always admired rock and roll, and I loved to play blues—especially string-bending. Jazz was always the first priority. I never confused the musicality and the integrity of jazz with the spirit and different rhythmic infusions of rock.

JC: Infusions, you say?

L: Yeah, because at that time, jazz was dotted eighth note and sixteenth note type of time—almost like a perverted straight eight. And I felt that one of the groovy things about rock was that it was more related to Latin music and had another kind of syncopated sophistication that jazz had kind of squeezed out of that dotted eighth and sixteenth thing. I felt it was only a matter of time before somebody who liked Elvin Jones could also like George Harrison.

JC: Was Jimi Hendrix a main influence on you?

L: Jimi was a main influence on everybody. The reason a lot of people compare me to him is because we both admired a lot of the same blues, and we were also the same age. He was really the best electric guitar player I ever saw.

JC: The Free Spirits was one of the earliest fusion bands to record (1966). Tell me about its inception.

L: The Free Spirits came about as a result of five tripped-out cats—Columbus "Chip" Baker, Jim Pepper, Chris Hill, Bobby Moses, and myself—from all parts of the world who moved into the same block of the same neighborhood. We felt that we would be ten years ahead of our time if we made the music we wanted to

JC: Which was what?

L: What later became known as jazz-rock.

JC: How was that music, which is so commercial now, received then?

L: Nobody understood it. As a matter of fact, the Free Spirits album was appreciated more in Europe, especially Denmark, than it was here.

JC: Electronics was an integral part of your music in the late sixties and seventies—is its use still as valid for you now?

L: Yes. What has happened is that I have transferred this "integration," if you will, from older techniques that were used *before* they invented things like the Mutron Bi-Phase, or all the various pedals, and so forth. What I used to do was take a hollow-body electric guitar, face it close to the amp, and squeeze feedback out of it, controlling it to various degrees by moving my body this way and that…But now I'm more inclined to push a button, or a combination thereof, to get nothing like the old effect, but a modern rainbow of noise-sounds over which I have much more control. To answer your question, electronics is valid to me. However, getting so extensively involved in it for the last decade has made me come full circle back to the purer form of guitar—acoustic guitar.

JC: When you finally made a choice to start pursuing the acoustic guitar—privately and publicly—do you remember this being a specific change, a dramatic change?

L: I remember very well because I had built up all this momentum as an electric player, and I saw that I couldn't go in and play acoustic one hundred percent right away. I was slowly going to have to break it in because I didn't know how to "get off" on the acoustic, to use a coarse term. I knew it would take me a long time to learn how to play it, so I didn't become a basically acoustic player until recently.

JC: Your role as a teacher has been steadily developing over the last few years. In addition to giving private lessons, you write a monthly column for *Guitar Player* magazine; you've made an instructional record for GPI. How do you feel about being an educator?

L: I feel very good because I liked learning things, and the best way to learn is to be a teacher because the teacher always seems to learn more than the student. I enjoy the experience of writing about music since I have always liked to write, but really didn't have anything to write about. Now that I have put in so many years as a musician, I feel qualified to write about my experiences in that so much is of an educational nature. So much of it is of a self-satisfaction in teaching someone something. It's a very good feeling.

al
dimeola

7/22/54

Jersey City, New Jersey

guitar

composer and arranger

producer

Al grew up listening to all kinds of music. He was especially influenced by his father, whose love for Italian classical music made a strong impression on him as he became aware of its melodic and emotional content. He did, however, find it very "unrhythmic," and was subsequently drawn to Spanish and Latin music, "to fill in that gap." He attended the Berklee School of Music in Boston for a brief time in the early sevenites before becoming a member of Barry Miles's quintet. In 1974 he joined Return to Forever, replacing guitarist Bill Connors. He left Return to Forever in 1976 to form his own band and record under his own name. Al, who travels to all parts of the world to gain inspiration and observe different cultures and lifestyles, says, "Going away to write has become very important to me" (*Guitar Player* magazine, February 1978). He has, to date, made yearly trips to France, Italy, Spain, and Brazil and has plans to travel to Egypt and Turkey.

A: I started playing when I was eight years old and began studying with a jazz guitarist. At that time I was introduced to many forms of music while listening mainly to the music of the Ventures, Elvis Presley, the Beatles, and so on. My teacher, though, had influenced me a great deal with his knowledge and ability and theory and technique. My style developed as it did because of the early introduction to different forms of music through formal training in the home where records of everything from rock and roll to classical and Italian were played. Later on I went through a period where country music was the thing to play. That helped me develop my picking technique, but then all of a sudden I fell in love with jazz, Latin, and classical music. That changed my approach to the instrument and my views on life. I later met Larry Coryell who influenced me because his approach back then was so unique. His approach definitely gave me confidence to continue in my direction. In that same period I ventured into New York City many times to see and hear Larry and many other jazz artists play. Hearing musicians that turn you on musically and then seeing them live was a real thrill. It was a great turning point for me.

JC: When did you start composing?

A: I composed on and off for years when I was in high school, but not seriously until I was nineteen. At nineteen I was asked by Chick Corea to contribute a composition for each album. By performing, recording, and rehearsing with Chick and the band, my ideas for composition developed rather quickly.

JC: How important was music school?

A: Extremely important. All of the classes were closely related and provided me with a thorough background in jazz and related studies.

JC: Has dealing with your early success been a problem for you?

A: Yes and no. I find now that the business end of music takes up a great deal of my time, but on the other hand, I'm getting educated in this area, and feel comfortable doing so. The successes have been rewarding and that gives me strength to continue with what I'm doing.

JC: What are your future musical goals?

A: One future goal I have is to compose and record a guitar concerto. Another goal is to make the music I play commercially acceptable to millions of people without sacrificing aesthetic quality.

JC: Is the road counterproductive or productive?

A: On the road I am performing and directing musically and I am meeting with musicians and people around the world in and out of the music business. Also my music is being played in front of new audiences and longtime fans. All of this can make touring a very productive experience. But you also have to get in shape for the road. It's not easy. You have to audition, rehearse, then tour. When that's over you have to write new songs, then rehearse again, and finally record. And since I'm the producer, I have to be there one hundred percent of the time. It's really four different occupations rolled into one, with each one being an extremely productive stage.

JC: It's a tremendous amount of responsibility.

A: Yes, but if you love what you're doing and you want everything you do to attain an extremely high quality, you must be there all the time. You have to overlook each stage to make sure there are no screw-ups.

JC: How do you feel about technology and the use of electronics in music?

A: If of course done well, watching a guitarist execute certain effects like ending notes or playing percussively without the use of any electronic device definitely creates a certain amount of excitement. A synthesist has to change a dial to create such a sound. On the other hand, when listening to a record, synthesizers can create beautiful colors, and their variety of sounds are multiplied due to the fact that technology has advanced in that area much more than it has for a guitarist. I feel that synthesizers are playing a major role in most modern music, and I feel that my music benefits greatly from the additional sound and color differences. Electronic hookups for my guitar don't seem to impress me right now too much, mainly because I prefer leaving my guitar sound natural.

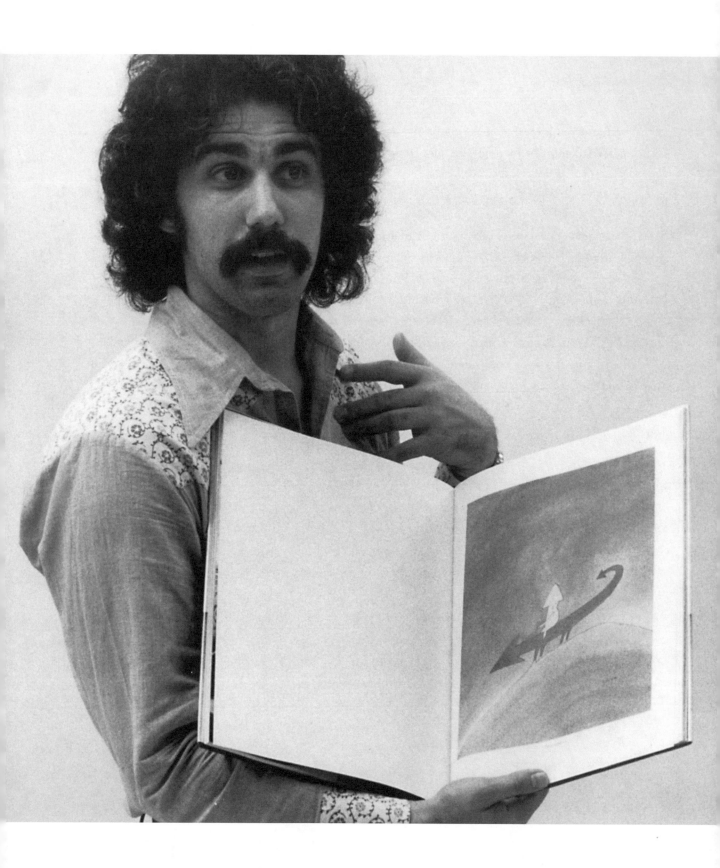

steve
khan

4/28/47

Los Angeles, California

guitar

composer and arranger

producer

Son of lyricist Sammy Cahn, Steve grew up in California and received his B.A. in theory and composition from UCLA in 1969. In January of 1970, he came to New York where he played with vibist David Friedman. Steve became active in the studio in the seventies while playing and recording with the Brecker brothers, Steve Marcus, and Larry Coryell, both in the United States and Europe. While continuing his work as a session player, in 1977 he toured and recorded with the CBS All Stars, a group that included Billy Cobham, Alphonso Johnson, Mark Soskin, and Tom Scott. He is presently working and recording under his own name as a leader. Steve, who teaches guitar, has transcribed the solos of the late guitarist Wes Montgomery and published them as the *Wes Montgomery Guitar Folio.*

S: I started playing the guitar when I was twenty. I was in college studying psychology and I suddenly realized that the guitar was my instrument and that I wanted to play, so I got a teacher and changed my major to music. I played the piano when I was five, hating every minute of it. I was a mimic and I'd sort of manipulate the teacher into playing the passage and I'd watch real carefully and I'd learn how to do it. I'd practice but it was like being in a concentration camp. I didn't really learn to read music until I changed my major to music in college. That's where I really started to have an association with quarter notes.

JC: What then is your opinion of music school based on your own experiences?

S: What I was learning in music school didn't somehow exactly relate to what I was hearing on the records. When I had teachers they didn't actually help make any more sense for me either. It's just the way classical music is taught. I mean classical music's A minor seventh doesn't have anything to do with John Coltrane's A minor seventh. The language they use, it's like they're two different things. So what I decided to do was take it upon myself and just make up my own system of organization for understanding and that's why I started putting together my own fake books of tunes and taking things off of records and really trying to understand the language; not disregarding classical theory but just to put it in some order that made some sense to me. It took awhile. It took a long time. It really started to make some sense to me. I was playing and I was very lucky; I got to play with some big people.

JC: Was it ever intimidating?

S: Oh, yeah, I was very defensive about music. I rejected a lot of things because I wasn't sure who the hell I was, what I sounded like, what I played like. I think in the last two years it sort of straightened itself out. I have my own worth and my own sound.

JC: Now that you have become a teacher as well as a player, what qualities do you notice most in your students?

S: Students will sort of always be the same, looking for the easiest possible way out, how can I get all this stuff and do the least amount of work. Also, some of them like to become perpetual students without sort of standing for whatever it is they are as individuals, whatever they are, their own worth as a person. My purpose was to try to give them as much information as possible in as scientific a way as possible so that they could take that information and play like themselves. Some of them fought me on it; like to some I was making it too simple, destroying certain mysteries about things…playing a D minor chord forever in a Dorian mode is generally the right one and these are the right notes, that's how you play them. Those are the same notes Coltrane played; here they are. Some people don't want to believe that's what it is, that it's that simple. The magic is in the way you play those things.

JC: What part do you think drugs play in music?

S: I think they probably play a bigger part than they have to. Maybe it's just part of the perpetual New York or musician mystique. That somehow is just part of it. I don't know if it helps or hurts. I always found that when I was high on any number of things that I had great ideas but I couldn't play them. I'd be hearing the greatest things, but I'd have no facility, no control. I couldn't execute anything. The way I feel about playing now is I love to play so much that when I get up there to play, it's like a real intense experience for me. Lots of levels of feelings come out when I play now and I'm happy that that's happening. I don't know if anything, a drug or a couple of drinks…I don't think they're going to help it.

JC: You've done a lot of writing. When did you first develop this part of your musical personality?

S: I think I really tried to write when I was in my last year of college. I used to think it was easy to write; writing was different then. Everybody played nine hundred choruses, those kind of tunes that were happening. Then everything changed. Generally, I find I write more than I have to. Just sit down and write.

JC: Do you write on the keyboard or guitar?

S: I sort of write a little bit on each. It seems more melodic when it comes from the keyboard because I have less facility. When I compose it just seems like there's certain things you should do and there's certain things you shouldn't do and I don't write things anymore where the tendency is to overindulge yourself as a player. I try to keep within the framework of the piece of music. There's enough room for a couple of people to stretch out into lots of different melodies and contrasts that are in the music that make it interesting to play. I try to make it a well-shaped thing where the solos are part of the whole. I guess I've learned by just listening to other people's writing, and if something sounds successful, I try to understand why.

earl
klugh

9/16/53

Detroit, Michigan

guitar

composer

Earl, who switched from the piano to the gut-string guitar at age ten, once described himself as an "unorthodox guitarist," in that when he plays sitting down he rests his guitar on his right knee instead of his left. Essentially self-taught, he credits Chet Atkins, George Van Eps, and Laurindo Almeida as early influences. Earl was sixteen years old and giving guitar lessons in a music store in Detroit when he was hired by Yusef Lateef. At seventeen he met George Benson at Bakers' Keyboard Lounge in Detroit and joined Benson's quartet shortly thereafter. "George really helped to bring time and swing to my playing," says Klugh (*Guitar Player*, July 1977). He remained with Benson for fourteen months, before leaving to play with Chick Corea's Return to Forever for two months. In 1974, Earl went on the road with George Shearing, before embarking on a career as a leader and recording artist in 1975.

E: My first introduction to music, I think, was really as early as three years old, when my parents bought a piano. I played it until I was ten, when I picked up the guitar.

JC: When did you begin to improvise?

E: When I was about sixteen. It's always been improvisation, because I learned how to play to a great extent from listening to records, which is sort of a haphazard way of learning. You get involved in a lot of things, but I think my first real experience of improvisation came after I met Yusef Lateef. I was sixteen at the time, and he was getting ready to do an album, including me on it. It was during that time that I figured I should become acquainted with something beside the way of playing that I had been exposed to, and I started listening to piano players, horn players, and more jazz-oriented guitar players—trying to play some of the things I was hearing. Up until that time, when I learned a piece, I would just learn it verbatim—I wouldn't improvise on it.

JC: Did you practice scales when you were learning to play the guitar?

E: No, I never practiced scales. You don't play scales when you're playing music. I never practice anything I wouldn't play. I practice lines, things that I would actually use. You're only going to do what you practice, so you might as well practice what you want to do.

JC: What about sight reading?

E: I'm not a good reader, especially when it comes to reading syncopation.

JC: How have you managed to get through gigs where there was a lot of emphasis on reading syncopation—for example, when you played with Chick Corea?

E: I just had to memorize the music. It was hard to do, but I could do it if I applied myself.

JC: You taught guitar when you were sixteen. Did you teach your students to play scales or to read?

E: Only basic things that everybody should know. I approached it the same way a folk guitar teacher would; that is, I would use diagrams to communicate what had to be said.

JC: How did your association with George Benson begin?

E: I met George through a friend of mine who he was staying with one time. I got together with him, and we sat down and played for an afternoon. George stayed in town for ten days, and by the end of that time, we were really good friends. When it came time for him to do his next album, he included me on it, and that's how my professional association with him began. Then, about a year later, I joined his band, and I stayed with him for about fourteen months. I would say that George was the most important person as far as my development as a player and performer is concerned.

JC: When did you begin to compose?

E: I became really interested in writing as a result of my association with Chick Corea, who I worked with for about four months in the early seventies.

JC: How do you compose?

E: Mainly on the guitar right now. Although in the next couple of years, I really want to get my piano together enough so I can compose more on the piano, just to give me another outlet. But, I think that basically I try to work with an idea. First, I try to work out whether it's a melody, or a series of chords, or a combination of the two.

JC: Why have you chosen the acoustic classical guitar as your instrument?

E: One reason is because I started on it, and the further along I went, the more I liked it. I really don't have any preference as far as listening to other players goes, but for myself, I think it's really allowed my personality to come through.

JC: There is a lot of emphasis right now on selling records, especially for the jazz-inspired musician. Have you ever felt any pressure in that area, or have you more or less felt in control of your own artistic direction?

E: I've felt pretty much in control of it. However, when I finally got my first record contract, it was something that I had been wanting for so long, I had to realize that my longevity in the business had something to do with the amount of records I could sell; so I think it was more of a consideration on my first album. Once I realized that I had sold enough albums to do what it was I wanted to do, while continuing to build an audience for myself, I became more comfortable knowing I could sell albums. There are other courses I could have taken to sell more records, I believe, but I think you have to be real with yourself and know there is a market for what you're doing, and if so, then to do that well.

john
mclaughlin

1/4/42

Yorkshire, England

guitar

piano

composer and arranger

producer

John, who is essentially self-taught, heard Django Reinhardt when he was fourteen and "started using a pick instead of just my fingernail. Immediately I tried to play like Django" (*Guitar Player*, February 1975). John had his first band in school when he was fifteen. Embarking on a professional career in music, he was exposed to all kinds of music from R & B to avant-garde jazz. In 1963, he played in the one club in London where "everyone played"—Jack Bruce, Ginger Baker, Mick Jagger (then the vocalist with Alexis Korner), and Eric Clapton (then with John Mayall). He also played with Brian Auger and with the late Graham Bond. In 1968 he emigrated to the United States to become a member of the original Tony Williams's Lifetime. He was also a main contributor to the historic Miles Davis fusion sessions in the sixties, *In a Silent Way* and *Bitches' Brew*. In 1971 John formed the Mahavishnu Orchestra, a group which originally consisted of Billy Cobham, Rick Laird, Jan Hammer, and Jerry Goodman. One of the earliest fusion groups to enjoy major critical and commercial success, the Mahavishnu Orchestra went through several changes in personnel before finally disbanding in 1976. McLaughlin was one of the first guitarists to utilize a guitar synthesizer, a device that provides a synthesizer for each string of the guitar. Additionally, Mahavishnu was one of the earliest bands to utilize multiple keyboards and the electric violin. In 1976 McLaughlin formed Shakti, and all-acoustic group composed of Indian musicians that embraced the essence of Indian improvisation, sparked by McLaughlin's work on a guitar he designed with raised frets for easier bending to simulate an authentic sitar sound. In the spring of 1978, McLaughlin disbanded Shakti and began touring with a new electric band, The One Truth Band, featuring John McLaughlin; Stu Goldberg, keyboards; Woodrow Theus (Sonship), drums, Tom (TM) Stevens, bass; and L. Shankar, violin.

J: When I was seven years old and I heard the last movement of Beethoven's Ninth Symphony [the choral movement] on a seventy-eight record, it made my hair stand on end and gave me goose bumps. That was the first indication of what music could do to someone—namely myself. It was a message to my heart and soul more than anything—just the fact that if music could have this kind of effect on me, it could have an effect on anybody. I was only seven, so I didn't stop to consider what was happening to me, but there was always music in the house, so fortunately the experience was repeated. It used to happen every time I listened to it, and when I started discovering Mozart, Schubert, and so on, and I realized that I could make music myself, that was quite a wonderful discovery. There was a piano in the house and my sister was learning piano, but of course when you hear someone else playing you don't get the impact that music is really magic; but when I was nine, I realized that I, too, could hopefully make music. So I started studying piano, which I continued to do until I was eleven or twelve. By this time, the guitar came into the house, which was the beginning of another story.

JC: So as far as your early education was concerned, were you primarily self-taught?

J: Yes. I taught myself until I was fourteen and heard flamenco music for the first time. It had a great effect on me. I saw similarities to blues music—a lot of it was improvised from flamenco, and the mood and motion were very clear-cut. I started sitting down and realizing I couldn't do too much on my own, so I began taking guitar lessons. I studied for about a year and a half, but by that time I had heard Django Reinhardt, Tal Farlow, and then finally, when I was about fifteen or sixteen, Miles Davis and John Coltrane, which was a revelation and really changed the shape of my direction. By the time I was sixteen, I was very deeply involved in the jazz movement and jazz music, and I got a job touring with a traditional jazz band, and that's when my professional career started.

JC: Would you say that when you went professional, you left your adolescence behind you?

J: I'm still trying to lose it.

JC: Your adolescence?

J: Yes.

JC: What motivated you to come to America?

J: I was motivated to come to America since I first heard blues—and later jazz. New York was the center of the world to me—jazz music is the real indigenous art form of America, the only real art form of America, it appears to me. The rest is sort of European-extended forms of art. But jazz is particularly American, and it's a so-called synthesis of African and European harmony. It's not just that, because it is a form in its own right, it's an art to me. For me, America was a dream.

JC: When you finally got here, how did the reality compare to the dream?

J: It was even greater than I dreamed. It was unbelievable—a fantastic country—alive and intense, vibrant, just dynamic.

JC: How did you feel about the music you were making then? Tony Williams being your first introduction to the scene at large—were you completely overwhelmed by the fact that this opportunity had been given to you?

J: Yes, but I realized, and I have realized since, that if you love something enough, it will come to you—sooner or later. That didn't take away my wonder and the sense of awe at being here. To the contrary. In fact, I don't think I really even thought about it; I just think about it in retrospect. But the fact that I was here was awesome, the fact that America truly existed as a continent and not just a figment of my imagination. I was very fortunate because I came over to play with Tony Williams who I considered then, and still consider, to be one of the great musicians of jazz—he's a real artist. Jazz is a much maligned word, but nevertheless, for purposes of simple classification, we use it. And so, through him, I met Miles Davis who was certainly one of my boyhood heroes.

JC: How would you describe your initial association with Miles?

J: Nerve-wracking—because I found myself after two days in the same recording studio as Miles Davis, and I was very nervous simply because this man had lived inside of my imagination, inside my record player for so many years—suddenly to be confronted with the actual reality, it was quite disturbing emotionally, but not in an unpleasant way.

While I was recording and playing with Miles, I was working with Tony Williams's Lifetime,* which was a completely new form and which I felt very happy about. It was a new direction which I was really a contributor toward, and this contrasted to working with Miles, where I wasn't a contributor except under his own terms. This was fine, because his own terms were very educational to me—so I had the best of both worlds. I learned so much in one year; it was astonishing to me. You don't discover it at the time; it's only later that you discover how much you moved forward in the evolution of time.

---

* A band which included Williams, McLaughlin, bassist Jack Bruce, and the late Larry Young on keyboards.

JC: So at this point were you consciously or unconsciously developing concepts that you would later use in Mahavishnu?

J: Absolutely. I think it was conscious. I think it works on both levels: I was conscious of the fact that what I wanted to do, the way I wanted to play, nobody was doing; but it took the years I spent with Tony and with Miles to give me the possibility of giving birth to the form that I wanted to use, which was, I guess, primarily expressed in the first Mahavishnu orchestra.

JC: In retrospect, looking back at Mahavishnu, could you describe that experience of having your own band, making your own music, going from the role of sideman to the role of leader—being totally in control?

J: Is one really ever in control? I wonder about that. I really wonder. It is good to be able to, at least, have things go your own way to a degree. It's very satisfying; it's a very growing process, too, because with your own group you have an idea, a conception of a particular piece; you can give birth to it quickly, and in the process of creative work, invariably the physical expression, the outer expression of the conception, falls far short. What actually happens and what you conceive are quite far from each other—the concept is always as perfect as possible, but how it works out is frequently imperfect. But because you have the opportunity instantaneously, more or less, of giving vent to your particular creative impulses, you very quickly learn the limitation of people, yourself, and your concept has a real possibility of growing because there are some things that you write when you hear them back, you don't like it at all. This has happened to me, but you don't discover it until you hear it come back at you. So it's really a very quick way of learning, evolving as a musician. You realize your dreams and find that your dreams are not too good, not too perfect—and then find that the articulation itself is even less perfect.

JC: What specifically motivated you, then, to go from one very definite image that you had created with Mahavishnu, to the acoustic Shakti?

J: It's not that I have gone about creating an image for myself; we all have an image. I have an image for myself, but it constantly changes. The fact that it crystallized in the media is something I can't even concern myself about. The image that people have of me is their business. That's up to them. My concern is what moves me from within, and what direction the music itself demands that it take. If I don't take heed of the demands that music makes on me, I am a fool. Furthermore, I don't think I am really being honest with myself, and so it is the most natural thing in the world, because the music is calling the shots to me and I just listen. The record companies—they don't know what the shots are. They know that I am just making what is to them outwardly a radical change. And really, it is not radical at all, simply a movement, a step forward in the right direction. But people—the world—don't change, even though change is absolutely inevitable for everybody. It's just the world—if it's something good, they try and hold it; but when you try and hold on to something, it turns to dust finally.

JC: How do you feel about competition in general?

J: Listen, I am like every other artist and like every other person—I want to be loved, admired, and respected, and given accolades and awards from everybody. That's one part of me. But there is another part of me that says, "That's absolutely ludicrous—your primary concern is to perfect yourself as a musician and to learn how to live more deeply and more profoundly and more clearly, in order that the music you do will become more profound and more clear." And so I realized that, in Shakti, just leaving an electric band and making an acoustic one is an example of how the two directions can work against each other as far as polls, record sales, as far as whoever is concerned—they see me as burrowing underground, becoming esoteric and all that nonsense. But I know what I need as a musician, and there are all phases of life, so many phases. It's like you talk to a Cubist painter, and he is a Cubist for about five years; then suddenly he moves and they say, "Why aren't you painting cubes anymore?" I mean, he says, "Why? I don't feel like it anymore." You just can't expect a man to continue, a man has to paint what he feels, and it's just like that. I can't help the fact that some people feel a little alienated because of the way I am moving musically. But that is their problem, not mine. The fact that it affects me financially is incidental and secondary. I think competition is healthy. I don't feel that anybody is competing against me. Quite frankly, I welcome competition. I mean, basically you go back to desire, wherever it is. If your desire is great, your achievement will be great, and a little competition can sometimes hone your desire quite acutely. If you apply that in a positive way, insofar as your work is concerned, it makes you work—that's good. Competition exists on a certain level and you cannot deny it. But it exists for a good reason and not for a bad one. People translate it into a negative fact of life, and I don't believe that anything is negative in life except what man makes negative.

JC: You were one of the pioneers in the jazz-rock movement. How do you feel about contemporary music now in the light of what you did?

J: How do I feel about jazz-rock? Boring! It bores me to tears; it just doesn't go anywhere. I haven't heard any since the original band. I am biased obviously. I listen to all kinds of music—I want to be moved—where are you going to touch me? On what level will you touch me—on a superficial level or on a deep level? Nobody makes the attempt to touch me on a deep or profound level, and I am dissatisfied and bored with the superficiality and mediocrity that comes out through the media. I am really bored with it; I never listen to it, never. I don't want to hear it.

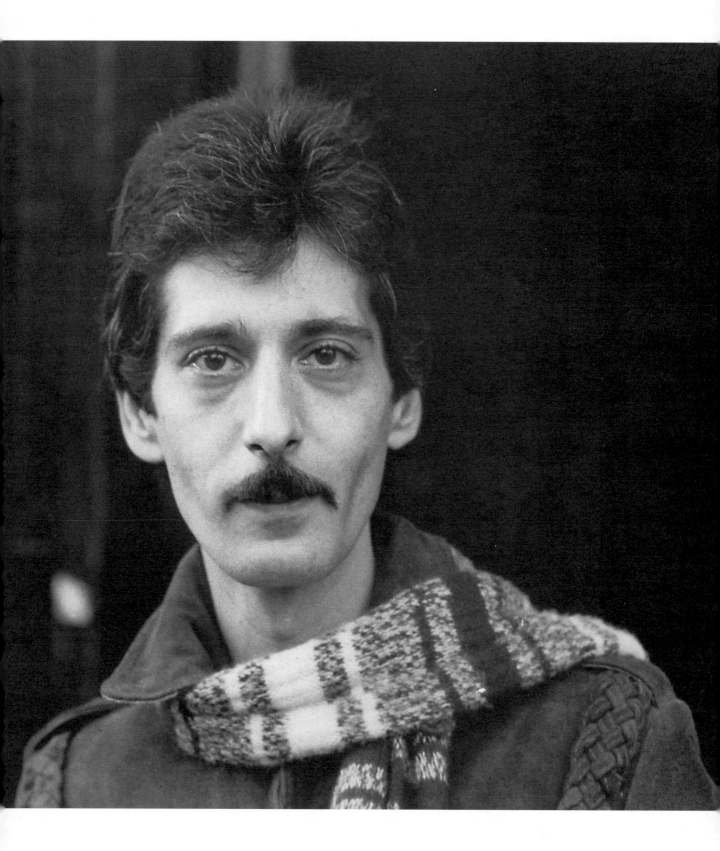

pat
martino

8/25/44

Philadelphia,

Pennsylvania

guitar

composer

Pat, a self-taught musician (except for some private lessons), has been on the road since the age of fifteen, having played with Willis Jackson, Red Holloway, Sleepy Henderson, Sonny Stitt, and Lloyd Price. During the sixties, he played with Jimmy Smith, Jack McDuff, Richard "Groove" Holmes, Jimmy McGriff, Don Patterson, and Trudy Pitts. In 1966, he spent eight months with John Handy. Since the late sixties, Pat has been leading his own groups and teaching guitar privately.

P: The first music that I heard was my father's music, music around the house. He was always into guitars and guitar players. He must have known that I had to be affected by that and I was. He used to play a lot of Coltrane and a lot of guitar players like Kenny Burrell, Charlie Christian, and Eddie Lyon. I felt that he influenced me in a subtle way. He allowed me to get at anything in the house, but his guitar. When I was about eleven years old, he finally said, "So you really want to play guitar?" and I said, "I've got to have a guitar." So he replied, "Well, I'll get you a guitar but if you don't play it, I'll wrap it around your neck." I got the guitar and I've been playing guitar ever since. The only teacher I can honestly say that I felt had an influence on me was a guy named Dennis Sendol. I was about thirteen or fourteen when I first started studying from him and I was so impressionable. I had no experience of notes of my own, at that point, and it was his that I was drawing from. The thing was that he was really very sensitive to art and different flows in the world of art, ballet and dance in general. He sort of sensitized me to a little bit more of the aesthetic at the right time.

JC: In general, what kinds of questions are music students asking you now that perhaps they didn't ask a few years ago?

P: The questions have changed because a lot of the questions that kids are asking now have been generated from things that I have said in print. If someone comes up to me and asks me a question, it's because they want to know what I possibly don't. But their questions have changed in as much as I suppose some of the images that I have generated have tickled their appetites in terms of wanting to know more about the formulative aspects of music, as opposed to what kind of picks I use, what gauge strings I use…There's always plenty of that. On the other hand, there's always a few kids that come up and say, "What can the guitar do for me? You look like you are getting something out of the whole experience; what is it doing for you?" I'm getting more of that, which is something that wasn't happening in the fifties, although it may have been happening, but I wasn't qualified to participate.

JC: How do you view your music presently and ultimately?

P: In the sense of its evolution, it has evolved in more ways privately than in the way it has evolved publicly. The majority of the growth in the evolution of my music has been done on a private basis. It's really very hard to put into words. When I was young and on the road with the organ bands, I'd do a tour and then I'd come back maybe for a week or two and I'd be so fired up that I would continue to create music for myself, alone. Suddenly I started creating a different kind of music than I was creating for those bands. So, there were two kinds of music formulated—music that was based upon my intellectual needs and the need to be concerned a little bit more with the basic nature of structure and true music, as opposed to just the creative experience as improvisation. So I continued to improvise and work as a player, and that music has evolved incredibly because, as a player, it satisfies my needs and techniques. On the other hand, this other hybrid form of music that is mostly stimulated by my composition is growing, too. It's just reaching a point where they are going to become one very shortly. It's very hard to say; they may be one already and I may not know it. It is something that I am working on and it involves multimedia. I am interested in dance and I'm interested in light. I'm interested in the senses more than I am interested in guitar players.

JC: You're actually incorporating life with art.

P: Absolutely.

JC: How do you feel about records versus live performances?

P: I feel that I haven't recorded my first album yet. I should add to that by saying that if I ever have the feeling that I have recorded my first album, it may be my last.

JC: Have you felt that as an artist you have had the freedom to express your ideals and ideas?

P: To some degree, yes. I have the perfect freedom to express all the ideas that I initially wanted to put into play when I was fifteen years old, now. I am at a point where I can live those ideas and prosper by them on a daily basis. In a way, it's comfortable to have created a place for myself, but the way I grow and the way I learn is a transcendental type of operation. As my goals reach maturity, suddenly they are no longer there and there is a completely different set of goals on a much larger basis. It's very hard to reach a point where I'm both stimulated and satisfied.

JC: You have a reputation for being extremely knowledgeable about your instrument, not just in terms of playing it, but the instrument itself. How did you develop this?

P: Curiosity. A need to escape a system that really didn't cater to my needs or to my talents when I was younger. I reached the point where I pursued my own ideas which I felt, at that time, to be just as valuable an experience creatively as any of the structure ideas. When I approached the guitar, it was in a total deductive framework, although there were certain inductive things around in the environment that I knew about. Some deductive processes have become inductive in the sense that a lot of kids in conservatories now are being told to get a record and transcribe it. In those days, I didn't have someone to say, "Well, get a record and transcribe the thing." If I heard a record that I liked, I did that automatically because I liked it that much. Now it's becoming an inductive thing. Then, for me, it was deductive. I'm very interested in bridging the gap between the two perspectives.

JC: Which type of dissonance do you prefer—do you favor certain ones and discard others or is your approach to atonality based on a single concept?

P: It's based on a single concept, movement, which encompasses for me tension and release. Dissonance, to me, isn't a group of notes, whether they are close or not, because over the years what was dissonant has become consonant. The more I am confronted by these groups of notes, the more pleasurable they become. So that, now, dissonance isn't the total phenomenon at all. It's something that occurs for me in the sense of nervous tension, metabolism, the time of day. These are all like dissonances, and when I think of dissonance, I think of it in the major sense of the role it plays in my life, more so that I do in the sense of the guitar.

JC: You are probably one in a thousand guitarists who use the right hand properly, that is, no right-hand finger contact with the guitar. Did this come naturally or did you have to work at it?

P: It came naturally. The only thing I had to work on were the ideas that I would produce with that talent. The concepts that I teach contain ideas that are related to technique, so that the technique is built into the music; therefore, if the music is realized properly, then the proper technique has been established. So, it is almost like the Zen concept at play. It's hard to pin it down in that sense, but I am interested in it in terms of the education of certain values with that instrument so that I can, for instance, take a student and in an hour and a half to two hours offer him an alternative to that syndrome that most students and teachers have symbiotically set up for themselves.

What I am talking about is the fact that many kids come to study. Kids that are maybe fifty years old, but nevertheless, kids, and they want to establish a relationship with me as a teacher and as my student. What I mean is that it is a never-ending process and though they are here on one tenet, searching for the answers musically, that's not what they want to hear. I found that in being able to give them those answers initially in an hour and a half, it's like giving them an alternative to a life-time of musical pursuit. It puts an end to the personal relationship, the need for the personal relationship, at that point. So, teaching is not totally information. I find that it goes much deeper and they need the personal relationship. The students need to know that someone is interested in their particular problem.

The information that has propelled me musically through my life and is still propelling me is just flat-out fact, and the guitar just proliferates itself on one of those facts and pursues it. As soon as you pursue something of that nature, then a door opens up and you're standing there looking at all the light at once. What I am getting at is that with the way people have been taught and educated, to some extent it takes a greater commitment for them to find those things and to pursue them once they have found them. I'm trying to be able to communicate not only the information but also the commitment, or at least enough stimulation so that a student can say, "Yeah, far out." Now I know where it is, now I know what to do.

To answer your question again about the guitar, what I am interested in is those values, being able to transmit them. For instance, Slonimsky has a book out and in the book are thousands of scales and patterns,* but not once did he speak of the formula that produced them all. What I am speaking of is one tiny little formula, something someone already knows, a system that they are already using. Put that into effect and suddenly there are thousands of patterns and scales and, in fact, thousands of Slonimsky books. That's the difference between deductive and inductive learning. The inductive student is confronted with these manual facts. He absorbs the facts and, therefore, increases his vocabulary. He now has the ability to respond in more ways. On the other hand, the deductive pupil, a student of art or anything for that matter, is going to do it himself. He's got his own ways of doing it. I think within the next ten years these things are going to really hit the street because there are too many inductive manuals, too many styles, too many ways, too many alterna-

---

* Slonimsky ,Nicolas. *Thesaurus of Scales and Melodic Patterns*, New York: Scribner's, 1947.

tives already. The thing is that it's going on in universities today. That's why the number of viable exponents in the system are slowly diminishing, because people are falling out, they're just peeling off. They can't absorb all of that information. I find that certain students have trouble perceiving music only because of the language. If they were shown that music is a language, like any other language, they'd realize it's only couched in different symbols. Then possibly they would understand that they knew things already, inherently.

JC: In other words, you're going beyond musical symbolism?

P: Exactly, because there are so many people that are totally intimidated by it. They should see that it's not really to be overcome, it's to utilize. Too many students are confronting this monumental task of trying to scratch the surface of this language on a daily basis. What's going to happen is that in another five years there's going to be no entrance into it.

ralph
towner

3/1/40

Chehalis, Washington

guitar

piano

French horn

composer and arranger

producer

Ralph, whose mother taught piano and played organ in church and whose father played trumpet, began improvising on the piano at age three. His "formal" training began when he enrolled at the University of Oregon and became a composition major and part-time trumpet player. In his last year of college, he began playing the guitar. By the time he graduated from college, Towner was immersed in the guitar and traveled to Vienna where he enrolled in the Academy of Music and Dramatic Arts, and studied with Karl Scheit. After a year in Vienna he returned to Oregon for the master's degree program in music theory, but did not complete his thesis. He then returned to Vienna for another year of study with Scheit. In 1968 he moved to New York City where he began earning a living as a pianist. Playing primarily jazz and Brazilian-oriented music, he worked with singer Astrud Gilberto, Airto (then on traps), Miroslav Vitous, Dave Holland, Jeremy Steig, and Jimmy Garrison. In 1970, he joined the Paul Winter Consort, which provided a steady format for his acoustic guitar, and learned to "integrate all those instruments in my writing" (*Guitar Player* magazine, December 1975). Two years later, the group Oregon was created out of the original Consort, with Towner, Paul McCandless, Collin Walcott, and Glen Moore.

R: My first formal training was in grade school on the trumpet at age seven. I improvised on the piano before that but never studied the instrument formally. My improvisation was limited to imitation of recordings and the grandeur of that prohibited me from playing the simple beginning pieces on the piano and also found me, years later, still without a standard and efficient knowledge of keyboard fingering and technique. I attended the University of Oregon and, after the first year as an art major, switched to music composition in which I obtained a degree. I then went to Vienna to study classical guitar with Karl Scheit. My interest in that instrument came in my last year at Oregon when I wrote some music for it. It became my major performing instrument after one year at the Music Academy at Vienna. I returned to graduate school in Oregon for two years and studied music theory. Then I lived in Seattle for a year and supported myself as a jazz piano player. I returned to Vienna for one more year of classical study, and then moved to New York.

JC: How do you develop your musical ideas—both improvisationally and compositionally?

R: I developed my current methods of improvising from an early interest in jazz piano trio playing and the rearrangement of standard songs that were necessary to know in order to work. Most songs of that era proceeded through an internal two-four cadence system, and the most effective solution to reharmonizing was to work backwards from the cadence points and provide new or different deceptive two-four cadences that still remained faithful to the original scales in the song. I realized that each substitution had a character or mystery inherent in itself, and I began writing songs that utilized some of the mystery and suspense of those substitutions. My notion of a song, including the improvisation on that song, is that from the first sound you establish a character, a sense of motion, and you are committed to develop a history, a miniature lifetime that is a faithful development of the original atmosphere stated.

JC: As an exponent of the classical guitar, could you elaborate on its incorporation into your music?

R: Concerning the classical guitar, the songs that I write attempt to bring out what sounds stylistically comfortable on that instrument. The first music I heard—improvisational on chord changes, that is—was Brazilian music. The national instrument there was a classical guitar, and they had established something more natural than a bebop style for it. I learned to play in that style and then extended it beyond its original identity as I had attempted with the standard piano songs in jazz or bebop.

The written long form music that I studied and played has served to allow me to play in a style that is not limited to quoting standard improvising styles.

JC: Your music is not especially commercially oriented—why have you not pursued a more lucrative direction?

R: I am fortunate to be able to support myself well, and each recording company has never interfered, only helped my musical conception. ECM Records is a small and private company that is interested in documenting the progress of each musician it records. I realize this is unusual for most companies. I was thirty-three years old when this happened and had only first recorded at age thirty. No other company had beaten down my door, and my anxiety to please had waned to a manageable level when I finally got an opportunity to record.

JC: Tell me about your history and preferences as a teacher of music.

R: I have taught both classical guitar and improvisation quite a bit until recently, when I became fortunate enough to perform most of the time. I preferred to use music, often short Renaissance pieces, to begin a student, and attached exercises to a difficult passage. This way the technical exercises had a direct association with what the student was trying to accomplish, namely, musical satisfaction. I often wrote or composed exercises as we encountered difficulty, and each student would have his lesson tailored to himself. Teaching improvisation has been difficult on this instrument, because the standard classical academic approach is the best for learning how to make it speak or sing clearly, and to also deal with the overwhelming focus on physical techniques. I isolated each approach from each other in blocks of several years, and still can't develop either one to a high-enough level to suit me. But this leaves me a fascinating amount of room for improvement.

keyboards

brian auger

7/18/39
London, England
organ and keyboards
composer and arranger
producer

Brian, a self-taught musician, started playing in London in the early sixties, listening to Oscar Peterson, McCoy Tyner, Miles Davis, Horace Silver, Art Blakey, Donald Byrd, Wynton Kelly, Bill Evans, and Herbie Hancock, to name a few. He put together an early fusion band in 1964 with John McLaughlin. In 1965, Brian began playing the organ and was part of the group Steam Packet, a band that featured Julie Driscoll and Rod Stewart. The music ranged from jazz to Motown, folk to blues. Steam Packet disbanded after eighteen months, leaving Auger and Driscoll to form the very successful Trinity in 1966. That group folded in 1969, because, says Brian, "the management spoiled the situation by working us to death and putting us under so much psychological pressure that, in the end, the band cracked apart, and after three years, disbanded." In 1970, Auger created the Oblivion Express, wanting a band that would go completely against the commercial tide. Around this time, he heard the Miles Davis record, *In a Silent Way*, "the first record in a long time to really turn me on, where somebody was making a stand." During this time, Brian incorporated two companies in London: Nasty Productions, his record company, and Omnibus Music, a music publishing company which also managed the band, the accounts, and set up the tours, affording Auger complete control. The original Oblivion Express disbanded in 1972, and in 1973, Auger—inspired by Marvin Gaye and Stevie Wonder—re-formed the band.

B: I began to play at age three. It seemed quite natural to me. There were pianos around the house and I used to play on them. I used to give little concerts, and the kids would come and sit on the windowsill. I'd open all the windows and play the piano, and they all used to smile—it seemed to make everybody happy. I think that was the motivation at that point, and the way they looked at me a little differently—as if I was somebody.

My father was a little musical. We'd play the piano a bit. He was also interested in player pianos, and this is the way I learned to play, in fact. We had a player piano. It had a roll of cylinder paper in it with holes for the notes of music, and pedals. You pedal the pedals, and the bellows draws the paper across this grid with corresponding holes in it, and to the keyboard—making the keyboard play. We had a whole cupboard full of these rolls of music—ranging from classical stuff to songs from shows, and some ragtime. I used to copy all the melodies with my right hand first—up until the age of about six—and then I started to play with the left hand, too.

JC: When did your introduction to the organ occur?

B: I started to become aware that there was a guy who played organ called Jimmy Smith, and the sound of that instrument I thought was extremely exciting. Eventually I got around to buying an organ and making the transition from piano, which I'd played right up to the beginning of 1965. I bought an organ and started an organ trio. If somebody had told me in 1963 that I was going to be playing organ in two years, I would have just laughed in their face, because, at that time, I was heavily into the jazz scene in London and was also traveling to many cities in England where there was an extremely frail and shaky jazz scene, consisting of a pub or a little jazz club here and there. I eventually made it up to the Edinburgh Jazz Festival in 1963 with my own trio. I made that group into a quintet in 1964 with John McLaughlin, and we started to play things like "Watermelon Man," and some Ray Charles stuff. That band in a way was a jumping-off point for a kind of fusion situation, or what has become known as fusion music.

The band folded, and toward the end of 1964, I was really beginning to listen to Jimmy Smith; I also heard Jimmy McGriff, Jack McDuff, and people like that. And so the organ became one of those things that I wanted to experiment with. There were many more underlying reasons for my transition to organ. Because in actual fact, the organ was synonymous with an R & B scene in London at the time, as distinct from the jazz scene. I had played on the jazz scene for about six years, and what was happening at that time was not too exciting. People were almost turning their backs on the audience, or had an attitude toward the public that was, if they don't dig it, it's because they're in some kind of a position down there and we're in another kind of position up here. I always found myself at odds with that kind of attitude, because I'd always play to excite people—to stir them up and to communicate with them. I wanted the fun I was getting out of playing to go across to the audience, and for them to be able to enjoy it like that, too.

I found the jazz club kind of atmosphere a little bit stifling. I'd heard records recorded live in American jazz clubs by people like Cannonball [Adderley], and it seemed to me that people were having so much more of a good time. Also, I found that rhythm sections in England generally were extremely capable in a technical way, but never played together. It was like three people playing as fast as they could—trying to impress the audience with what they could do—and therefore there was never any real rhythm section playing the way I would like to play. I mean, I'd listen to the East Coast hard bop—that's what I was weaned on, I suppose—people like Art Blakey's Jazz Messengers, and Miles Davis and his rhythm sections. For me, they had a totally different concept of playing in the rhythm section. They definitely listened to one another and played together as a unit, and therefore the excitement and the swing and power that came off it was just a spirit of the music that was different. That had always been lacking on the English jazz scene. And, I began to realize that on the R & B scene, there were people who didn't have all the technique, but who could definitely put a groove down that was exciting to play in. Therefore, my attention began to switch toward that area to find rhythm sections to play with, once I had established myself on the organ.

JC: Having had no formal music education, what are your feelings about the self-taught musician?

B: There's no substitute at all for the playing experience. That is something which, if you're going to be a musician and be on a spot where you've got to come up with the goods, there is no better learning ground than that particular time for learning how to communicate what you know to your audience. That's the whole point of the exercise; otherwise we might as well all sit back and just play for ourselves. The live experience for me is the thing that makes music. I find a studio atmosphere just a totally different work avenue. But to play live is an art that anybody who's going to be a musician is going to have to learn. Music school can help you with your technique and with your musical knowledge, but it can't help you to put on a great show, because you've got to learn how to do that. Jazz calls upon you to express the core of what you are musically, and it leaves you open to express the sum total of everything that you've become—mentally, musically, and culturally. It is also, in a way, a guide—well, it's been for me anyway. It tells me when I'm lazy, when I've got to really sharpen myself up; it tells me all sorts of things about myself which is the fascination of the whole thing, the whole kind of journey into music for me.

JC: How has technology affected your musical concepts and execution?

B: I'd say it's revolutionized my whole concept of music and my playing technique. The reason for that relates back to the days of the piano. I'd be asked to go and play in various clubs, and the standards of pianos in England range from reasonable to diabolical. One was never sure that one could put on a reasonable performance, simply because playing that kind of instrument is not a thing you can carry around with you easily. The first thing I noticed when I switched to organ was that the organ was the same every night. At least that was something I could deal with on a night-to-night basis and get to know. I also realized that you can't play the organ the way you play piano. It requires a different technique. It requires different chords, because the organ has so many more harmonics, if you play extremely close harmonies, and they tend to get pretty muddy. It also gave me a great range of sounds to play about with, and so my ideas on sound—where it should go and what it should do—were affected by that. Also, it dragged me into the world of electronics—a thing I never bothered about before—and I began to learn about amplifiers, mixers, synthesizers, and all the gadgets that go with them, like flangers and echo units, and it just goes on and on now.

JC: Do you think that fusion music is generated by the jazz musician's need to cross over into commercial markets, or is the music a creative reflection of the times?

B: I think music is in a pretty healthy state. I think the fusion movement in particular over the last three years has made incredible strides and has opened a huge market. The media is still geared more or less the same way unfortunately, though it's not so bad in America as in Europe. I regard the fusion movement as today's music, today's jazz. Looking back, I think I've always looked at our bands as a situation in movement forward, pushing forward: pushing out knowledge of jazz harmony, pushing out knowledge of rhythms, and using not only rock rhythms, but Latin rhythms, Afro-Cuban, Brazilian—anything to enrich the whole situation. I think that rhythm is one of those things that more subtly reflects the times than probably harmonic content in music. If you look back to the twenties and thirties, when people were dancing the black bottom and the Charleston, that society was very rigid, they weren't loose. So they danced in that particular way, and the music that reflected that period was a very tight kind of syncopated stuff which maybe some of us would laugh at now. Rhythm is a reflection of the times, our present music, and the musician's essential desire to express himself in this idiom.

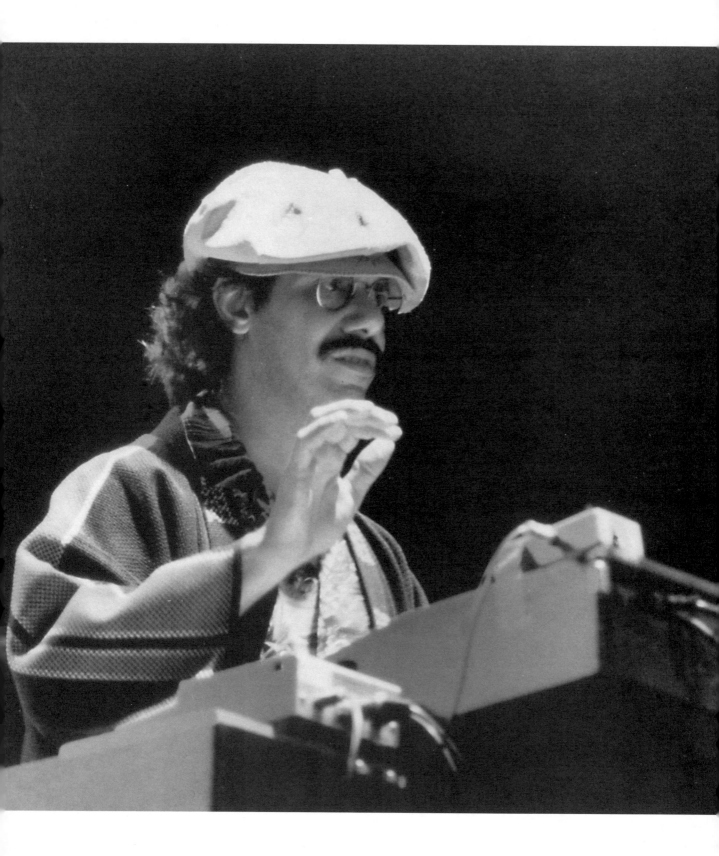

chick corea

6/12/41
Chelsea, Massachusetts
piano and keyboards
synthesizer and organ
composer and arranger
producer

Chick began studying classical piano at age four. His father Armando, a jazz trumpeter, bassist, composer, and arranger in the thirties and forties, provided Chick with early direction. Chick played at country clubs with his father around Boston and Cape Cod while still very young. In high school he worked with several bands and was thus introduced to Latin music, which remains an integral part of his own music today. After finishing high school in 1959, Chick moved to Manhattan to attend Columbia University. He returned to Boston after two months and spent eight months preparing for a Juilliard audition. Once at Juilliard, he became dissatisfied with his formal studies and left to pursue a full-time career as a professional musician. His first major appearance was in 1962, with Mongo Santamaria. He then played in the Latin band of percussionist and singer Willie Bobo. Chick went on to play with Herbie Mann, Blue Mitchell, and, in 1966, Stan Getz. In 1968 he worked with Sarah Vaughan in Las Vegas for two months before joining Miles Davis, with whom he remained for two years. Working with Miles, the then acoustic player Chick began to play the electric Fender-Rhodes piano. After his tenure with Miles, Chick formed the avant-garde group, Circle, with bassist Dave Holland, drummer Barry Altschul, and reeds player, Anthony Braxton. In 1970 Chick formed his own group, Return to Forever, and began to employ multiple keyboards. Although Return to Forever has experienced personnel changes, it remains one of the strongest and most popular bands of the seventies. In addition to his activities with Return to Forever, Chick and Herbie Hancock did a series of duo piano concerts together throughout the United States and Europe in the winter of 1978. Chick also writes a monthly column for *Contemporary Keyboard*. He has received several Grammys and numerous other awards.

C: I began to actually play the piano when I was four. My father has been a musician all his life and he gave me my first introduction. He was really kind and gentle. He got me off to a real safe start. My parents were both always very encouraging and allowed me total freedom to pursue music. I think that was a real nice safe space that was created for me in the beginning. My motivation has always been simple it's been because I really loved doing it. Piano was my first instrument and has always been my main instrument. Through the years I've picked up various degrees of facility on the trumpet and the drums especially and a little bit on the vibraphone. But piano has always been my main instrument.

The only real formal education, musically, that I have had, or what could be considered formal, was a six-year stint that I spent with a great classical pianist who lives in Boston whose name is Salvatore Sullo. He taught me the basics of real proper piano technique, Italian classical style. That teaching has really stuck throughout my life as a pianist. He also introduced me to classical repertoire and I played a lot of classical music when I was studying with him. I began to study with him when I was about eleven, twelve years old and stayed with him until I was about sixteen or seventeen years old. Bach, Beethoven, and Chopin were prevalent in my classical music studies on the piano, along with a little bit of Mozart and Scarlatti. Since then, I guess, I've been influenced by every good piece of music I've heard, both by famous composers and musicians and nonfamous composers and musicians. The list is endless. My favorite contemporary composers are Bartok and Stravinsky. Also, I admire Eric Satie's music an awful lot.

Some of the first music I listened to was bebop music, the music of Dizzy Gillespie and Charlie Parker. I was interested in that and later on, in my teens, Horace Silver was the first jazz pianist that I actually listened to closely enough to begin to study some of his songs and copy some of his solos and his licks. His music was actually influential in getting me started composing.

When I left high school in 1959, I began working as a professional musician throughout the sixties. I worked with numerous bands and generally all of it was real good learning experience for me. I got to play with a lot of very excellent musicians in a lot of different fields of music, mostly jazz, commercial music, and Latin music. I was always a good student; I was able to pick out the strong points of each leader and musician that I worked with and kind of learned from them and made them my own. I think that one of the main things that formulated for me in those early days, the fifties and the sixties, was a real ability to spot the musicians and artists who were real dedicated to their life as an artist, their music, and their art. They would always outshine the dilet-tantes. One of the most rewarding gigs I did as a sideman was a three-year stint with Miles Davis's group. I got to play with some fantastic musicians during that period—Wayne Shorter, Tony Williams, Jack DeJohnette, and Dave Holland. I even got to play with Keith Jarrett, another pianist. I began to use the electric piano around the time I worked with Miles. At first I didn't like it very well because mechanically it's a far inferior instrument to a regular acoustic piano. It still is, but I enjoyed being able to play at a louder volume, mainly so that I could play more comfort-ably with the volume level of drummers like Tony Williams and other young drummers who were putting out in those days. After that I started liking the timbres of the electric piano and other elec-tric keyboards and just naturally began to use them in my playing, my composition, and my groups.

JC: To what extent has Scientology affected your life and your music?

C: It's hard to express in a few words to what a fantastic degree L. Ron Hubbard and the subject of Scientology and Dianetics that he developed has helped me in my life. One of the things I always knew, even before discovering Scientology, was that the main reason why people, say marriages or groups or companies or countries, had such a hard time coordinating with one another and had so much strife in their interactions was basically because the individuals that made up these groups were so encumbered by their own problems—physical illness all the way through emotional uncer-tainly—and this can create enough turmoil to stop an individual from really pursuing and clinging to his own purposes.

Some of the first things I gained with the applied philosophy of Scientology was a greater under-standing of myself as an individual and the ability to get rid of the personal barriers that I had created for myself so that I could much more freely operate as an individual. Since then I dis-covered the enormous amount of literature in Scientology that exists on the interaction of groups. I have been studying and applying that to great advantage within my own music group and my own administrative group.

JC: How do you relate to the music business at large?

C: I have a certain opinion about the music business. To live a complete life anyone who creates something, or who has a product, has to be able to be responsible for the administration of his own product. Otherwise, when the creation leaves his hands it will get altered by others, either with good intentions or with bad intentions, it doesn't matter. Although one could find fault with people in the music business and in the record industries and so forth, I personally think that artists are going to have to take stock of their responsibility for what happens to their music after they create it, in an effort to change it for the better. As beautiful and needed as art and art forms are on plan-et earth, their value is only to the degree that they can affect people. And so the administration of any artist's music becomes ultraimportant in his being able to cause any effects on the society around him. The only answer I found to that is to be a source, myself, of an administrative group that handles my own business and to be involved to a degree where I can set up my own business atmosphere businesswise for what I do, and gradually begin to encourage and even demand agreement from those business people who are outside of my own group, such as record companies, booking agents, promoters, and so forth. The result for me is a much freer atmosphere that I have self-determinedly created around me with my primary purpose, which is to create great music for people.

So far as inner peace goes, there is nothing more calming than operating with utter honesty and having the knowledge and the ability to encourage, and also demand, that same kind of honesty with the people one works with. Studying Scientology has helped me define these subtle areas, and it has taught me how to handle them a whole lot better. I personally like a lifestyle of very high production and lots of positive energy.

JC: What advice, if any, would you give to the serious music student?

C: To an aspiring musician there's only two bits of cheap advice that I always give, or lately have been giving. One is to really find out what your own true goals and purposes are. Once having begun to see them, there is nothing else to do but make an uncompromising decision to actually become an excellent musician and be willing to work incredibly hard at it. Don't let the crazies in the world stop your beautiful creative purposes.

JC: In what direction are you moving now in terms of your musical goals?

C: I have lots of plans and projects musically and lots of goals that I'd like to fulfill as an artist. Personally, my desire as a composer is growing and growing, and I have plans to do extensive writing of piano music, of small chamber music, string quartet and piano, orchestral music, and various experimental forms that I think of from time to time. I would say that one of my main goals is the rehabilitation of people's artistic desires. The more I see this happen, the saner I see the society getting around me. I also have a desire to help artists become aware of and be able to control the ways of the nitty-gritty world around them enough so that they can continue to create their music in a controlled atmosphere.

george duke

1/12/46
San Rafael, California
piano and keyboards
synthesizer
vocalist
composer and arranger
producer

George received his B.A. in composition and trombone from the San Francisco Conservatory of Music and his masters in music composition from San Francisco State University, where he taught classes in contemporary improvisation and jazz in American culture. From 1965 to 1970, he led his own trio at the Half Note Club in San Francisco, then went on the road with the vocal group, the Third Wave, for whom he played and composed. In addition to leading his own band, George worked with Gerald Wilson, Dizzy Gillespie, Bobby Hutcherson, and Don Ellis in 1968 for six months. In 1969 he performed with Jean-Luc Ponty, with whom he eventually recorded. He became a member of Frank Zappa's the Mothers of Invention in 1970 and began to experiment with the synthesizer. Staying with Zappa until 1971, he then joined Cannonball Adderley's band, where he remained for two years before returning to Zappa. George stayed with the Mothers until 1975 when he left to form the Cobham/Duke band with Billy Cobham. Since 1976, he has performed and recorded under his own name.

G: My first instrument was the piano. I was six years old. My mother took me to a Duke Ellington concert—at least, so she told me—I didn't know who it was. She said I went ape—I went crazy. I was running around the house saying, "I can do that!" It evidently really took me out. I don't remember it, but she told me I just went crazy—I mean, I didn't want to go to school or do anything. I just wanted to hear that music.

My mother scraped up enough money to buy me a little piano about four or five months later, because I just kept on her. I eventually started just tinkling around with the piano, so she said, "Maybe I'll give him some lessons." She found me a teacher and I started taking lessons, and I've been playing ever since.

JC: Your fundamental education, then, was mostly classical?

G: I was strictly classically oriented, because there were no jazz teachers and I didn't understand it. But I always looked at it and said, "Hey, I would really like to be able to do what they're doing, but I don't know what it is." So I stayed away from it, but as I gained more knowledge of theory and the whole bit, I began to try things, and by the time I was in high school, I got this little Latin band together. Latin music I could understand, because it felt good; and I was into Les McCann. I could dig his music because it had the church feeling, so it all sort of melted together. Rock and roll, at that time, I could not stand. I thought it was the saddest stuff I ever heard. I've since changed my tune, but at that point in time, it drove me up the wall.

I graduated from high school, but I couldn't get into the college of my choice because I was a grade short of grade points, so it forced me to go to music school, which was fortunate. I still didn't know if I could make a living playing and I was scared. My cousin, Charles Burrell, was playing the bass at the time in the San Francisco Symphony. We got together and he heard me play and said, "Listen, you have no business playing classical music."

JC: Was he the first person who said that to you?

G: Yeah. I heard some of those people play over there, and I said, "I'm seriously lacking as far as playing classical music." I mean, to make a living playing classical music was not in me. I just didn't have the facility. Besides that, I wanted to be free, so my cousin more or less made the decision for me. He said, "Listen, don't do that. You're a much better jazz piano player. Improvise and do what you want to do." At that time at the school, they didn't allow anybody to be playing any type of improvisation other than people like John Cage, which is great, too—but they didn't like that anyhow. They did have a new artists' ensemble that played some new stuff, but as far as playing jazz—uh-uh. They used to run me out of the room.

JC: Who introduced the synthesizer to you?

G: I was playing with Frank Zappa, and Ian Underwood was playing synthesizer with Zappa's band. I was interested, but not really. Finally Frank said, "Hey, man, you'd be great. And I said, "No—there's too many knobs. Just let me play, I'm happy." So he said okay, but it went on and he prodded me a little. Then Ian left and Frank needed a synthesizer in the band, so he bought one and put it in front of me and just left it there. As time went on, during rehearsals I kept looking at it, and Frank would look over at me smiling. Eventually I took it home with me one night. But I brought it back and said, "Frank, I'll never learn how to play this thing." He took it on the tour and I still looked at it—it was sitting with me on the tour, and finally I started playing it. Then, he bought a minimoog and put that in front of me, and eventually I learned how to play both.

JC: You played with Zappa for a long time—actually participating in two different bands of his—how would you sum up your experience?

G: The second Zappa band was great, an incredible band! If that band was still together, I'd probably be there. I felt like I wasn't a sideman, I was really a part of that band. Everybody contributed to the overall thing, but it was all under Frank's umbrella. After we learned how to be free within that context, we could do anything we wanted to do.

JC: Have you ever felt manipulated?

G: Well, we're always being manipulated, I guess. I haven't felt manipulated to the point where I couldn't manipulate myself out of something, or manipulate an event the way I wanted to have it manipulated. In other words, you can be manipulated, but you can still be the manipulator in the end.

JC: You are a composer of great diversity and versatility—what sources in particular do you draw from?

G: What I do is look at the world around me, compiling a sort of information bank within my mind to draw upon at any moment. Basically, I'm just playing or composing and feeding off of whatever I see through my eyes, and I write the way I feel about it.

jan hammer

4/17/48

Prague, Czechoslovakia

piano and keyboards

synthesizer

drums

vocalist

composer and arranger

producer

Jan attended the Academy of Muse Arts in Prague where he majored in composition and piano from 1966 to 1968, after winning the International Music Competition in Vienna in 1966. In 1968 he won a scholarship to the Berklee College of Music, where he remained for a brief period of time. He worked around Boston from 1968 on, playing at the Playboy Club for a year. In early 1970, Jan began playing with singer Sarah Vaughan for a period of thirteen months, touring the United States, Canada, and Japan. In 1971 he worked with Jeremy Steig and Elvin Jones before becoming a member of John McLaughlin's Mahavishnu Orchestra, with whom he remained from May 1971 to December 1973. It was during his stay with Mahavishnu, on the record *Birds of Fire*, that Jan first recorded with the synthesizer: "I was searching for a melodic instrument, and the synthesizer was perfect. Synthesizers gave me a new lease on musical life; once you get down to serious business with the synthesizer, you realize that the possibilities are endless, yet only a few will lend themselves to your music" (*Contemporary Keyboard*, August 1976). Hammer recorded and toured with rock guitarist Jeff Beck until the late seventies, when he began traveling with his own group.

J: My first recollection of hearing music is very foggy. I must have been about two years old. I can remember hearing a bebop group with my parents in it rehearsing in the next room. My mother is a jazz singer and my father is a doctor by profession, but his major love is music and he plays bass and vibes. Obviously, if music surrounds you every day, you can't help but get into it, to try doing it yourself. So I started playing at around four. When I was six I started taking lessons. It is a necessary step for anybody who wants to play. You have to take lessons to actually advance your technical skill, but, at the same time, you're running a risk of losing perspective of the whole purpose of it all. I mean, of why we play. It happens to so many musicians that it's frightening. That's why there are so many frustrated classical musicians today because they never actually got a taste of being one with the creation of music, not just being a tool in the hands of composers, but also being an improviser and creating spontaneous music on the spot—which saved me later on.

Originally, when I was little, I was putting things together for myself, but then later, on, all of a sudden, I really got into the classical piano. It wasn't until I was about ten or eleven when I rediscovered improvisation somehow, I guess thanks to my father who would spend some time with me and we'd play four hands and play just anything and I would end up improvising on top of whatever he would do or I would play background for him. Ultimately, I found fun again, which is the only reason I can see for doing anything, really. I mean, if you're lucky, that's what it would be about. It's what children ask, you know—not how much do I make, but is it fun? Obviously, not everybody is capable of improvisation, and there are a lot of classical pianists who derive tremendous satisfaction just out of performing the classical repertoire as close to perfection as possible—or their idea of perfection. Obviously, it works for them.

Later on, I started to see the technical side of practicing and actually learning classical pieces, much more as a necessary discipline, and also as a means to sharpen my skills so I'd be ready for inspiration when it came. Ultimately, what really sank in the deepest, I think, was the music of Eastern Europe—the folk music and the folk-influenced classical music. Growing up in Czechoslovakia, this music was all around us and you just couldn't escape it. The only other thing was some jazz music from records, scarce as they were, and the Voice of America broadcasts late at night.

JC: When did you consciously decide to pursue music as a career, and what steps did you take to expand your horizons academically?

J: When I was fourteen, I was in a band with Miroslav Vitous and his brother. I was getting ahead. I was starting to play and be recognized. It was all great and everybody was into it, but I still saw music as a hobby. I was going to be a doctor. That is what my father is, and my grandfather, and I was really going to be a third-generation doctor. It wasn't until I was seventeen that the change came. I had written quite a lot of pieces that we were performing, and a friend of my father's—a great composer—came over and listened to some of the tapes I'd been working on, and in one day he completely talked me out of becoming a doctor—just by logic and explaining to me how I would feel; that it really wouldn't be right, and I would feel out of place if I wasn't among my own kind of people. I had to break it to my father, but it worked out fine because he saw how deeply I was involved in music. It was much more than a hobby at that point, and there was no turning back. I think the most important ingredient in my studies was when I left high school to study at the Prague Academy of Muse Arts, which is what they call it. I spent two years there studying classical composition, and this enabled me to put my improvisations and my approach to music in order so I wouldn't just shoot off ideas. My music became much more coherent. I'm not talking just about composition, which it obviously helps, but ultimately, it really helps improvisation. There is an underlying sense of form that you learn and that sinks into your system, and you almost forget it except in your subconscious. It's still shaping everything I do right now in music.

JC: As an original member of the Mahavishnu Orchestra, how would you classify its contribution to the contemporary fusion music?

J: I don't know what to say other than what's happening now really testifies best to the gravity that the band had when it started, because at present there are so many bands that are complete copies and derivatives—it's just amazing. That, to me, speaks louder than anything I could say about it, except that we felt that we were on to something big at that point. It was a very high time, and it's affected the music scene quite profoundly.

JC: What about your involvement then with the electric keyboard?

J: I was in Boston. We were jamming and playing all this far-out music, every time I played piano, I couldn't quite get up to the level of volume and intensity of the drummer, so I finally gave in. I had been a diehard; I didn't want to hear about electric piano. Finally, I tried it and I was hooked, because you can stand right next to the drummer. When I play with a drummer, I don't want him to hold back from me at all—I want him to be as free as he would be with any other instrument. So, electric piano was the only alternative. After that, the next step in the same general direction was the synthesizer, except ten times more expressive. Electric piano is fairly one-colored; it doesn't lend itself too much to expressive playing. But the synthesizer is quite the opposite—it's endless. You really can go anywhere, and I think I have really found the closest thing to my true voice with that instrument.

JC: Your approach to the synthesizer has been characterized as guitaristic. Is this, deliberate?

J: I think that's a misconception that a lot of Western listeners have. It's not truly the guitar that's influencing me, as much as it is Indian music and folk music of Eastern Europe—a mixture of all that. Basically, Indian music was what really influences guitar in the first place, especially the way we were playing it in the Mahavishnu Orchestra. There was a very heavy Indian influence, and that's where it comes from. It's not truly via the guitar. I think it's more or less a direct line to Indian music, but to Western ears the only instrument we immediately associate with that kind of playing is guitar. That's why people assume that it sounds a lot like guitar, and I can understand that.

JC: How does the lifestyle of a musician generally affect you?

J: I got up against the wall toward the end of the Mahavishnu Orchestra when I could not truly create, as far as writing music, or even make a coherent statement as a player, because I was jammed. You know, it's an overload—too many gigs and too little satisfaction, too much pressure between members of the band. When all those things collide, you have to get out, and that's exactly what we did. I moved to the country and finally silenced everything that was buzzing in my head. I started hearing things that were truly me and not just conglomerates of all the things that were jammed into my ears and my brain by the incredible amount of information that was flying around in New York City. Finally, I could start writing something that was different, but, as far as the lifestyle of a musician—there is no such thing. I went through about four or five different lifestyles in five years—from a jazz musician playing in a club every night until three in the morning, to a touring sort of rock musician, when you play one show and you're back in the hotel at ten. What I really prefer most of all is change, not being stuck in one particular lifestyle too long, so I can appreciate the different times.

herbie
hancock

4/12/40

Chicago, Illinois

piano and keyboards

synthesizer

composer and arranger

producer

When Herbie Hancock enrolled at Iowa's Grinnell College in 1956, his major was engineering. Within a short time, however, he had become immersed in music, composing and arranging for the seventeen-piece concert band he had created. Changing his major to music composition, Herbie remained at Grinnell from 1956 to 1960, but fell one credit short of graduating. He completed the course sixteen years later at UCLA and received his B.A. He was also awarded an honorary Doctor of Fine Arts from Grinnell in 1972. In the winter of 1960 Herbie began playing with Donald Byrd with whom he remained, except for brief stints, until he joined Miles Davis in 1963. During this time he made his first record, which contained the now classic "Watermelon Man," popularized by Mongo Santamaria in the early sixties. When Herbie left Miles in 1968, he formed a sextet which began to incorporate more and more electronic devices. In 1972 Hancock moved to Los Angeles, disbanded his sextet, and set out to play "funky" music with a new band. Impressed by the commercial success that his friend Donald Byrd was enjoying, Hancock soon found himself in a similar position when his record *Headhunters* was released in the fall of 1973. "Chameleon," one of the tracks on the album, became an AM hit. The record subsequently enjoyed unprecedented sales and Hancock began to attract a large audience of pop, rock, and R & B fans. A prodigious composer, Hancock wrote the scores to the films *Blow-Up* and *Death Wish*, and Bill Cosby's TV special, *Hey Hey Hey! It's Fat Albert*. In late 1976 Hancock toured extensively with V.S.O.P, a group that reunited the members of the earlier Miles Davis quintet—Ron Carter, Tony Williams, Wayne Shorter, and Hancock—adding trumpeter Freddie Hubbard. An all-acoustic band, it was received enthusiastically by jazz and fusion fans alike—a phenomenon that prompted Hancock to remark, "I think it shows another side of the value of jazz-rock. Not that crossover music was done for this purpose, but it has had the virtue of being the first type of jazz the general public could relate to. Listening to fusion jazz served as a stepping-stone to hearing mainstream" (*Contemporary Keyboard*, November 1977). In early 1978, Herbie and Chick Corea did a series of duo acoustic concerts together—further bridging the gap between mainstream jazz and contemporary music's audience.

H: I first started playing when I was seven, out of envy. My best friend had a piano, and just because he had his, I had to get one. I got the piano in April on my seventh birthday, and I started taking lessons in September. We were going to this church, Ebenezer Baptist Church in Chicago, and they must have asked the church organist to give me lessons—her name was Mrs. Whalum. She taught me for about two and a half years. I learned to read and I was a pretty good reader. She taught me nothing about sound, about touch, or about the character of music—just mechanical reading. After that, I studied with another teacher, Mrs. Jordan, for about three years. She heard me play the first time and said, "You're a fantastic reader, but you don't know anything about playing music." Just with her hands she would show me different ways of touching the keyboard to get different sounds. She said, "Did anyone ever show you how to get a note soft?" I said no. Then she got me into Chopin, Mendelssohn, and some music that has more nuances in it. I'd never even heard of the word nuance.

JC: When did you discover jazz?

H: As far as jazz is concerned, anytime I heard it on the radio, I would usually turn it off because I couldn't make heads or tails out of it. It didn't appeal to me at all, and it didn't make any sense. I couldn't relate to it in any way, shape, or form. The chords sounded like they were off the moon. The melodies sounded like they were off the moon, and there was no rhythm—I mean what I considered rhythm. There was a beat, but it was real weak by comparison to the other stuff. So I usually turned it off. But there was one tune that I really liked that I heard on the radio. It was "Moonlight in Vermont" with Johnny Smith and Stan Getz. I kept hearing it and hearing it and then pretty soon I loved it, and then it got to the point where I was waiting to hear it. When is he going to play that record? I didn't know what it was, it just had some kind of magic for me. I was about eleven years old and then I knew it was jazz. But the other idea I had in my head was that jazz was a kind of music that had to be played by somebody who was older. You'd have to be at least twenty. I felt I wasn't mature enough for that kind of music.

At the Senior Variety Show in my second year in high school, I was thirteen, and they had this jazz trio—the Don Goldberg Trio. He was the one who showed me how to play the blues. I heard this music at the variety show and I said, "Well, I'll be God damned. This guy is playing jazz and he is my age." I couldn't believe it, and again it sounded like music off the moon, but it was cohesive. I knew that the bass player and the drummer and the piano player were playing together. It made that kind of sense, although I had no idea what they were playing. It was together, and I was fascinated by it, and plus all the people in high school that were into jazz seemed to be a little cooler than anybody else: they were more together, they were kind of hip. You know, they seemed to be more adult, more suave and smooth. So I started hanging out with them and they were telling me about Chet Baker and Shorty Rogers.

The first jazz I listened to was George Shearing because that's what my friend Don Goldberg was playing; then I heard Erroll Garner. Most of the kids in high school that were listening to jazz were white, and they were listening to the West Coast jazz, and I remember one guy said to me, "The West Coast jazz is cool and hard bop is not happening." One time I was thumbing through jazz records in a record shop and I ran across a record; the name of the record was "Hard Bop" and I said, "Oh, maybe he was talking about this record." I didn't know; I didn't know he was talking about a whole school of music. So I put the record on. It was Art Blakey and it was so high. I said, "Whoa, wait a minute!" and it completely turned me around. I said, "I gotta hear more of this." So then my taste moved directly from the West Coast to the East Coast. Then I started listening to Horace Silver, Art Blakey, and Max Roach, and then I got into Miles. The first thing I heard… actually the first thing I heard Miles do, I think, was "Birth of the Cool," which was already a collector's item by then because it was recorded in the late forties. It had West Coast people and East Coast people, and it was cool jazz, but it had something else in it. It was weird, but I liked it.

After that, I started to get involved with jazz again. I played a gig for the YMCA. This was fascinating because I was learning to create—the thing that fascinated me was that this guy [Don], fourteen years old, was creating music out of his own head, on my instrument, the piano. I had been playing for six, seven years. If he could do it, I could do it, too. So I started hanging out with him. I was always yanking him out of class and saying, "You don't have to go to that class. Let's go upstairs to the band room and play some music." I'd watch him and ask him thousands of questions and he would turn me on to different records. The funny thing was after getting exposed to George Shearing through this guy, after maybe, I don't know, three or four months, I went home and I told my mother. I said, "Mom, you gotta give me some George Shearing records. I gotta check it out." She said, "You have some George Shearing records." I said, "I don't have any George Shearing records. What do you mean?" She said, "I bought you some George Shearing records a year and a half ago and you listened to them and told me that I should never have bought that garbage and that you didn't want them." I said, "No, I don't have any." She said, "Come here." She went into the records and there they were—she pulled out this album of seventy-eights—George Shearing.

My mother was the first person that actually bought me jazz records, before I was even ready to hear them and that was weird. I got the record out, and I put it on, and I was in ecstasy. It killed me. It was real funny. I was trying to find out what the hell he was doing so I put on the record and I tried to find the first note he played. When he got to the solo, no way was I going to figure out the chord. So I figured if I took the single line, maybe I could figure it out. I taught myself theory and harmony from doing that. So by the time I actually got to college to study theory and harmony, I knew it. I even had arguments with my teacher in college about what to call certain chords. There are certain chords that we have—for example, we might have the fifth in the bottom, but it isn't really the root. Now, I could hear that it wasn't the root, but the teacher said if the interval on the bottom is a fifth or a fourth, the root is the bottom note, the base note, and I said, "Wrong. It wasn't like that." Or even if you could have an interval of a fifth on the bottom, the bottom note is a fifth, the next note could be the ninth. Like I could play a C chord and have G, D, E, G, and C. that's a C chord. You could hear the C chord and the root is on the top, but he said, "Wrong, because there are certain rules."

So the first major seventh chord I ever played was one I heard the Four Freshmen sing. You know, major sevenths and minor sevenths. I played a dominant seventh because I could play the blues, but the major sevenths I didn't know anything about. Major ninths and a couple of voicings I got from the Four Freshmen. I'd pick them out from listening to records and figuring out who was singing what. That's how I developed my ear…because I didn't know where else to turn to learn what they were doing, see, but the thing is, when you learn from experience like that, you never forget. Then by the time I actually heard the Hi-Lo's, I started picking that stuff out; my ear was happening. I could hear stuff and that's when I really learned some much farther-out voicings—like the harmonies I used on "Speak Like a Child"*—just being able to do that. I really got that from Clare Fischer's arrangements for the Hi-Lo's. Clare Fischer was a major influence on my harmonic concepts…he and Bill Evans, and Ravel and Gil Evans, finally. You know, that's where it really came from. Almost all of the harmony that I play can be traced to one of those four people and whoever their influences were. And, of course, Miles.

I listened to Miles more than I listened to anybody—I mean, Miles and Trane as instrumental-

---

* Blue Note, 84279.

ists, and I always wanted to be able to phrase like Miles. I loved Bill Evans's chords; he really influenced me, but the phrasing that Miles would do and the way he played real simple melodies on top of some stuff that would be burning—he'd play just a few notes—it would just kill me.

JC: How did working with Miles's band affect your future concepts as a leader of your own?

H: My years with Miles were really formative years. The third record I did on my own was when I was with Miles. It was called "Inventions in Dimensions" with Paul Chambers and Willie BoBo on drums, and a guy named Chihuahua on percussion, and myself. The last record I did, I think, was "Speak Like A Child." You know, it's funny, when I did that record I knew that was the sound I wanted for my own band. That's when I knew I was going to switch from Miles. I said, that's it. That record was a surprise. I had in my head that I wanted to use the least number of instruments and get the most sound, fullness, and range out of them. So I figured for lower instruments the bass trombone has got the greatest range; for high instruments, I figured flute. Then I thought, well, alto flute, because it goes real low, too. Then I figured the trumpet sound would be too hard, so I got the flugelhorn. When we first started rehearsing and had that sound, I thought—that's the one. That was maybe 1967 when we recorded the album. I guess it probably came out in 1968 and I left Miles in August.

JC: When did you start to utilize the synthesizer, and why?

H: That was because of producer David Rubinson. When I was doing my album, *Crossings*, we had recorded the tracks, and David suggested the synthesizer since it was kind of a new thing, and kind of hot on the pop scene. You know everybody was into acid—it was kind of associated with acid and freakiness and all that. David said, "I know this guy, Pat Gleeson—he's really into the synthesizer. Why don't you let him do something on the record?" I said, "Okay—let him overdub something on another track and if I like it, we'll use it." So I gave the tape to Patrick and I said, "Here's an empty track—do what you want and we'll see what it's like." And what he put on killed me. It just blew me away. Right after that I hired him. It was so funny because the synthesizer was still such a new instrument. It was only used on recordings; there was no precedent for him to follow. He had nobody to listen to to figure out how to play it. You know, with jazz, where the music is constantly moving and changing intuitively, and we were "out," too, he really had a hard job. He was like a pioneer playing the live synthesizer, and after that, when I broke up that band, and I was doing the *Headhunters* album, I decided I was going to try a synthesizer myself—and I did it and it worked.

JC: When did you consciously incorporate the funk element into your music?

H: I listened to James Brown and Sly. I said, "Look, I want to find out what this is, and I'm going to go as far as I can." That's why I got some cats who can play funk, and it was really funny. I knew that I had never heard any jazz players really play funk like the funk that I had been listening to. Instead of getting jazz cats who knew how to play funk, I got funk cats who knew how to play jazz. So that's what it was; it was just by listening, because I've always been really good at being able to find something that can fit. If I hear something, I can kind of figure out what goes on there even if it's something I'm not familiar with.

JC: How has Buddhism affected your life?

H: Buddhism has had a profound effect on my music as well as my life. The more you do the practice, the more you begin to find out about yourself. Not that I didn't know anything about myself before, but it accelerates the process of learning about yourself. At the same time, it accelerates the process of learning about life in general—the world—the universe that we live in. It sounds like two different things, but actually it's the same thing—your life and the universe are really the same thing, and the basic thing behind both is the same: life, vitality, the law of cause and effect, and the universe. They are all really the same thing, but by learning about the law of cause and effect, you learn about life, because you can see by changing the present, you can change the past and the future. You can change your character and, at the same time, change your fortune. And what happened is that through changing, I began to find out more about myself, and the reason I'm playing this music is not because chanting told me to play it; it's only because I discovered that this is really the music I like to play.

bob james

12/25/39
Marshall, Missouri
piano and keyboards
synthesizer
composer and arranger
producer

Bob received his B.A. in composition from the University of Michigan. He then went to work with Sarah Vaughan for four years until 1968, acting as accompanist, musical director, and arranger. Leaving Sarah, James quickly became one of the busiest arrangers in the music business, working with some of the more celebrated soul vocalists in the field—Dionne Warwick, Roberta Flack, and Aretha Franklin, to name a few. In 1973, assisted by his friend and colleague, Quincy Jones, James was signed as arranger, composer, and conductor for CTI Records, and worked with, among others, Hubert Laws, Eric Gale, Stanley Turrentine, Ron Carter, and Grover Washington, Jr. Bob contributed several original tunes to Washington's *Mr. Magic* and *Feels so Good*—both crossover albums that went gold, in addition to his work as arranger and conductor. In 1974, James began to record under his own name for CTI, and started to receive recognition as an artist in his own right. In 1976, he joined CBS as director of progressive A&R, and became involved with the more commercial pop-oriented artists at Columbia, where his activities included arranging, orchestrating, and producing for Paul Simon, Neil Diamond, and Kenny Loggins. Bob now heads his own label, Tappan Zee Records, created in conjunction with, and distributed by, Columbia. In addition to these activities, he has explored other media—composing the score for the Broadway musical, *The Selling of the President*, and arranging and conducting the music for the motion picture, *Serpico*.

B: I started taking piano lessons when I was four years old. It was a result of hearing my sister play the piano. She was three years older than I was, and she started, I think, at five or six. I was very jealous of her being able to take these lessons. I thought, if she can do it, I can do it. I had perfect pitch and I picked things up very quickly by ear that my sister was doing by reading. That was the beginning, and I stayed with it—studied classical piano all the way through high school and college.

JC: So there was never any doubt that you would pursue music?

B: Yeah, in high school I pretty much knew. I went through a period when I was eleven or twelve years old when the boys didn't want to have anything to do with anybody who wanted to be a musician, and I hated practicing. I wanted to play baseball, basketball, and be a normal kid. So I begged my parents to let me stop taking lessons—which they ultimately did after I harassed them for a long time. Then I realized very quickly after that that I was already hooked on the piano, that I wanted to play. So, on my own, I started to go back and play a lot. I ended up asking my parents for permission to start taking lessons again. That was, I think, a really big turnaround in my life. I fought back and forth in high school as to whether to play on the basketball team or play in dance bands at night. Not being able to do both, I ultimately chose to quit the basketball team. From there on out there was not too much question about what I was going to do.

JC: Did you do any writing at that time?

B: I was writing a lot. I had a very good teacher who believed in teaching theory, in addition to just learning how to play the piano. I think even before high school I was noodling around trying to write little pieces, and during the time I was in high school, I was doing a lot of writing—not too much that was actually ever played, though. I did some simple dance band type of things which were really the only thing the musicians I knew could cope with, and I fantasized a lot about writing classical music—symphonic. I wrote some symphony-type things that I still have in my files, that were not destined to be played. They were the kind of things that looked good on the page. I was studying classical scores at the time, and I liked the way the big scores looked; they had lots of notes all over the place, so I would get these real big pieces of manuscript paper with twenty-four staves on them, and fill them up with an incredible amount of notes.

JC: What composers were you particularly attracted to?

B: Hindemith was the composer who, at that time, I was interested in the most, and I was really trying to copy his style—just from having studied the scores. I related a lot to him. And at the same time, I had become interested in jazz mostly because of records. I remember there was a lot of Stan Kenton I was interested in, because I liked bigness, and some Charlie Parker and Miles. I got very hung up on the West Coast movement of jazz at that time—Chet Baker, Gerry Mulligan, and those kind of arranged things. I was always interested in complicated arrangements; also, Oscar

Peterson. I lived in Marshall, Missouri, and there wasn't much jazz activity there—a few, maybe half a dozen at the most, musicians who were even interested in jazz, so the level of playing was not extremely high. We dabbled around with it, but most of the exposure I had was from records.

JC: So needless to say, because that element was missing, it probably motivated you to go out after school and play.

B: Absolutely. It motivated me to go away from Missouri to school, period. I went to the University of Michigan, which had a terrific music department, and I kind of assumed that there would be a lot of jazz going on there, too. When I got there, I found that things were happening in jazz, but very much under the table. The university wouldn't have anything to do with jazz at all at that time. There were some professors who were so adamant about it that they refused to allow jazz to be played in the music building under any circumstances.

JC: How extreme.

B: Yeah. So I spent a year there, and again begged my parents to let me leave, because by that time, I wanted to play jazz more than anything else.

JC: Do you think that that was a reaction?

B: Sure…a lot of rebellion going on in all kinds of ways at that time. And I had read in *Downbeat* about the Berklee School of Music, which sounded like utopia to me, because they indicated that you had the opportunity to study classical music and jazz. So my parents agreed to let me go there, and I went for three months—that was in 1958. It was an interesting school, but it was far below the level of classical training that I had become used to at Michigan, and again, I was already more caught up in that than I realized. So I ended up asking to go back to Michigan, which I did. I majored in composition and got my bachelor's degree there. And I think I liked the jazz environment better the way we did it at Michigan, which was all on our own—all in off-hours—with a group of very interesting, creative musicians that I met away from the academic environment. So I spent my days involved with classical training, and weekends, nights, every other time heavily involved in jazz writing, playing, sessions.

JC: You have your own record company now. What motivated you to do that? Business and art are two different things.

B: They are, and yet I've had the feeling for a long time that it's possible—not for everybody; I don't think it's right for very many musicians—but I think it is possible to have music as an occupation, and have it be a very good one, and to be very successful not only in a musical sense, but also in a business sense. And I think, too, many musicians apologize for that aspect and are kind of afraid that becoming a businessman in any sense is a bastardization of their talent. I don't feel that.

There are people like Charles Ives* who strangely felt that music and business should be totally separated, and he became so obsessed with that that he refused to allow anything that had to do with his music to come in contact with anything financial. So he went into the life insurance business, and became a millionaire, and actually gave up performing music. He just didn't have time for it anymore, but he definitely hated the idea of letting business interests corrupt his music. There are a lot of people who feel that way today. And there are a lot of people who feel that those of us who are involved in the kind of music that has become commercial, and salable, and financially profitable are in some way corrupted as a result of it. The only thing I would say about that is that if you accept as a goal the challenge of trying to reach a wide audience, there is a simplification process that takes place—there are intellectual kinds of pursuits I might have if I were writing music for a highly selected intellectual audience that I don't really pursue as much, because I do try to find universal musical values that work. And I don't think of it as a bastardization; I think of it as a more direct kind of communicating.

I love the fact that jazz has opened up in a direction that is so broad now that it's very difficult for people to define it and talk about it, and for me it's extremely healthy. I love it, and I'm not in any way bothered by the fact that there are those of us who are supposedly jazz musicians, and that we've been criticized or accused of not playing jazz anymore. For me, the basic ingredients that jazz has had from the beginning—those of improvisation and creativity—make it mandatory that you explore, and that it changes. Jazz is never going to stay the same. The bebop players of the fifties could have been accused of not playing jazz because they weren't playing Dixieland. And the same thing is true, I think all along the way—the jazz of the sixties, which, I guess, was our most advanced, progressive, and serious jazz, reached a plateau as far as striving toward the serious music world is concerned. And for me, somewhere along the way, that direction lost something on the level of spontaneity and a kind of "lightness." But the roots of jazz that appeal to me the most are those that were connected with dancing and nightclubs, with no bigger desire on the part of the soloist than to make somebody fall in love, or to appeal to our base emotions, which, to me, is not a bad thing at all. I still have a whole different world that I respond to in classical music, and primarily the twentieth-century classical music that I'm very interested in—starting with Stravinsky and onward. I think the greatest of the classical composers were able to make music on such a refined plane intellectually, and plan it, and spend a year to complete a composition, or two years, or three; whereas a jazz musician has three minutes to do that. And he's doing it on the spot, and spontaneously, and he's doing it to reach an immediate audience, not an audience forty years from now. We now have records that will make it possible for people to listen to our music forty years from now, but I don't know how well our music will stand up, and I don't even know if it's

---

* Twentieth-century American composer.

that important, because it is something that is an emotional thing that happens right now, and it's supposed to be heard right now. The most exciting jazz music to me is the stuff that's heard live.

JC: Do you feel that there is, in fact, a dichotomy in this life, in this life of music, where the musician is put into a lifestyle which may, in fact, be counterproductive to his music—like there's some kind of a myth that in order to be great, you've got to live a life of debauchery?

B: I think one aspect of the myth, at least I felt it real strongly when I first came to New York, was the "white" myth, the myth that the white player who starts out without soul, must acquire it in order to be "black." And the easiest way to do that is to become an addict, or an alcoholic, or completely screw up your life to the point where you're a mess. And after doing that, theoretically you would have all these highly emotional memories that would translate themselves in your music. But I thought then that that was bullshit, and I still do. There are people who are brilliantly talented but don't understand their talent, and don't know what it is about their talent that people like. It can lead to a very neurotic personality, which, once you have it, and once those gremlins are strong enough, there's always the world of drugs, or booze, or whatever to try to pull you out of it. It's the person who is scared, who's afraid that he's not going to make it, and it's magnified in the arts, because you're dealing with people who want you to perform magic…

JC: …transform their lives.

B: Yes. And you don't know what that magic is. You can practice, you can learn the technique, but the inspiration for that next song that's going to make people fall in love with you, or the inspiration for that magical improvisation that can happen at a concert, is not found in the practice room. So, if you don't walk into that concert, or into that studio, or sit down at your desk to write with confidence, then I guess for a lot of people, it's easier for them to walk into it in a blurred state of one kind or another. But for me music is a very intense thing, it's a very mental thing, and I feel I'm at my best when I have all my faculties going for me.

JC: You are now an executive and are in a position to change the power structure. How does it feel?

B: So far, all right. It's a lot of pressure and a lot of risk that I'm taking by doing it, and I won't know how worth it it's been until we have some successful records, which I hope we will have. The main reason I did it was because I wanted more control over artistic choices, which is really impossible to have with a big company. There are just too many people who have to be involved in the decision. The development of new artists is something that a large company is less willing to do. I think in many cases they would rather pay a little more and get a guy who's at least off and running with his career, than to start from the beginning. For me, it's more of a challenge to take a guy who's in the formative stage, and take him to that next level, and then to take him all the way to the top.

keith jarrett

5/8/45

Allentown,
Pennsylvania

piano

soprano saxophone

composer and arranger

producer

Keith began playing the piano at the age of three. At seven, he was composing, improvising, and performing at solo recitals. He began formal studies in composition at fifteen, and later received a scholarship to the Berklee School of Music where he remained for a year. Keith worked locally in Boston before moving to New York in 1965, where he played with Art Blakey and Roland Kirk. He joined Charles Lloyd in 1966, touring with him in Europe and Moscow. In 1969 he formed his own trio with Charlie Haden (bass) and Paul Motian (drums), and embarked on a long European tour. In the early seventies, he recorded and appeared with the Miles Davis band, while continuing to perform with his own trio. In 1972, he added reedman Dewey Redman to his group. Also, in the mid-seventies, he received a Guggenheim Fellowship in composition. A dedicated proponent of the acoustic piano, Keith has done much to acquaint the public at large with the beauty and purity of the instrument.

K: I think everyone's introduced to music when they are born. In my case there happened to be an old piano in the house that I fooled around with, but I also played with celery sticks on the tabletop. I wouldn't say that's an introduction to music. That was music coming out in that particular way. Everyone is musical. I don't remember any particular musical charge that suddenly made me conscious of music; I think I knew it ever since I was born. I did play some classical concerts when I was a kid, professional recitals in small places. I had perfect pitch, so my parents did the logical thing which was to give me piano lessons at the very early age of three.

JC: Something led you to the Berklee School of Music. What was it?

K: Yeah, being ignorant of what it really was and also there were no other paths to take for what I thought I wanted to do. A lot of people go there because there is no other place that says they do what Berklee says they do. But no one, including them, does what they say they do, because that's impossible. Actually, though, they are shrewd enough to realize that they can't do what they say they'll do. So they say they produce professionals, totally professional musicians, which is true, in a way, in the sense that a professional musician is someone who is just like a professional executive. I mean, someone whose profession is music and who doesn't have any particular strong feeling or need, someone who can write a jingle or a chart for the sound track of a TV movie or something like that. Still, the only school ever connected with the word jazz, at that time, was Berklee, and all the other schools were mostly stiff. Anyone who didn't want to see that stiffness around them ended up at Berklee.

JC: I understand that you didn't complete your tenure at Berklee.

K: Yeah. I kind of got kicked out because I had a trio made up of two other people who had dropped out of Berklee and I had a pretty large reputation in the school. I think some of the people at the school were afraid I was starting some kind of anti-Berklee campaign. Once I was in the school jamming with some other people and I played inside the piano. One of the administrators must have been waiting for this chance, he jumped in the door and said, "Out," and that was it. I said, "Thank you," and left. He tried to apologize years later when I was at Newport with Gary Burton. He said, I really have to tell you that I have wanted to say this for a while; we are sorry about what happened," and I said, "Don't say that because I built my reputation on that."

JC: I'd like to talk a little bit about the various situations you participated in after music school.

K: Well, more interesting than after was during because I had to pay for my schooling, or rather for my living expenses. I had every kind of job I could find in Boston and unfortunately became successful at doing cocktail gigs and things. I knew it was total insanity. On the other hand, at that time, everyone was putting that down. You were supposed to starve and only play what you wanted to play. These were the people that couldn't get jobs. It wasn't that they couldn't get jobs because they were idealistic, it was that they couldn't get jobs because they couldn't play. So naturally they had to rationalize it. But there were only a few people among us that worked. As far as interesting jobs, those were the strangest assortment of things I have done. I can't think of any kind of music or any kind of job that exists that I haven't played up to now.

JC: You wouldn't single out any one specific experience, for example, Charles Lloyd or Miles Davis?

K: No. actually, I may have learned more playing cocktail piano at Dingy Moors in Boston than I did with Charles. Who knows? It's hard to say what the learning process was. In Charles's band, because of the fact that I was doing what I wanted, maybe I wasn't learning as much as when I was doing what I didn't want to. But I would imagine that the learning experience involves the things you are most uncomfortable with, not the things you are comfortable with. But there isn't anything that I have done that I have regretted doing so far. If there was, I would tell you about it—and certainly I didn't regret my experience with Miles. Although, for a few years, I resisted his attempt to ask me to be in the band because I didn't want anything to do with electric music. Actually, more than the electric thing, I couldn't stand his preceding band and I wondered if I could do anything, if I could save anything, and if I couldn't I'd leave right away. It turned out very well because the whole band kind of changed around the time I joined.

JC: Was it a comfortable experience then?

K: No, it wasn't comfortable. It was what I wanted to do at the time. Mine is my own music. Whenever I have worked with people, I have realized that I have accepted to be in their organization. Whatever music I can get out of it I will, but I am not going to be an inside threat to the overall feeling the band has. So with Miles, fortunately, I liked his playing throughout the change of personnel he had. The time I had heard the band that made me feel bad about it, the only person who I thought was playing music at all was Miles. So I realized that, if I would play with the band, at least I would have that camaraderie with him, that I could trust his playing and maybe he could trust mine.

JC: Would you say that compensated for the fact that you were playing an electric keyboard?

K: Definitely. In fact, his music, at that point, was totally based on having electric instruments so that, because it was him playing it and he didn't lose track of his own past playing and because the music wouldn't sound like anything at all with acoustic instruments, at the time I didn't mind. But I knew it was temporary and I told him it was temporary.

JC: You have maintained the same band for an unusually long time. What do you attribute this to?

K: I don't know. Maybe it is the difference between an elephant's lifetime and a moth's. There was just enough music to be played between the three or four of us that there was never any reason to change personnel. There were thousands of people who thought I should have hipper people in the band, the so-called drummer of the hour and the bass player of the year. Those are the people I would never be able to deal with in a band because those people get to be the bass players of the hour because they have been playing that music the way they play long enough to be identified as doing a particular thing a particular way. When they do that and they come into my band, they'd have a style and my music doesn't have a style. It may have a style, if you look at it and analyze it, like there is no other sound that sounds exactly like that band. But that was an accident. Everybody is still playing fresh music most of the time.

JC: You have indicated that you compose away from the keyboard. Could you comment on this?

K: Composing a piece for piano should not be done away from the piano. But if you are a pianist and you are writing for strings, you are too tempted to use the piano to test what you have written for strings. I almost threw away an entire movement once that I wrote for a brass quintet because I was testing it on the piano and the piano just didn't sound like a brass quintet would have sounded. In fact, it sounded incredibly boring to me on the piano and I thought, "What is this that I wrote?" But some inner confidence in what reason I had told me I should keep it and it was the best part of the whole piece with the brass quintet. So piano is not an instrument to overuse when writing for another instrument. The piano can be a crutch. Of course, if you can't look at what you wrote and hear it then, if you are intelligent enough not to believe the way the piano sounds, you can just listen to the notes you wrote. I mean, I check out my pieces on the piano at some time, but not while I am writing, because I just found that it's very dangerous.

JC: You once said, "I rarely see myself as a continuation of a pianistic tradition except to the extent that I use the piano."* Could you elaborate?

K: The whole idea of influences is based on the egotism of the human race; man is so great that the obvious question to ask someone who does something very well is "Who?" It's never "What?" or "How?" and, anyway, none of those questions are really answerable except "Who?" if there is a "Who." But, in my case, there isn't. So what I meant was that, if everything is continually in a state of change or things are in continuous process, then there are no "Whos." Then if you ask me who I was influenced by and I gave you an actual name, I would be making something solid out of something that is essentially fluid, and the poor guy that I had mentioned would be suddenly turned to stone. It doesn't make any sense. In fact, it's very related to the word eclectic. The word itself means something that could be interpreted in so many ways, but in the sense of a continuous process, everything is eclectic—hopefully. But if I was afraid to sound a certain way because it made me sound a little bit like something that happened before, then I would no longer be an artist. Then I would be a politician. And that's what I think most artists think they have to do. They have to make sure they sound like themselves, as though they know who they are. So, for example, in

* Lyons, Len. "Keith Jarrett: Pianist and Composer," Contemporary Keyboard 2, no. 3 (May/June 1976): 23.

the last few years, fourths on the piano are hip; if you play thirds, you sound like too many other people and with sixths you sound like Chopin. If you play tenths on your left hand, you are playing old music; if you play a triad, you're Beethoven. I mean, it's unbelievable. I would say that ninety percent of the contemporary, so-called improvising artists that I know follow the rule that they think they are doing something positive when they are actually doing something completely opposed to the process of creativity. They are eliminating everything that might sound like something other than themselves and ending up with what they think is them, when actually they have erased themselves. And yet, when they erase themselves, millions of other people who erase themselves all the time acclaim them because they always sound the same. It's a mutual "erase yourself" program.

JC: What does the word "eccentric" mean to you?

K: It is something I have been accused of very often, being eccentric on the stage, which translates to the people that know what's going on up there, not to the audience and not to the promoters, but to the few people that sometimes help me get things together, who are now also called eccentric, although some are businessmen. The word translates onstage into knowing what you need. Pianists are a good example. Most of them don't know why a piano is bad, what is wrong and what is needed. So they go to their gig and play the piano and complain. Someone says, "Well, they are just crybabies, they don't know what they want." I go in there and I know what's wrong with it and I say, "I want this done before the concert." The promoter answers, "No one has ever told me that before. God, what do you mean, before the concert, there are only two hours?" I reply, "I am sorry, I need that. If it's not that way, I am not going to play the piano." Well, that's terribly eccentric behavior. Or telling the audience at a university, an audience composed of students, with a big music program, that the piano is kept in such a bad condition that I think they deserve to know that because they are going to the school. They are paying money to have these things presented to them and I am there willing to give them what I can give and yet I can't because no one at the school really knows how to take care of an instrument and after that, getting flack from those same students for an hour and a half about, "What did you mean?" Isn't it clear that the problem is that I was supposed to be up there saying, "You have been a great audience, folks, and this is the name of my first tune…?" I mean, you are allowed to say those things but if you go any further than that and say anything that doesn't fit that schedule of events, it is eccentric behavior. At Newport I said that this was not a jazz event, it was a music event. Well, anyone who was at least half intelligent could realize that music included jazz, but what everyone said was, "How can he say that? This is the Newport Jazz Festival and we want to hear jazz here tonight."

JC: You have said that people are asking too many questions. What do you mean by this?

K: What I was saying is that the questions they ask, they ask to cover the real question they have. The other thing is that asking questions is a substitute for answering them. But now, the event in America is to have questions, which is better than not having questions. Any good teacher will tell you there aren't any answers. An average students will say, "Oh, wow, fantastic, that's a fantastic answer." There it goes. It wasn't an answer.

JC: Another quote, "Playing is the least important thing; it's the waste product, the activity of being musical."*

K: Well, it's a good parallel to explaining why and how I learned to play. That's why I said birth is probably a major musical experience. Playing the music is relating the experience; having the experience is bigger than relating the experience because relating the experience is further away and more interpretation can be put on it. So the actual experience is more important than the fact that I play the piano to show the experience. I could not say a word or not play a note and somehow the experience could be conveyed; it just wouldn't be conveyed to that many people. But it also wouldn't be so diluted. I know my son Gabriel doesn't play the piano, but he is a perfect example of being able to communicate his experiences anyway.

JC: But you also said that music is the medium which comes the closest to projecting harmony with oneself. Obviously there have to be other ways, or musicians would be the only people living in harmony with themselves.

K: But when I say music, I am not talking about musicians. Musicians are the last people to know this. The first people to know it, very often, are the people who say, "I don't know anything about this, but I like it" or "It's way over my head." Those are the people who would know it; if you could shock them at the right time, they'd know it. There are too many shock absorbers in artists, based on their ego workings, for them to be shocked properly even when they really have to be for their own good. A so-called average person doesn't have all that and as a result they can have "realizations" much quicker and much more directly. But, when I say music, I'm never talking about music as played by musicians. I'm talking about music as maybe the balance between rain and nice weather.

JC: Why have you chosen to record so much of your music in Europe?

K: Okay, if we talk about specific things, all the record companies in America are based on politics and big business. You can't be too naïve and say, "Well, why isn't there a company that…?" because the whole society is based so much on money. You could say it, but if you were the one that was going to try it on the scale and on the quality that you'd like, or the highest quality attainable, you might find certain things are impossible. But in Europe there is a good quality level and just a higher standard. It's funny. I mean, they don't even think about it. In America I haven't done a single session where there hasn't been a comment like, "Oh, I forgot to turn the machine on," or you'd listen to the playback and there'd be this terrible flutter and they'd have to get a repairman in to work on it.

JC: How do you relate to the changes you have noticed in your peers in regards to their musical directions?

K: Well, I would just consider it weakness, but I wouldn't say I'm mad at them. I am mad at a certain possibility that somebody who seemed to have potential sensitivities of a certain kind could go that crazy and just jump out of the process to somewhere else and expect to come back, anytime, when they've made enough money or they feel like it, because it's possible to jump, but the streams don't just keep waiting for each other. You make that jump only when two streams are pretty close to each other, so that you can get to the other one. The chances of those two things getting close enough again to jump back is very, very small. Mostly, I think I feel sorry for the feelings they must have when they think about the way their music used to sound—if they still remember that feeling. It's got to be a sad thing to think about. They can't just go back and get it again.

patrice
rushen

9/30/54

Los Angeles, California

piano and keyboards

vocalist

composer and arranger

producer

Patrice, one of the first female musicians to receive major recognition in the seventies, grew up in Los Angeles and attended USC, majoring in music education with a minor in performance. Unable to finish the last semester as a regular student, Patrice taught seminars in contemporary music for three summers to obtain her degree. More recently, she has studied privately with orchestrator teacher Dr. Albert Harris. Patrice first appeared with trombonist Melba Liston's big band, and subsequently played with Abbey Lincoln, Hubert Laws, Lee Ritenour, Harvey Mason, and Jean-Luc Ponty. Patrice is also a busy studio player, contributing her talent and skill to numerous jingles, sound tracks, and records.

P: I started playing when I was five. My parents had been informed early in my life that I had a gift, a musical ability that should definitely be paid attention to. My first musical involvement was at three—in a program for young gifted children over at the University of Southern California. After that, it was suggested that I study the piano, because that's a pretty wide-open basic instrument.

JC: Did you have a normal childhood?

P: Yes. I wasn't treated special so that I could grow up like a normal kid. I was forced to practice, to develop the habit of practicing—first fifteen minutes a day, then fifteen minutes twice a day, later thirty minutes, and finally one hour.

Eventually I would find myself practicing longer just because I'd feel like I wanted to—to fulfill myself. By the time I was seven or eight. I had started composing, and had acquired quite a good musical vocabulary. I had actually started to compose when I was younger, but wasn't yet able to notate, so my folks taped a lot of it and had teachers transcribe the tapes.

JC: What kind of music were you listening to then?

P: Everything. My folks are fans of all different kinds of music; the radio was always on and that was an influence. As far as classical music was concerned, I listened to it, too.

In junior high school, I became aware that the piano was not an instrument that you could play with other people all the time, because there was no piano choir or trio where I could play. So I got bored. Then it occurred to me to learn another instrument that I could play with other people, so I learned to play the flute, and in doing that, I was able to play in a band for the first time in my life. Getting involved in ensemble playing really made a tremendous difference insofar as my understanding of music was concerned. The piano took kind of a back seat for a while after I began playing the flute. I was still going to my lessons, but all my activities in school were with the flute. That experience allowed me to observe first-hand the other instruments and their roles in a band or orchestra, and how the choirs of instruments are put together, and how they sound separately—their textures, colors, and so on. That's when I began to write things that were more oriented for woodwind players.

By the time I got to high school, I started writing seriously. I was part of a marching band that was playing Top 40 material, and one of the band directors told the students who could handle it to try to expand the repertoire. This was when I began to learn different transpositions on an instrument, and some of the ranges of the instruments. That whole thing got me into arranging. My second year of high school, I became involved in a workshop that was sort of a jazz lab. It was a vocational orchestra where the teacher was trying to give the students alternatives to just going into music as a hobby, so if you didn't go to college, you could get a gig. That took me back to the piano, but now I approached it from a different perspective and started playing music that called for improvisational skills, which I had not developed playing classical music.

JC: When did you encounter the electric piano?

P: I encountered it then, because that was one of the keyboard doubles I had to learn. This orchestra trained the student to understand what was expected of the studio player, 'cause in Los Angeles that was one of the main alternatives to playing in the Los Angeles Philharmonic or playing in clubs.

JC: At that point, did you start having a specific goal in terms of your own career?

P: Definitely. I began to understand that if I was going to be really successful—that is to say, financially stable—that I should always be aware of these alternatives and prepare myself to do whatever I wanted to do. So I concentrated on improvising well, and I learned certain leadership abilities that would be required of me in the event that I should have my own group. I knew that I didn't want to play classical music for a living, because I didn't have that kind of discipline. I was much more fulfilled by writing my own music and playing music of a more spontaneous nature, where I felt like I was contributing in a different way than interpretation. So I just knew that contemporary music was where I wanted to be.

JC: Were you learning other electric keyboards besides the electric piano?

P: Yeah, synthesizer—an instrument which has to be at least understood, by any keyboard player.

JC: Have you officially studied orchestration and arranging?

P: I kind of dabbled in it on a trial-and-error basis, asking a lot of questions as I began to meet more and more professional musicians. I left USC before I got into that, because I wanted to study privately. At school, when I was in class, the teacher would tell me, for instance, that a trumpet could only play up to a high C. I knew through personal experience that that was not true, so for him to make it a class assignment to understand the range of the trumpet is from here to there, and I knew players who can play higher, it just didn't seem realistic to me. So I began to study privately with Dr. Albert Harris, who is a master orchestrator. He is aware of a lot of things, including certain studio techniques that can be used to your advantage when you have to write for different-sized ensembles, and then make the music sound bigger than it is, if it has to be revoiced for live performance.

JC: Has being a woman had a positive or negative effect on your career?

P: Mostly positive. I am probably one of the few female musicians in the field getting notoriety who can say that. I think that women who are involved now have a better chance of not having to encounter negative attitudes that are going to keep them from doing what they want to do. I was lucky, because by the time I got into music professionally, the women's lib movement had kind of mellowed out to the point where it was no longer unusual to see a woman doing something "unusual." I didn't have to break down doors, although I did turn a few heads around. If there were any strange vibes that existed, they always ceased when we started playing.

JC: To what do you attribute the scarcity of female instrumentalists?

P: A lot of it has to do with the attitude of the women themselves, I think, because many were just too self-conscious. Also, a few years ago the whole field of music was a very ugly situation. You had people who spent half their lives becoming craftsmen at the art of making music, and where were they going? Jazz musicians were rarely respected by anyone other than themselves and their peers. If I had been a woman coming up, say ten years ago, I would have probably limited myself to being a music teacher.

richard
tee

11/24/43

Brooklyn, New York

piano and keyboards

organ

vocalist

composer and arranger

Richard had twelve years of classical training on the piano before attending the High School of Music and Art in New York, graduating in 1961. He went on to study the bass at Manhattan School of Music, but dropped out after a year. He began playing for twenty-five dollars a night with a weekend band before becoming a pianist for Motown, where one of his first recordings was with Marvin Gaye. Soon after that he became a staff arranger. He also discovered the virtues of the Hammond organ while working at Motown, and would spend time at the studios at Broadway Recording where he would, "mess with the organ, seeing how many stops I could get and learning what everything did" (*Contemporary Keyboard*, November 1977). Through his contacts at Motown, Richard was able to secure work as a studio player. Since the mid-seventies, he has become one of the busiest and most sought after players in the studio, working with a vast cross section of artists, including George Harrison, the late Roland Kirk, Doc Severinsen, Melanie, Carly Simon, Paul Simon, Burt Bacharach, Tom Scott, Joe Cocker, Ashford and Simpson. In the late seventies, he became a member of the group Stuff, along with Gordon Edwards, Cornell Dupree, Eric Gale, Chris Parker, and Steve Gadd. Beside the early influence of classical music, Richard points to Ray Charles and Oscar Peterson as sources of inspiration to him and his music.

R: I first realized there was a piano in my house when I was about two and I started messing with it. It was an old upright with half the keys missing. I played it for about two years before my mother got me another piano. She wanted to make sure I was going to play the instrument. She bought me a Knabe spinet when I was about five years old, which I've still got, and I started taking lessons. I took classical lessons until I was about seventeen—scales and exercises.

JC: Reflecting upon your early academic training—has it affected your present music?

R: It pays off. All the exercises give you your finger dexterity. And classical music helps your reading, so you can read anything the first time down.

JC: Did you contemplate going into the studio full time?

R: No, I was thinking about having my own band and I didn't even know what the studio was. I remember coming from my first record date—it was fun. There were a couple of notes to read, I looked for more notes, but all they had written down were the chord changes. That was an early taste of being inside a studio. It looked weird, but it was fun to play with a whole bunch of guys, playing music I'd never seen before. From there, Eddie Singleton got me a job at Motown as a pianist. Then I became a staff arranger and started writing. Meanwhile I started doing other dates in town.

JC: You write for the group, Stuff. When did you start to compose?

R: I started writing songs when I was singing in 1959, but not that many. At that time I didn't consider them that good—not until about 1964 when they made sense to me. I'd write a passage and that's as far as I'd get. I wasn't writing complete tunes. I would write the verse and leave out the bridge and everything else till later on.

JC: You've said of your classical studies, one of the composers you were most attracted to was Debussy, while Bach was less interesting to you. Why?

R: The feeling of Debussy's music, the prettiness of it—the chords and progressions—was much more interesting to me than Bach, who seemed sterile and very rigid by comparison. Chopin and Debussy and even George Gershwin were more to my liking and my personality.

JC: Stuff is a band with a strong group identity. Was the inception of that band deliberate?

R: I really don't know. We just got together and played. We played so often in the studio, and we liked it and we just kept doing it until someone said we all should record as a group. We turned around and laughed and said, "We don't have the time—we're too busy doing other people's sessions." But they got to be kind of persistent so that's how we got a record deal. I still look at that band as a group of guys, part of a rhythm section that plays together a lot in the studio.

JC: For you the studio is really the central aspect of your life. I don't mean financially, but creatively, because what you did with Stuff is really just an extension of that. How would you compare the studio with live performances?

R: When you do gigs, you don't have a chance to do it over if you mess up. Everything is spontaneous. But in the studio you can do it over until you get it right.

JC: You mean there's more pressure in live performance?

R: Yeah, but it's also a lot of fun.

JC: You have not as yet gotten into the synthesizer or multiple keyboards. Why not, and do you ever intend to?

R: I might, but my favorite keyboard is the acoustic piano. I'm still learning some things on that.

JC: You once said, "Chords and rhythm are my meat; even my solos are mostly chords. I try to be an orchestra and I feel most comfortable playing everything I can with 10 fingers."* Can you extrapolate a little bit on that?

R: If I'm playing by myself, I want it to sound like I'm playing with a band. The only thing I can't sound like is the drummer. Everything else I just want to incorporate into my own playing. So, when I play by myself, I'm comfortable. Some people choose to play a horn—they can only play one note and they can't feel the chords. I'm fortunate enough to play piano, and I can play all the orchestration and play the lead line and everything else. That's the way I like to play.

I play a constant rhythm that doesn't really change, and I try to keep it simple so that it gives other people a chance to put their two cents in. When you start playing a whole lot of things, no one can relate to it, because you haven't played the same thing twice; you've played it differently.

JC: What would you say to young musicians who are trying to play music?

R: Listen and try to be aware of what you're playing, and don't try to play everything you know in four bars. Take your time; a song goes a long way—maybe five minutes. Don't play everything you know in two or you'll have nowhere else to go after that. Take your time and you'll get there.

---

* Stix, John. "Richard Tee from New York Session Work to 'Stuff,'" Contemporary Keyboard 3, no. 11 (November 1977): 46.

joe zawinul

7/7/32

Vienna, Austria

piano and keyboards

synthesizer

composer and arranger

producer

Joe grew up in Europe during World War II. He attended a conservatory before enrolling at a gymnasium or college where he remained for seven years. In 1959 he came to America and played with Maynard Ferguson, Slide Hampton, and Joe Williams before going with Dinah Washington, where he stayed from 1959 to 1961, when he became a member of Cannonball Adderley's band. He stayed with Cannonball until 1970. Joe was the first musician to record jazz on the Fender-Rhodes electric piano; the composition was his "Mercy, Mercy, Mercy," which became a hit in the early sixties. He composed the title track for Miles Davis's *In a Silent Way* in 1968, a landmark in contemporary music. In 1971, Joe and Wayne Shorter, along with Miroslav Vitous, Airto, and Alphonse Mouzon formed Weather Report, a group that was to undergo many personnel and musical changes to become—in the late seventies—one of contemporary music's most significant groups. Joe plays both the synthesizer and the acoustic piano in Weather Report.

J: The first music I heard was my father and my mama singing, and they can sing good. I grew up in Vienna where they played folk music—it was country music and street music.

JC: When did you start your formal musical training?

J: When I was six, I started out on the accordion. I studied for about a year with a teacher, and then I got a scholarship for the conservatory—Third Reich time, if you know what I mean.

JC: I bet you could really feel it.

J: I felt good, you know. I went to school, got a scholarship, and started playing piano, but I didn't have one, so I had to go once or twice a week to a friend's house to practice.

JC: You really had to be motivated to do that.

J: I didn't have any motivation. I didn't want to do it. I did this for my folks, because they were always saying that they never had the opportunity. But I didn't ever really take it seriously until I got older. Things just happened kind of naturally. I started playing the piano, and by the time I was eleven, I was really into it. I had to go to the conservatory every week, and I started enjoying it. I was learning new coordination things and exercises, and I had a very good teacher.

JC: How did the war affect your life at that time?

J: This would take an entire book to cover, but as far as the music was concerned, lessons were very sparse because the bombs were falling and everything was very heavy.

JC: How did you spend your formative years, your adolescence?

J: I spent a lot of time in the country and in the fields. Then, in 1946, I went to Vienna and started going to what is called over there, "gymnasium." It's actually like college. I went there for seven out of eight years—then I started to become a professional musician. I was about seventeen years old.

JC: What music were you listening to then?

J: Well, there was no contact with America until about 1947. That's when they had military stations playing some jazz music. And that was the first time I connected with jazz. At that time, they played mostly George Shearing's music, and that was one of my first real influences in playing. They played Erroll Garner's music, who was also one of those idols we all had. Later on, I heard Oscar Peterson. But mostly George Shearing was my hero. After that, everything kind of started opening up. However, there were no records available, but we did always go to the English Reading Room and read *Downbeat*. We all dug America—that was what was happening. I saw a movie, *Bathing Beauty*, with Esther Williams, Red Skelton, and Harry James—I saw it many times. After that, I saw *Stormy Weather* (twenty-four times), and this was the most influential thing in my life up to that point.

JC: So America became a dream to you.

J: I really became obsessed with wanting to go to America and learn how to play music, and it took me until 1959 to bring this to realization.

JC: How did it happen?

J: Well, first I had to get on a boat. It was very difficult to do because we were still occupied by four nations—Russia, and I was living in the Russian sector, and the British, the French, and the Americans. So it was rough. I mean, you had to go from one district to another, and you had to have an ID. It was like you had to have a pass just to go from 52nd Street to 42nd Street. Anyway, in 1959, I got a scholarship to the Berklee School of Music.

JC: In retrospect, did America live up to the expectations you had of it?

J: Yes. Absolutely. As a matter of fact, the first day I arrived here, I had a fight with this cabdriver because he wanted to mess with me with my money, and I wasn't going for it. So I started out correctly on my own terms.

The first day I stayed on 54th Street and Broadway, and I walked down Broadway. It was a cold, clear January day, and it was about two in the afternoon. The sun was already setting, and all the big lights were on, and I knew in my heart that my parents were really suffering a lot because I went away. When I was walking, I had this feeling and it made me kind of sad, because I knew I was never going to leave America. I mean, I had found it here—right here. I didn't know a person in America—no relatives, no friends, nobody—not even an acquaintance. I just went out and said, "I'm going to start from the beginning," and I felt sad because I knew this was where I was going to be. That first night I went to Birdland and it all just started. In the years following, I paid a lot of dues, but so what—everybody does that. I wanted to learn…to suck in, to inhale all that life— Birdland, Harlem—all a part of the growing experience of living, 'cause play—I always could…In order to express yourself you've got to get the knowledge to do it. I was tired of searching. I was ready to find things.

JC: What contribution has the synthesizer made to contemporary music?

J: What it has really done is to replace all the many, many instruments you find, for instance, in a symphony orchestra, which a small group of musicians (for example, a quintet like Weather Report) could never accomplish before. It gives you, according to individual taste, the opportunity to do as many things as you can think of, producing an incredibly full and versatile sound. Any sound I hear in my head, I can reproduce with a synthesizer, and this is its greatest blessing. It's like dream world.

JC: Weather Report—a band which has gone through a lot of personnel changes and managed to survive them all over the years—have these changes in any way altered its direction and conception?

J: Not really, because the initial concept was Wayne's [Shorter] and mine. It never mattered, because we're always forming as people. That does not mean that we haven't changed, or that we don't learn from others, because everybody plays differently. It makes you change automatically. If you know how to adjust, you change and put strength into that change, of course. Any little thing or any big thing will change events, but the concept of the band—that was always there.

JC: You've really been unusually lucky—how do you account for this?

J: There is no luck; you've got to make your luck. You've got to always be prepared—without trying to. That's what we wanted; therefore we joined Columbia Records. We had a reputation before we joined; we had made a record with Miles Davis for Columbia called *In a Silent Way*, for which I wrote the title track. It was the biggest-selling record Miles had at that point, and that had a lot to do with everything. Then we recorded *Bitches' Brew*, and Columbia was immediately interested in us. A record company doesn't do anything for an artist in the sense of luck, and I learned this. As great as Columbia is, the main hard work always comes from the artist, and then the interest of the record company starts growing. Most of the people in the recording business know very little about music, ours in particular. But more and more of these people learn by just checking out the reaction of the audience, even though they themselves don't understand what the group is doing. There are many people of all walks of life who really feel what we're doing, and then the record company finally gets aware, and we finally get support. Weather Report was one of the least-played groups on the radio. There has to be a reason for that.

JC: How did it get played?

J: The people demanded it. The record company finally woke up to what we were doing, which was good because there's a big difference now. We're selling a lot of records, but we could have sold a lot a long time ago. The people were ready, but what you don't hear, what you don't see, you don't buy.

JC: You have to be very tough to survive it.

J: Goddamned right! That's why I don't like the word "lucky," because it's no good. It is hard. You have to fight every day to get them off their asses and realize that this is a gold mine—this group is a real gold mine, and we're going to go farther. We're going to take this all the way. We're going to bring this music to a lot of people. People who are on the streets are ready for all this—people want to hear it. There is something happening in the world for the young other than a backbeat.

JC: You're really an optimist then?

J: I'm going to make it happen. The revolution started a long time ago. If it takes a few years more, it's going to be happening—nobody can stop it.

percussionpercussion**percussion**percu

airto (moreira)

8/5/41

Itaiopolis, S. Brazil

percussion and drums

vocalist

composer and arranger

producer

Airto, who grew up in the small village of Curitiba, had his own show on a local radio station while still a child. At sixteen, he moved to São Paulo where he played the trap drum with various groups in local clubs. In the early sixties he lived in Rio de Janeiro while he played in cabarets all over Brazil for about three years. He then joined the Brazilian group Quarteto Novo before coming to the United States in 1968, when he began studying with Moacir Santos in Los Angeles. Soon after, he moved to New York and began to record and perform. During the sevemties, he recorded with Miles Davis, Herbie Hancock, and many others and became a member of the original Return to Forever in 1972. Airto has performed and/or recorded with countless other musicians, among them Lee Morgan, Stan Getz, and Gato Barbieri. Since 1973, he has been leader of his own group and works and records with his wife, singer Flora Purim.

A: When I was three years old, I used to go out in the woods and play. I had no lessons; I just grew up playing and singing. When I was five, I had a program every Saturday on the local radio station in the small town in Brazil where I grew up.

JC: Do you think that you were aware then that you would pursue music for the rest of your life?

A: Yes I was.

JC: What made you come to America?

A: Flora Purim.

JC: That's a very good reason. How would you compare the musical and social attitudes in general between your country and America?

A: In Brazil the musicians—and everybody—are much more repressed than here. Here other musicians help you and listen to you, and it's much easier to sit in here than in Brazil.

JC: There was a period in your life when you played traps, before you really became known as Airto the Percussionist. I think people have a strange concept of a percussionist as one who is really an accessory, or perhaps an embellishment to the music, but not really important. Would you agree?

A: I think it's the same thing as black and white—any kind of prejudice. Before I played with Miles, I used to play congas and maybe some bongos and maracas. But after I started to play with him, everybody began to see all kinds of things that they could do with percussion instruments, and percussion became a category—became an instrument instead of just background, as you said. So, percussion became much more important, and people who play music with percussion today see that it is not just banging things—there are a lot of sounds and a lot of different approaches.

JC: From about 1974 on you were a very busy studio musician; you don't do that nearly as much anymore. Why is that?

A: Recording is a whole different thing; it's a whole different approach. When you go to the studio to record, and when you go up onstage to play for the people, it's a whole different thing. When I started out, I was not really familiar with studio recording, and I gained a lot of experience and knowledge during my time in the studio. I learned about microphone techniques and a lot of other things that have become very valuable for me. But then I had to go and play for the people again, because that's my thing—I am a player. I have to see the people's faces from time to time in order to recharge my battery or whatever.

JC: You've had bands, but never one that has lasted for a very long time. What ingredients are necessary to keep a band together?

A: Number one is money—especially here in California. The musicians don't want to play unless they get paid. It's because the business is stronger than the art. So, really the main ingredient is to get the money to back you up, and then call the musicians you like and say, "How much money do you want?" Because that's what is happening in the United States. Of course, you have to have a good reputation, especially as an artist, as a musician, so that other musicians would like to play with you. I know a lot of leaders who can't put a band together because they are not strong enough. You have to be a strong leader, and you have to play real good. You have to play better than the whole band put together.

JC: As a listener as well as a player, what elements in music really move you emotionally?

A: I am a percussionist, so for me the first thing that really moves me or grabs me is the rhythm, and then the melody, and then the harmony. But the first thing is the rhythm—in everything. Sometimes even in free-form music, I feel the pulsations, the rhythm from that music, even if there's not a real downbeat there.

JC: What are your future goals?

A: I'm doing something right now that is very important—maybe the most important thing that I have done—I'm writing a percussion book. It's a book on percussion method—not like the way to handle the instrument or this or that, but the way that I approach music generally speaking. Also, I'm talking about all kinds of percussion and sound—mellow sounds, wooden sounds—all kinds of different qualities of sound in percussion.

JC: What is your "approach"?

A: You never come to a jam session, for example, and expect to start playing right away. Even if everyone else is playing and somebody says, "Hey, do you want to play a little bit?" you sit down and listen to the music first. You don't grab a tambourine right away just because you know what the rhythm is. First you look and listen for your own place in the music—your own space—and then you start to make sounds in that space because the music is like a map that you can see. It's like a picture; it's not like just a sound.

ralph
macdonald

3/15/44

New York, New York

percussion

writer

producer

Ralph began playing conga as a child and was soon working in his father's band. While still in his teens he went on the road with Harry Belafonte, with whom he remained for ten years. While working with Belafonte Ralph met bassist William Salter and orchestrator/writer/producer William Eaton and formed a songwriting team. After leaving Belafonte, Ralph supported himself by working in the studio, doing record dates, and playing ad jingles for McDonald's, Budweiser, Chevrolet, and others. In 1970 he joined singer Roberta Flack, staying with her for five years. Roberta, along with Donny Hathaway, recorded the MacDonald/Salter composition, "Where is the Love?" which has sold more than ten million copies. Ralph left Roberta in 1975, and along with Salter and Eaton formed Antisia Music. The three principals collectively have written eight million-selling albums. Rosebud Recording Studio, owned and operated by Antisia, is where Ralph produces himself and others, including Joe Farrell and Bobbie Humphrey. To date, he has co-written tunes on seven gold records, among them: "Mr. Magic," recorded by Grover Washington, Jr., and "Trade Winds," recorded by Rod Stewart.

MacDonald, who has played everything from telephone jacks to toy hammers, was the first player to introduce the syndrome, a percussion synthesizer consisting of four pie-tin-sized, blue-plastic drum heads attached to a central synthesizer console, a device which allows him to produce every sound achieved by standard percussion, plus the additional element of melody.

R: My father was a musician. He had his own orchestra and band, and I had six uncles who played drums, so it was inevitable. It wasn't looked upon, or considered anything spectacular in my family, 'cause everybody played them. I didn't have any ambition to be a musician; it was just a hobby. From traveling around with my father from the time I was small, I was in a position to just sit down and play drums—I wasn't even conscious of it. When I was seventeen years old, I joined Harry Belafonte, and really began to develop. It was a fantastic learning experience for me. The first year I spent with him, I played West Indian steel drums. It wasn't until the second year that I started playing percussion. I just looked at the percussionist who was there and saw what he was doing, and I said, "Hey, I can do that, too…I've been doing that all the time." So I began to play percussion in the show. Bill Eaton, who is one of my partners now, became the musical conductor.

JC: This is an understatement, but you've spent a lot of time in the studio; did you foresee that as a lifestyle then?

R: Yes. When I worked for Harry, I was on the road all the time. It's nice for a while, but then you say, "Hey ,I'd rather stay in town, in the studio, and work and see my family." So I think every musician's aim—or mine anyway—is to get into a studio. When I stopped working with Belafonte, it was about 1968. I was already doing a few sessions, but when I decided to stay in town for a complete year, I started to do a lot of record dates as more people found out I was around. And just about when I felt comfortable with that, I decided to get into the jingle business. I wanted to do commercials because I knew that that paid a musician over a long period of time, so I got into that.

JC: You make it sound so easy.

R: It was easy for me. If you have an ambition or a goal and you strive for it, then you'll complete it and say, "Right—this is it, I knew I could get it."

JC: How did you get your songs recorded initially?

R: When we left Belafonte in 1968, we wanted to establish ourselves in the business—we wanted to establish ourselves in a way that, when we couldn't play anymore as musicians, we would still be able to work. We liked being in the music business and we were looking way ahead. So we figured, "Hey, we've got all these songs." We tried to give them to somebody else to handle, but we didn't get any satisfaction. So we decided to start our own publishing company. Then the problem was, "How are we going to get these tunes to the producers?" So I said, "Well, man, it's easy—I'm on everybody's albums…they call me…I'm right there when the timing is right, when the situation is right. They respect me and my musicianship, and when I say, 'Hey, I got a song to play for you,' they say, 'Let me hear it.'" See, I approached this whole thing from an angle that was never, ever done before. It was the easiest way for me, instead of writing and sending people letters, I would be right there on the scene, playing the music. I know if my song is better than another song—not necessarily meaning they have to do mine, but I know that my material is in the ball game. All I have to do is tell them and everybody wants to hear it. People say, "Oh, you write?"—unaware of all the songs I have written already. They don't associate Ralph MacDonald, musician, with the songwriter. My music doesn't sound black at all; our stuff is done by Ray Conniff, Shirley Bassey, Jerry Vale, Liza Minelli, Helen Reddy…We call ourselves songwriters. Any legitimate singer can sing a good song.

JC: You seem to be a really well-balanced person who has everything in perspective—your music, your life, your sense of business and reality.

R: You see, I came up with Harry Belafonte who had a tremendous organization. He came up through legitimate theater, with Broadway rules: If a show was at 8:30, he was there at 8:00—thinking he might not get to go onstage because there was already somebody ready to take over his part, always plenty of talented people waiting in the wings who had come at 7:30. I hear people talk about paying dues—I don't know what kind of dues they're talking about. All I know about is putting on a show. It takes organization; it's a profession and you've got to have some pride in what you do.

My parents came from Trinidad and they have a different kind of pride about themselves. They have a different kind of feeling of who they are; they have a sense of being. And when they looked at America, they saw it as a great place of opportunity; they felt they could come here and get into something and make something out of their life, as opposed to the black American who's been here all his life and doesn't see any of this.

JC: Is there anything you've tried that you haven't been able to do?

R: Basketball—I wanted to be a basketball player. That was my whole ambition, my aim in life. If you had asked me what I was going to be, I'd have told you basketball. But I didn't get along with my high school coach. Well, I didn't get along with school to be truthful. I hated school with a passion.

JC: You were a rebel.

R: No. They made me a rebel. I was bored. There was no purpose for me in school—what they were teaching me and what I had to deal with—none whatsoever…"See Dick. See Jane. See Spot run…" Run, run, run—where? I was dealing with rats and roaches; I didn't know what they were talking about. I just couldn't relate to that whole thing. You don't get the logistics of what real education is about until you go out into the real world. At the age of seventeen I traveled with Harry Belafonte, and that's where I got my education!

braphonevibraphonevibraphonevibraphonevibraphor

vibraphone vibraphone **vibraphone** vibra

roy ayers

9/10/40

Los Angeles, California

vibraphone

vocalist

composer and arranger

producer

Roy was a piano player until his senior year in high school, when his parents bought him a set of vibes. He attended Los Angeles City College for a year in 1959, studying music, before leaving school to begin his professional career. Ayers first became known in the early sixties through his playing with Chico Hamilton, Jack Wilson, Gerald Wilson's big band, Phineas Newborn, Jr., Teddy Edwards, Curtis Amy, Leroy Vinnegar, and Hampton Hawes, with whom he co-led a band. Roy had his own quartet in 1965 for a year, before joining Herbie Mann, with whom he remained until 1970. He then formed his own band, Roy Ayers Ubiquity, and toured America, Europe, and Japan. Roy also composed the music for the motion picture *Coffy*.

R: My mother is my greatest influence and inspiration. Because she plays piano, ever since I was five years old, I've been able to play boogie-woogie-style piano. My older sister played piano, and I had a great piano teacher who lived two doors from me. I used to go down to her place and study and practice with her. The person who really made me want to play music and get into an instrument, especially the vibraphone, was Cal Tjader. Although my parents took me to see Lionel Hampton when I was real young, the main influence was Cal, then Milt Jackson. I grew up in Pasadena with Bobby Hutcherson, who is still one of my favorites. We used to hang out together and occasionally practice vibes together. I played piano from childhood on up until 1958, although I had four to six years of playing the steel guitar through elementary and junior high school.

JC: As far as the vibes go, are you pretty much self-taught?

R: Yes.

JC: When were you first introduced to the vibes?

R: I got into them in 1958, my senior year in high school. I had a group which I called the Jefferson Combo; later we changed it to the Latin Lyrics. After I left high school, I had my own band, but I had a problem leading it because most of the guys got into smoke and pills. They'd fall asleep on me; they were trying to find themselves. Everybody tries to find themselves in different ways, but these habits they had took away from the quality of the music, and I couldn't deal with them anymore. It was very difficult for me to be leader, so I said, "In order for me to be a good leader, I have to become a follower," and I then became a sideman with Curtis Amy. I worked with Curtis for three years. After that I worked with the Jack Wilson quartet and the Gerald Wilson Orchestra, and finally Hampton Hawes who I co-led a group with. A great turning point occurred when I left L.A. to join Herbie Mann's group, which first of all allowed me to get away from my family and meet more exciting musicians. It also gave me an opportunity to get some good exposure. I got to work with some great musicians like Reggie Workman, Jimmy Owens, Chick Corea, and Larry Coryell.

The next turning point was when I formed my own group. I had learned everything I had to learn from being a sideman. I took all the qualities from each leader I had been with, and I used them. You have to realize that each musician is a separate voice, a separate person, and each person has to respect him- or herself. I've been working with men and women which I think is fairly unique. I've tried to innovate, while at the same time trying to change my style considerably to a total music spectrum, instead of just being limited to one facet of music. I feel that musicians who have the ability to play every bag are unique in their own right because a musician who can play inside and outside can play freedom, jazz, blues, rock, classical—can play everything—is a total musician, not just limited to one aspect of music. I'm not really putting down the musicians who are limited, or let's say, who are dedicated to one aspect of music, but I'm saying that I am capable—my musicianship allows me to play everything. It allows me to be versatile, and being versatile enables me to get into many different financial brackets, begin able to keep a consistent work pattern going. I also looked at a certain thing, and I saw many musicians who were older than me as I continued to grow in the music industry and go with different people and play with different people. I saw many musicians who had been out there longer than me who I had highly respected and still respect. I saw many of them falling by the wayside, many of them dying from drugs and many times just dying of maybe a lost dream. I think many musicians have a dream of accomplishing something in their life, other than just their contribution to music, and I started to get drugged because I saw musicians not having anything after putting twenty-five to thirty years in an industry and pleasing millions of people just by playing their horn or playing their drums and not reaping any benefits—not having a house to live in or a car to drive, not having a place to go or a place to lay their heads, and I think that that still exists today in certain areas of the music field.

JC: Beautiful. Now, how do you feel about the use of electronics in music?

R: I think that electronics is going to go even further than it has gone. I still have yet to go as far as I want to go, but I'm going to get more into it, because I think that electronic sound is very strongly needed with the space age and with the new dimensions in music. I think it enhances the sound. I think it can grow and be stronger. But I think that acoustic music is very valid and very important also, and it should remain within the total music structure because of its purity of sound. Music is free. I think it's the freest art form in the world. The music is the message, and the message is the music, and people need the message, which is the music, because within my mind, it's a never-ending magnitude of infinite strength, wisdom, and will.

gary burton

1/23/43

Anderson, Indiana

vibraphone

composer and arranger

Gary began playing the marimba at age six and the vibra-phone a short while later. Essentially self-taught, he is today considered to be the leading exponent of the four-mallet technique. He attended the Berklee College of Music in Boston, where he later taught. His professional debut was in 1960 in Nashville where he worked with, among others, Chet Atkins. He first achieved national prominence as a featured soloist with George Shearing in 1963. He remained with Shearing until 1966. The Gary Burton Quartet was formed in 1967, expanded to a quintet in 1974, and recently returned to the quartet format. Between 1971-1975, Gary toured Japan, Australia, England, and the Continent, including Communist-block countries. In 1971 he became a member of the Berklee staff. Gary also performs lecture-seminar-concert programs at universities across the United States.

G: I started playing music at age six with marimba lessons in my hometown. Within a couple of years, I was also playing vibes. I became interested simply because of seeing someone give a recital on these instruments, and it looked attractive to me, in a visual way, I think. My family was very encouraging and helpful. All my brothers and sisters and my parents played one instrument or another at home, so it was very much a family thing. The only formal training I had was two years at a music school in Boston, Berklee College. Vibes was a difficult instrument to study, officially, so mostly I took piano lessons and tried to learn from my experience. My main influences were the major players of the late fifties and early sixties. In my quest to approach the vibes as a keyboard instrument, Bill Evans became a major conceptual influence. Other major players of the time, Miles Davis, Jim Hall, and Sonny Rollins, were big favorites, each for different reasons. There were a few influences among my contemporaries, namely Mike Gibbs, the composer, Carla Bley, and Steve Swallow.

JC: Please describe the evolution of your music, conceptually and instrumentally. What do you look for in terms of a total synthesis of idea and concept as expressed by your music and the musicians who play it?

G: In retrospect, it is obvious that I found a sound and format that fit my musical personality well and that I have essentially stayed within this format. I feel that the quartet instrumentation I have provides an ideal setting for the vibes and for my particular concepts of group interplay. We have always viewed the quartet as a group featuring interplay, as much as a classical string quartet, for instance. There is a great deal of variety and flexibility available, plus a strong continuity from the consistencies that are present. It has meant that I haven't exactly changed with the times, as the times went through changes. I would change in a few minor ways in response to what I was hearing around me, but mostly there are times when we've been in vogue, and times when we haven't just as jazz weaves its drunken path through music history. Our music is undeniably lyrical, and designed to feature primarily players' skills in improvisation and with their instruments.

JC: As an educator, what do you think of the present standard of jazz education in music schools?

G: Jazz education in the schools is very uneven. Some schools offer impressively enlightened programs and playing opportunities. Very few, however, live up to this higher level. Most, unfortunately, range from total naïve foolishness to sickening commercialism. I'm actually very critical of jazz education at the moment.

JC: Is it possible, in your opinion, for a self-educated musician to assimilate as much information on his or her own or to be as technically proficient as the music school graduate without the structure of a formalized music program?

G: Self-education for a jazz player is always a possibility. I think the musician who has some formal training will be more versatile and will find getting into the business easier. But many will always succeed and become important players from sheer experience and private studies.

JC: Can one suffer from too much education, thus stifling the natural organic process of creativity?

G: I don't think a talented musician would become stiff or unnatural from studying or over-studying. This misconception is fostered by the fact that so many near-talented people turn to extensive studying in an attempt to somehow succeed. And they set a bad example. The natural player is a natural player, and nothing short of mental incapacity can take it away from him or her.

JC: Why, in your opinion, are there so few vibes players receiving recognition and making a name for themselves?

G: I have often wondered about the state of vibes playing today, myself. It's a curious pattern. First, there are many players of my generation who have dropped out for various personal reasons (health, strain, commercial careers, and so on), leaving several gaps, which ought to be in hot competition. But in spite of the fact that I know of literally dozens and dozens of aspiring mallet players, none seem to be breaking into the scene that much. This may be due in part to the nature of the instrument. Today's amplified music doesn't work so well for the acoustic vibes. It's no doubt, fortunately for me, that I got established just before volume levels and new instruments arrived. Most likely some new players will receive prominence in the next few years.

JC: What are your future goals as an educator, player, composer?

G: There are no "things I've always wanted to do, but never got the chance" type items left at this point. Mostly, I'm enjoying playing a lot these days, and I enjoy the occasional special project recordings alot. Goals are not really so much a part of it now, as it was when first starting out. My goal now is to get to keep on playing and enjoying myself until I'm old enough to retire. I feel like I'll want to be at my most mature and developed by the time I'm another fifteen or twenty years older. Guess I'm about halfway there.

mike
mainieri

7/24/38

Bronx, New York

vibraphone

synthi-vibe

keyboards

percussion

composer and arranger

producer

Mike, who learned to play the vibraphone at age ten, was performing in clubs at twelve, and by fourteen had learned over a thousand standards. He performed in children's shows, and after attending Juilliard briefly, went on tour with the Paul Whiteman Orchestra. A protégé of Buddy Rich, for whom he worked during the sixties, Mike more or less abandoned live performing and devoted most of his time to session playing. In 1970 he became president of Gnu Music Inc., a New York City musical production company that supplied composers and arrangers for television, radio, and record production projects. Having a recording studio as his principal working base, Mainieri was able to offer musical refuge to some of New York's most talented—though still unknown—studio players, among them the Brecker brothers, Steve Gadd, Tony Levin, Barry Rogers, Warren Bernhardt, Joe Beck, and others. A band, Red Eye, for which Mainieri contributed most of the music, emerged from Gnu. That group subsequently became known as White Elephant, made one "historic" record, then went on tour and disbanded. Eventually, Mike relinquished his position as president of Gnu Music and formed a quartet, L'Image, with Steve Gadd, Tony Levin, and Warren Bernhardt. More recently Mike has toured and recorded with his own band, an offshoot of L'Image with the same personnel, except for the additions of Michael Brecker and David Spinozza. Mike is the creator of the synthi-vibe, "a vibe 'controller' which allows him to play electronic sounds through any synthesizer. A five-octave instrument, it replaces the keyboard on any synthesizer, allowing him to trigger its oscillator with mallets instead of fingers" (Leonard Feather and Ira Gitler, *The Encyclopedia of Jazz in the Seventies*). At various times, Mike has performed with Charlie Shavers, Roy Eldridge, Joe Jones, Coleman Hawkins, Erroll Garner, Harry "Sweets" Edison, Eddie Vinson, Benny Goodman, Chico Hamilton, Sonny Stitt, Billie Holiday, Morgana King, Philly Joe Jones, Elvin Jones, and Laura Nyro.

M: My family was involved in many levels of the arts. My father was a vaudevillian dancer; my aunts and uncles were composers, dancers, musicians, and singers. Our house was constantly filled with singing, dancing, songwriting, and jam sessions. So from an early age, I was exposed to a constant exchange of musical ideas.

JC: What was the first instrument you played?

M: At first I just experimented with all of the instruments that were available in the household—congas, drums, sax, guitar, and piano. My father and uncle were jazz fans, and they would take me to Harlem to hear bands at the Apollo Theatre. After the shows, we would go to clubs and jam or go uptown to my grandfather's barbershop and play all night. I was also exposed to another form of music through a friend of my uncle's who was a Cuban conga player. Percussion bands were very popular in Spanish Harlem and in the Bronx where we lived, so I would hang out with him and listen to him play in social clubs, dances, and basements. The rhythms were amazingly hypnotic and I would dance and play cowbell until I'd collapse.

One night at the Apollo I heard Lionel Hampton and became fascinated with the vibes, so my mom saved her pennies and bought me my first instrument—a pre-war Deagan, two and a half octaves, with cardboard resonators. What a beauty! I still have it.

I began playing professionally within a year, and at the age of fourteen, I went on tour with Paul Whiteman. I had a trio and we played TV and radio shows with Whiteman. I continued touring during my teenage years and was tutored some of the time, but managed to get home enough to gig locally. When I was sixteen, I discovered the joy of playing with an organ trio in a neighborhood Negro Baptist church. At seventeen, I auditioned at the Village Gate for Buddy Rich. He and the audience were so impressed with my playing that he hired me on the spot. He fired his band three weeks later, asked me to write some new charts, and that marked the beginning of a relationship that lasted six years.

JC: What happened after you left Buddy?

M: I formed my own band and went on tour for a couple of years. I became disenchanted with the road scene—after all, I had been doing it for ten years. I had performed in every major country in the

Far and Near East, Europe, South America, and also had the opportunity to jam with just about every musician I idolized as a youth. Frankly, it all seemed quite boring for me at an early age. So I turned to other forms of expression and explored other areas of music, which brought me to the New York studio scene. There I got involved in writing for films and TV, radio commercials, and, of course, playing on albums, and so on. At that time, rock 'n' roll was happening, but not in the studio scene; especially on Madison Ave. there was nobody writing R & R music for commercials. That's when I became involved with David Lucas who I met while touring with Buddy. Lucas was an excellent songwriter and singer, and we tackled the job of writing and producing rock 'n' roll commercials for TV and radio. We were also responsible for introducing many rock 'n' roll musicians into the studio scene. It was a risky venture because these new players posed a threat to the Establishment. I did help break down some barriers that existed between the agency people and musicians, and between the established musicians and this new breed. Believe me, there was a lot of resistance!!

At the same time I was working gigs with Joe Beck in the Village and, while we were playing at the Café à Go-Go, we had the opportunity to jam with Hendrix, Havens, Zappa, and many other players on the scene. Larry Coryell and Randy Brecker had arrived, and so had Jeremy Steig and the Satyrs. I joined that band and learned about a kind of freedom in playing that was new to me. I also was introduced to the music and poetry of Tim Hardin who I also toured with occasionally. Things were starting to happen!

JC: What was starting to happen?

M: The fusion of all these musical styles. I then organized a rehearsal band with the late Sam Brown, Don MacDonald, Tony Levin that attracted many players. I wrote the charts, and the rehearsals became an oasis for studio players. The music was experimental and very free, mostly playing on vamps for hours on end—strangely reminiscent of my early experiences in Spanish Harlem. The band grew in size and the talent was overwhelming: saxes—George Young, Michael Brecker, Frank Vaccari, and Ronny Cuber; trumpets—Jon Faddis, Randy Brecker; trombones—Jon Pierson, Barry Rogers; rhythm—Steve Gadd, Don MacDonald, Tony Levin, Joe Beck, Dave Spinozza, Warren Berhardt; and singers—Ann Sulton and Nick Holmes. The band recorded a double album under the name *White Elephant* for Sunshine records, made its debut at Alice Tully Hall [New York], toured sporadically for six months, and disbanded. It was a fantastic experience for me, for I felt I served as a meeting place for musical and social exchanges. Many careers were launched immediately thereafter.

JC: Why are there so few vibes and mallet players around? The instrument still seems to suffer from underexposure.

M: There are two major reasons: first, the expense. The parent of a child interested in the vibes must commit to a major investment which is risky. Secondhand or used sets are almost impossible to find, and they are expensive. Second, acoustics. The vibraharp or vibraphone cannot compete with amplified instruments, making it unattractive to contemporary players.

I experienced this problem for many years. In the past, to perform my music, the sideman would have to play a mezzo forte passage at pianissimo just to hear me, while I was playing the same passage at triple forte, just to hear myself. I had to face the fact that the acoustic vibe was virtually obsolete on the contemporary scene. I needed an instrument that did not limit my musical expression, which led to my pioneering the electric vibes. I've been working with J. C. Deagan for about ten years and just recently have come up with an instrument that responds beautifully.

I experimented with many pickups and amplifying devices as long ago as 1964. In fact, on the album *Journey Through an Electric Tube* [Solid State], I used fuzz tone and wah-wah effects. With this new instrument, I can bend notes or use any of the electronic phasors that guitarists and keyboard players use. I have also developed a new instrument called a synthi-vibe [a synthesizer with a vibe keyboard]. It can be heard on my debut album for Arista, *Love Play*, on the tune "Magic Carpet." Unfortunately, the new electric vibe was not available for my first album, but I will use it and the synthi-vibe on my forthcoming album on Arista.

Most vibe players are not interested in the electric vibe. That's cool, but to answer your second question. [Gary] Burton could have taken the instrument out of the closet, which is what I am about to do.

JC: How would you describe the present state of contemporary music?

M: As for the future, I believe that the arts are an expression of the needs and imagination of not only the artist, but of the masses—whether they be social, political, or spiritual. I am not insinuating that an artist be a puppet, but he must realize that he is a part of the whole expression, not separated. Therefore, if the inner needs are anxious and compelling, then the music will reflect them dramatically. If those inner needs are tranquil and reflective, so will the music be, and change will come slower. Now we are experiencing a climate of reflection and exploration of direction. But I feel we are on the brink of a musical explosion.

violininviolininviolininviolininviolininviolin **violin** violi

jean-luc
ponty

9/29/42

Avranches, Normandy

France

violin (acoustic

and electric)

violectra

keyboards

composer and arranger

producer

Jean-Luc began classical studies at the age of five. By the time he was thirteen, he had left school and was practicing the violin six hours a day. At fifteen, he entered the Conservatoire National Superieur de Musique de Paris, from which he graduated two years later, receiving the Premier Prix. The following year, he joined the Concerts Lamoreaux Symphony Orchestra, and remained for three years. In 1964 he decided to play jazz exclusively. He appeared at the Antibes Jazz Festival in France that year, and subsequently played all over Europe until 1969 when he came to the United States for recording and club dates, working with the George Duke Trio. He returned to Europe in 1970, and by 1971, had created the Jean-Luc Ponty Experience, a group which included guitarist Philip Catherine. It was during this time that he met Elton John, with whom he recorded the record *Honky Chateau*. In 1973 Ponty returned to the United States, becoming a member of Frank Zappa's Mothers of Invention. He stayed with Zappa for nearly a year, leaving in October of 1973 to pursue his own recording projects, in 1974 he joined the Mahavishnu Orchestra, with whom he stayed until 1975, leaving to form his own band and record as a leader. Jean-Luc was the first artist to exploit the potential of the electric violin and pioneered its use in jazz and rock. He explains: "What I'm interested in is creating sounds that can be made only with the violin. Using the various devices, the sound is very different from what it would be using the guitar with the same devices" (*Downbeat*, December 1, 1977).

J-L: My father gave me a violin when I was three. He was a music teacher and had a school in a small town in France where he taught clarinet, piano, everything; but his main instrument was violin. He gave me a violin just to fool around with. Then, when I was five, my father started me on serious violin lessons, and my mother started me on the piano. When I was thirteen, I decided to become a professional musician, so I left regular school and my parents sent me to another violin teacher in a bigger city. I started practicing six hours a day, and from then on I had a different childhood. First of all, I was kept from all my friends because I didn't go to school anymore. I took private lessons and I was at home every day practicing.

JC: When were you first exposed to other kinds of music?

J-L: Later on when I was an actual student in the conservatoire at Paris, I heard jazz for the first time, and the very first jazz album I ever heard was by Chet Baker with strings. The phrasing really impressed me. I really loved it. I could recognize that it was improvisation, but I didn't know anything about jazz in general. At that time, there was a jazz band in Paris looking for a clarinetist, and since I was playing a bit of clarinet on the side, I joined. This was when I was seventeen. I really started playing jazz on the clarinet, because I knew the instrument, and that's how I learned the rudiments of jazz. Still, at that point, jazz was just a hobby and classical music was my main thing. I spent two years at the conservatory and got my degree at the end of that time.

When I finished my studies, I entered a symphony orchestra in Paris. I started working right away and there I played a lot of music. I stayed about three years, during which time I played everything from Bach and Beethoven to Stravinsky and Bartok. While I was in the orchestra, I started looking more into jazz and going to clubs in Paris. That's when I started meeting local musicians as well as American musicians like Bud Powell, Johnny Griffin, Kenny Clarke—musicians who at that time were living in Paris.

At twenty-one I left the symphony orchestra and I started playing regularly in clubs and began my professional career as a jazz musician. I played in a club called the Blue Note and stayed there for two months. Then I got a deal to make an album—a solo album; it was really bebop—kind of Charlie Parker. It was called *Jean-Luc Ponty: Jazz Long Playing*.

JC: How did you get such an opportunity at so young an age?

J-L: It really was a new thing for people to hear me playing modern jazz on the violin. So there was a lot of excitement. I got my name in the magazines and reviews very quickly.

JC: What about the violinists who had come before you, like Stephane Grapelli?

J-L: He was already very established. He was not too much of a musical influence on me, more a psychological one. I met him pretty quickly after starting to play in Paris, because everybody told him about me. He was very encouraging. I would go to his place in Paris with violin exercises and we would practice together and have a few Scotches, and that's about it. But the fact that he—an established, recognized, great jazz violinist—would tell me that I was talented and that I had something original to give and should go on was extremely encouraging to me.

So, to go back to that year when I was twenty-one years old, that's when I did my first solo album, and I did my first appearance in a big festival in Antibes in the south of France. That was very important because it was a triumph, and people from all over Europe—from radio and TV stations, producers and critics alike—were all there. At that time, it was the only real big jazz festival in Europe. So I became known to all those people at the festival and I got contacts and proposals for playing from all over Europe. Right away, from that first year, I started going to Germany, to Sweden, to make radio concerts—all the jazz gigs that exist in Europe.

JC: When did you come to America, and how did it happen?

J-L: I came to America in 1967 for the first time. John Lewis knew of me. He organized a violin workshop for the Monterey Jazz Festival in 1967 and invited me to go. I played at the festival and was brought to the attention of American producers and critics, and I was offered a few record deals. In 1969 I went to California again, this time for a longer period of time, to record. I recorded three albums altogether in California, and I played some clubs.

JC: What was your impression then of the American musical scene—was there a cultural shock for you?

J-L: Yes. For one thing, jazz was a very exotic style of music to me because of my whole background. I was raised with traditional music and concepts, and everything fit in with that. All the music I heard on the radio or the TV in France and Europe was extremely inspired by traditional music. So jazz was totally exotic. But, since I did have a passion for it, I just learned through albums and through American musicians. I learned jazz like I would learn a foreign language, and it was very hard in the beginning to adapt my technique to jazz, but eventually I did. When I went to the States, it was funny seeing jazz in its context—where it comes from—the whole literal background in relation to the music. But more than anything, I realized that the ideas were changing faster in America than in Europe. Here they had already begun to incorporate electric instruments, and that was really the thing that didn't exist in Europe very much except in progressive rock.

JC: Were you developing your writing then?

J-L: No. I didn't have any confidence in my writing then, because I was writing with more lyricism than anything being played at the time in jazz, and it didn't fit at all. So I very seldom used what I was writing. Now I write all the material for my band. I just realized that, finally, the style is not that different from what I was writing when I was twenty-one years old. There's still a strong sense of melody which comes through in anything I write. The thing that happened was that I came back to Europe and had a band. I began to realize that I had a lot of affinities with the progressive rock musicians in Europe, or musicians using more of the tradition of Europe in the music, while dealing with electric and electronic instruments. That was what separated me from many jazz musicians—that curiosity I had for electric instruments. So I started playing with those kinds of musicians in Europe. I incorporated electric guitar into my band and made the whole band electric, instead of me as the only electric instrument. Then I went into a much more experimental form of jazz which was really called "free-form" or "avant-garde," where we wouldn't have material or structure. I experimented with that kind of free form for two years. Then I realized that it was not a creative way for me. I believe I actually pursued this dierction because I didn't feel any maturity yet as a musician, and I was searching for the proper form that would feel the most comfortable. So I tried that, but then realized it wasn't the one.

I broke up that band and again did different things. But I didn't feel very comfortable anymore in Paris, and I was looking to move. I considered London first, which was close, but realized that there was not much going on in London which really attracted me. And then I thought that the United States would be the only place where the musical values made sense to me and there was real stimulation. So I moved to Los Angeles, because that was the city I knew best in the States, and the one where I knew the most musicians. Frank Zappa heard about it and asked me to tour. I did four tours with him, and then I started writing more and more. I realized I had found the form of music which would be a good one for me—where there was no barrier between jazz and rock, and I could incorporate my classical experience into it. So, I started writing and rehearsing to make a band for a record. But in the meantime, John McLaughlin called me to join his band, the Mahavishnu Orchestra. I spent a month of deliberation and finally decided to do it.

JC: Comparing your experiences as a sideman with those of a leader—would you say that the role of leader is infinitely more satisfying?

J-L: No doubt, but you have to be ready. When playing somebody else's music, you have to concentrate to understand the concept and the feelings of the composer who conceived of the music, and it's very challenging. I think this kind of experience makes everyone stronger, because what happens is that you have to play things you would never conceive of yourself, and therefore are more difficult for you to play. But the thing is, of course, once you really have a concept of writing, there's no doubt that the role of leader is best; and having to provide your band with music is fantastic, because then it's you who can expand your concept, and that's what happened.

JC: What do you think about the current musical trends?

J-L: I think the music that is growing the most is the one which lets the ideas flow from other forms. It seems to have reached a point where musicians grow by opening their ears and minds to other musicians from other fields—like between classical, jazz, rock, and music from other parts of the world. That's where I see the newest things happening.

JC: What do you think of the caliber of the young musicians who are coming up now?

J-L: As soon as someone picks up an instrument—even if he's fifteen or sixteen—if he's a talented musician, you can hear it right away. It has always been that way through centuries. What is a new syndrome is how quickly young musicians are getting their music together. I guess it is due to the fact that we are living in a century of media. Compared to my childhood, for instance, a kid now, wherever he lives—Europe, Australia, New Zealand, or anywhere in the States, as long as it is in the Western rich world—can find albums; he can see concerts on TV and tours that go all over the world. Only ten years ago in France, most of the big concerts were happening only in Paris and now they go all over France—even to small cities of a few hundred thousand people—so a kid living in a small town is as lucky and informed about what's happening today in music as a kid in Paris or New York.

JC: Based on your own very theoretical education—started by your father—would you definitely say that music school is the place to get it together?

J-L: No. this is a very delicate point, because sometimes it can kill the spontaneity—creative spontaneity—that there is in some people. There are so many cases of great musicians who became famous who were not in school and who were self-taught. Somehow, their style would have been different—maybe not as creative—if they had followed a sort of training. In my case, it helped because I played the violin, and for me, especially in France, there was no other way to become a violinist. Maybe now in the States there are a few places where a string player has a chance to learn things from it—just the basic technique—in order to play whatever music he likes. In my case, everything helps me now. I had kind of put aside everything I learned when I started to play jazz; everything I had learned in classical music I tried to forget so that I would find the spontaneity to improvise and the looseness of coordination. Now, after many years of overcoming this difficulty, anything and everything I have learned in my life is useful. It is just a matter of knowing how to use it for what you want to do, but every musical experience I had was useful.

stsvocalistsvocalistsvocalists vocalists vocal

al
jarreau

3/12/40

Milwaukee, Wisconsin

vocalist

composer

Al, who earned his master's degree in psychology from the University of Iowa, was working as a rehabilitation counselor in San Francisco in the late sixties when he began singing in area clubs. Soon after, he quit his counseling job and began to pursue music full time. He recorded his first album in 1975 and toured Europe for eight weeks in 1976, acquiring a large following. He has since traveled through America, and has appeared on national television.

A: I think becoming aware of music was prenatal for me. I had a first recital when I was seven years old. It started before that in church, but that is an occasion I can remember quite well—a little garden recital and benefit for the church. It began there and it hasn't stopped. It's only been in the past ten years, since 1968, that I decided to do it full time professionally with no other commitments. Before that, school was my major vocation.

JC: Your major vocation being—?

A: Psychology. I got my master's degree and then I went to work in counseling and in rehabilitation for four years until I was twenty-eight, and that brought me up to 1968 when I let all of that go and started to do music full time. Until that point it had been something that I did after hours after work— doing it seriously, but it was always my second vocation.

JC: Were there any particular styles or eras of music that, growing up from adolescence into adulthood, you responded to?

A: Yeah. The era for me was definitely big bands and bebop. That was the music my older brother and sisters brought into the house. It was on the radio, and there was just no question for me that that was the music to pursue. I suppose it could have been classical or blues—just simple down-home blues. If that had been the music in the house, I would have gone with that, but it was jazz, so that is the theme that probably runs through most of all I do. Up until about seven years ago, most everything that I did was written by other people; and most of my life I was the typical jazz singer— you get up and you do the thing with the trio or with the quartet that's working in the club, and you stand there and sing your solo right along with the horns and all. I've done that all my life, and it's only recently that I'm starting to do concerts. In 1970, or maybe a little before that, I started trying to write some. I was writing for a group of us who were working together and we needed some original things, and I just picked up the pen, so to speak. I don't really know how to use the pen as a writer, because I don't really play an instrument—I don't know the technical part of writing, but I just hear.

JC: You've got a very unique approach to singing, although it certainly is in the tradition of the "Jazz Singers." Did you ever consciously develop any kind of technique; have you ever, for example, taken voice lessons?

A: Well, I studied voice for about three or four months, three or four years ago, and I wish I had done it before, and I wish that I had continued it. There is some very valuable stuff going on there that I didn't get, and I think sometimes I have difficulty vocally because of it, because I didn't learn some of the real roots about singing. I think I sing pretty correctly, but still there are some real fine things that I should have taken time to learn that wold be a big help to me right now. That's really the only formal training I ever had. Everything—the style and technique that I've developed—is something that's evolved over a long period of time. I didn't sit down one day and decide that I was going to do this other thing. It's something that just kind of grew out of needing to contribute more to the music than people standardly tend to do as singers. I didn't think of myself as a singer. It didn't matter what name to apply—I was just a living, breathing, creating thing up there onstage, and the melody was okay, but there were other things to do.

JC: What motivated you to get into counseling and psychology to that extent—to the point where you would actually get your master's degree and then suddenly decide to leave it?

A: A large part of it was just a thing that was instilled by my parents—the importance of going to school, coupled with the upward-black-mobility thing. I didn't really have to think about it so much, but when I analyze it and break it down, some combination of those things made me want to finish school, get a master's and have a practical gig that I could do. And it was something I enjoyed. I think that some of the same things that are involved in wanting to be in a helping profession are similar to some of the same things that an artist has—a sensitivity that I think I shared. I don't know if there is anything more important than to help someone direct his life. That's really an art.

flora purim

3/6/42

Rio De Janeiro, Brazil

vocalist

percussion

guitar

composer

Flora grew up in Rio, the daughter of a Brazilian mother and a Romanian-born father. Her parents played classical music and also listened to jazz. The street music of her native country also contributed to her general musical awareness. Flora appeared with the group Quarteto Novo which included Airto and Hermeto Pascoal. Arriving in the United States in 1968, she learned to read and write music under the tuition of Moacir Santos. She earned a degree in music at California State University at Long Beach, and later studied drama in Los Angeles. In the late sixties, she moved to New York and started working with many bands, among them Duke Pearson, Stan Getz, and Gil Evans. In late 1971, she became a member for the original Return to Forever, along with her husband Airto. Since the mid-seventies, Flora has been performing with Airto and also as leader of her own group.

F: I was first introduced to classical music when I was really young—about five years old. My father and mother were both classical musicians and they played all the time. The first instrument I studied was the piano when I was six, and then at twelve I took guitar, and from that point on I stayed with acoustic guitar. I began singing when I was about seventeen.

JC: What kind of music were you singing?

F: The music of my country, Brazil, which I grew up with. My mom used to hear jazz music quite often—piano players like Oscar Peterson and Erroll Garner, and sometimes she would bring home Ella Fitzgerald or Billie Holiday. She also like Frank Sinatra and Nat King Cole.

JC: So it was all there: Brazilian music, classical music, and jazz.

F: Right.

JC: What made you come to America?

F: A lot of things started happening for me in Brazil and I wanted to stretch, but I couldn't because they didn't have the right conditions there and not much work either. So I decided to come up here to learn something. I came to America and I stayed.

JC: When did you start writing words?

F: When I was working with Chick Corea, although I already had my own songs at the time in Portuguese. Stanley Clarke was a neighbor, and he was writing a song that was so pretty, it inspired me to write lyrics for it. We decided to call the song "Light as a Feather," and from that point on, I couldn't stop. I did some of McCoy Tyner's music, some of Chick's, and some Airto and George Duke—most of the people I worked with I co-wrote music with.

JC: As a mother, how have you managed to grow as an artist and become successful and artistically fulfill yourself while raising a family? Has that ever been a problem?

F: My oldest daughter is sixteen and my youngest is five. They both have a really nice understanding, and they've been on the road quite often with us. They miss us but they know we are working, and from time to time we have family problems, so we stop and talk to everybody and take a couple of days off. I never knew how difficult it was going to be, because as they grow up, they become more demanding. Now I'm kind of trying to reconcile both roles. I'm singing less than I used to. I've been on the road for less time—I only go out, say, twice a year—and I spend most of my studio time after five in the afternoon.

JC: Are you writing much music now?

F: Yes.

JC: How do you compose?

F: I write on guitar or piano. Sometimes I write music and lyrics together, and sometimes they bring me the music, give me a title, and ask me for my views, and we work together—it depends on the situation.

JC: How do you incorporate electronics into your music?

F: In the past I used electronics often, but now I'm moving in another direction with less emphasis on that aspect. It's still electronic but not as much as before. I was experimenting for a couple of years and now I've got certain sounds that I'm using more often. I use electronics only for effect, which is more tasteful, and not all the time as a personal sound.

JC: When you are performing what elements within yourself are you most aware of—other musicians, the audience?

F: I am aware of the exchange that happens between me and the band and back to me, to the audience and back to me and the band. I'm a sort of bridge between the music and the people.

JC: Communication.

F: Yes, that's the key. Of course you cannot leave technique and intonation and certain other technicalities out, but they are things that you can work out through the years. True emotion is something that is inside of you, and you cannot work that out—you have to have it or you don't.

JC: What are your future goals?

F: I never had a real break that I didn't make happen for myself. And right now I'm looking to give the same opportunities to other musicians who are not known and who are looking for spaces to express themselves, and stretch out and contribute.

JC: So one of your goals is to really help other people.

F: For sure, because with Chick I finally got to a point where I felt a responsibility—like my lyrics say "open your eyes and you can fly"—and this is a statement, and people know what I mean. Every song I sing means something; it has to do with human growth, and it reflects my personal attitudes and philosophy of life. A lot of people find affinity with my way of being, and this is helping me to understand that more and more there's a need for space for younger and newer people who are willing to experiment and give of themselves.

woodwinds

gato barbieri

11/28/34
Rosario, Argentina
tenor saxophone
composer and arranger

Gato began studying the clarinet at age ten at Infancia Desvalida in Rosario and went on to study the instrument privately in Buenos Aires after his family moved there. He switched from clarinet to alto saxophone at age fourteen, playing lead alto in orchestras and studying composition and harmony with Argentinean composer Juan Carlos Paz. One of Gato's most influential teachers was Alberto Herbier, who helped him develop a technique that allowed him to play high-pitched tones. He was introduced to the tenor at age twenty-two. After becoming one of the most important players in Buenos Aires, he was urged by his Italian wife and manager, Michelle, to leave Argentina and expand his horizons. They moved to Rome where Gato was introduced to film by Michelle who was a script girl for Bernardo Bertolucci. Once in Rome, Gato's reputation grew rapidly. In 1965, he met Don Cherry in Paris, forming a close association with the man with whom he was to create some of the more avant-garde music of the sixties. Gato moved to New York in 1965, recording his first album as a sideman with Don Cherry for Blue Note, *Symphony for Improvisers*. During the seventies, Gato's reputation as an innovator increased, and in 1972, he composed the sound track for *Last Tango in Paris*, for which he won a Grammy. In 1973, he toured and recorded with a group that consisted of South American musicians mainly from Argentina and Brazil. Since 1976, Gato's records have increased dramatically in sales—a phenomenon Michelle attributes to the change in his music which, she says, "is less Latin and dramatic, and easier to enjoy."

G: My introduction to jazz was through my uncle who plays the saxophone. I grew up in Buenos Aires and listened intensely to the music of Charlie Parker, Dizzy Gillespie, and Miles Davis. Brass was very special to us in Latin America. When I was about fourteen, I started to play in jam sessions. Later, I became a professional musician and played with an orchestra, playing the rhythms of my country—the mambo, samba, and cha-cha.

JC: Was music always the most important thing in your life?

G: No, soccer was what I loved and still love the most. Music was always the most anguishing thing in my life. In soccer, you are a part of a team, but when you are a leader of band, you have so many responsibilities, there is so much pressure (and I hate anything that has to do with pressure). I am always very anxious about my performance, because I know that it's up to me to create the quality of the music and stimulate the other musicians.

JC: When you are involved with other media—film scoring, for instance—is it more enjoyable?

G: Yes, film is different; it's more quiet. You do what you have to do and everything is written down. When you improvise, everything is in your head. Some musicians think that improvising is easy. I think it is difficult. Making records, for example, is for me very abstract; a film is there for you to see, so it's completely different.

JC: Is the process of composing for a record especially "anguishing"?

G: Yes. I am very slow. There is so much to structure when you write arrangements for an orchestra; everything has to be very clear. I used to play with small bands, five or six musicians, where I could just write out the tune. Now it is much more complex.

JC: How do you regard the advent of electronics in music?

G: For me, there are only two kinds of music—good music and bad music. The most important thing for the musician to do is to not lose his or her integrity. A lot of people try to make "crossover" records and they become very stupid. Miles Davis succeeded because he was never banal.

JC: Do you recognize the concept of music as a business?

G: No. I don't understand that and maybe never will. It is why I am now going to an analyst.

mike
brecker

3/29/49

Philadelphia,

Pennsylvania

tenor saxophone

flute

drums

piano

composer and arranger

producer

Michael studied both at Indiana University and privately with Vince Trombetta and Joe Allard from 1965 to 1969. He made his debut with the R & B band Birdsong, in New York in the late sixties. With his brother Randy, Billy Cobham, and Barry Rogers, he formed the early fusion band, Dreams, 1970-1973. In 1973 he joined Horace Silver for a year. He left Horace to play with Billy Cobham from 1974 to 1975, touring extensively throughout the United States and Europe. Since 1975 Michael has co-led the Brecker Brothers Band with Randy, and is one of New York's busiest studio players. He has recorded with James Taylor, Carly Simon, Paul Simon, Laura Nyro, Phoebe Snow, Ringo Starr, Bruce Springsteen, Larry Coryell, Elton John, Charles Mingus, and Mike Mainieri. He has also appeared with pianist Hal Galper and his quintet, which includes Randy, and with guitarist Steve Kahn.

M: I started playing clarinet when I was seven. My father used to play every once in a while at our house, and one day someone came over with a clarinet and I liked the way it looked and that was it. My musical interest was a combination of my parents' influence, because they were musicians, particularly my father, and also my brother Randy, and my sister were playing ever since I can remember. It seemed to be the natural way things went. I just assumed when I was a kid that everyone played an instrument and I heard a lot of music when I was young; music like Clifford Brown, Oscar

Peterson, Dave Brubeck. I switched to saxophone when I was in junior high school. I started out on alto and later changed to tenor. But I never learned anything about music in high school. I learned most of the theory from analyzing tunes and taking the solos off records. When I was at high school in Philly, I played with various jazz groups and then I went to college at Indiana University. I originally intended to major in music, but I switched to pre-med right before I went there because I started to think that I wouldn't make any money playing music. I got worried. Then I realized it was too late. By the time I got to college, all I did was play and listen to rock, "acid" rock. You know, Jimi Hendrix, Eric Clapton, Cream, and the Beatles and the Stones. I never went to any classes. I spent a lot of time in the woods in Indiana getting in touch with myself and then decided to move to New York.

JC: Was moving to New York a catalyst in your musical development?

 M: Absolutely. It was the best thing I ever did because I got to be around a whole city of musicians and we were all kind of growing in our own ways. I really got into R & B when I came to New York. Randy had been here and that made it easier when I first came here to get some work. I did a lot of playing when I came here.

JC: Did you do any writing when you were growing up?

 M: Very little; it's still difficult. It really depends on how you write. A lot of good players, like Coltrane, for instance, wrote specifically with their playing in mind. His writing was a vehicle for his playing, which to me is still the best way. I haven't gotten my writing to that point. I think my writing would be better if I could keep that in mind, even though it never works out that way. I still write at the keyboard. Actually, a lot of people don't write like that. Randy, who I consider to be a great composer, sometimes writes tunes that don't really lend themselves to solo on, and we have to figure out how we're going to play on them.

JC: Are you a very ambitious person?

 M: Well, I'm musically ambitious. It still comes down to what I like to play and what I don't like to play.

JC: Are you concerned with your peers? Do you feel it's good to have that competition around you with the possibility of there always being another great player who will emerge?

 M: I don't look at it necessarily as competition. It's a good motivation. But the motivation isn't to try to sound better than somebody else, it's just that when I hear somebody playing and it sounds good, which unfortunately is not that often, it makes me feel like playing. You like to hear something beautiful. It reestablishes your belief that it is possible.

JC: What, in your opinion, is the present state of contemporary music?

M: In the last few years music has really advanced, particularly with respect to drummers and the concept of a rhythm section in the area of R & B. It has grown and I don't distinguish jazz from R & B in a lot of ways as far as playing on it. A lot of people think that I'm a purist, but I have been playing both jazz and R & B all along, and I've been playing almost the same thing, in a way, except that I do alter my sound a little bit. It may be a little bit less complex, harmonically, although not so much anymore. But, you know, R & B doesn't have a lot of chord progressions.

JC: What are your feelings regarding the use of electric devices?

M: I feel the necessity to play electric, if I'm with an electric band. So now, a lot of the time, unless it's a very mellow kind of music, the sound of the acoustic tenor alone doesn't really sound right to me. It doesn't blend unless I use some electric gadgets. I don't know that much about electronics. I just plug in to the box and if it sounds good, then I use it.

JC: Why do you think so many musicians fall victim to excessive lifestyles—drugs, alcohol, and so on?

M: If the talent is there, it's there, and in certain ways I'm not one to rule out drugs completely because sometimes they can be therapeutic and can help a person. It's actually a common syndrome among musicians. It's a question of loosening up, sometimes. It's a state of mind. It's definitely a mental thing. I think it has to do with a lot of personal things within the individual musician—things he can't face, areas that the person can't confront, which we all have.

THE FOLLOWING INTERVIEW WAS CONDUCTED WITH MICHAEL BRECKER IN 1999, MORE THAN TWENTY YEARS AFTER THE PRECEDING CONVERSATION WITH JULIE CORYELL

JC: It has been said that jazz is dead. Radio does not favor or promote real jazz today.

M: The music is anything but dead. It remains a vital form of expression not only for myself but also for hundreds of musicians I'm in contact with and gratefully, the audiences I play for.

JC: Are you satisfied with your role today in the jazz world, and have you achieved what you set out to accomplish years ago?

M: I feel good about the music that I've made over the years and believe that I have at least partially achieved what I set out to do when I first ventured into music years ago. There's still so much to learn.

JC: Most of the musicians interviewed years ago for this book are now very cynical about the lack of attention jazz currently receives, especially as it has impacted their ability to make a living. How has your own career been affected by this change? Do you find your music better appreciated abroad than in the States?

M: I certainly do seem to spend quite a bit of time in Europe and Japan. I'm grateful to reach an audience there that is not only appreciative of the history of the music, but also open to innovation. It's true, there is room for growth in the U.S. in terms of the awareness of the history of jazz and appreciation of the art of improvisation. I don't really have time to be cynical, though—I simply continue to perform here and abroad and I teach when and where I can.

JC: How have you changed as a person since our original interview? Are you still excited by music and the creative process?

M: Hopefully, I've grown up a bit since the original interview! Actually, I'm probably more excited than ever about music and the creative process. I'm optimistic about the future and have come to appreciate the fragility of life. I try to be thankful for every day I have on the planet, and I feel blessed to have the ability and the opportunity to play, write and share the music.

JC: Is there anything new to say musically or is it just a recycling of the old? Do you feel there is anywhere left to go with the 12 notes we have, or have we exhausted all the possibilities?

M: For me, it's always been a bit of both. I'm constantly recycling, trying to learn from what's come before. One the other hand, ideas come out of this process occasionally that are fresh. Music is and has always been much more for me than just 12 notes.

JC: Are you still as ambitious as you once were, or have other priorities taken over?

M: I'm still dedicated as I have ever been I still try to be the best I can, and at the same time, I also now have other priorities—most importantly, a family whom I love very dearly. The fact that music doesn't overrule everything has hopefully made me a more mature and compassionate player.

JC: What was good and memorable about the period known as fusion? One musician interviewed remembers it as a great period for arrangements, compositions, and the use of funk.

M: My favorite time in the period known as fusion was before the music was *known* as fusion. In the early seventies, when we had no real name for it and when the barriers between rock and jazz were becoming blurry, I found myself, along with my brother and our contemporaries, interested in finding ways to apply jazz harmony and sensibility to funk grooves. It really hadn't been done much up until then, and it felt like a blank page that hadn't been written on.

There was an enormous sense of freedom to pursue paths that seemingly hadn't been traversed. Out of that grew Brecker Brothers, my brother Randy's fantastically original writing and great times of real musical joy and creativity. There were many other groups inspired by this same freedom, including the great Mahavishnu Orchestra, Weather Report, Chick Corea and the legendary Miles Davis. It certainly was a time of great arrangements as well, and it was a portal through which an endless array of new sonorities and fascinating and visceral harmony and rhythms came.

JC: If you could go back and change anything about those times—in terms of lifestyle or music—what would it be?

M: I wouldn't change a thing.

JC: Do you think the fusion movement was created out of a need? Might it have been a need for expanding financial possibilities for jazz musicians, a need for something new artistically, or a combination of both?

M: At the time I didn't see it as any kind of movement. For me, the music was born of a genuine desire and need to do something new and exciting, while coming out of past musical traditions. It was so exhilarating to play this music for a large audience and really feel that it was being heard, understood and felt. I had never experienced that before.

JC: How do you think fusion will be viewed twenty or even fifty years from now?

M: Good music is it's own legacy; it not only stands the test of time but is, ideally, a contribution to generations to come.

JC: Have the record companies changed in respect to artists?

M: It's difficult for me to comment. Personally. I've been given a tremendous amount of freedom by the various record companies I have had the privilege to work with over the years. I have also always been given the freedom to grow artistically.

JC: Music today seems to have become very impersonal and soulless. It's all about money and "product," with little attention paid to art. Do you agree?

M: Again, I can only speak from my own experience, which has been pretty positive. I've had a large degree of support from most of the people at the record companies with whom I've worked.

JC: Do you have an overall opinion of today's rock, R & B, and jazz? Do you still have the same idols or mentors who influenced you as you were growing up?

M: It's always difficult for me to comment about today's music because there's just so much out there; I'd wind up generalizing. I still have the same idols as I did when I was growing up; the only difference now is that I've added many, many more to the list. The older I get, the more I seem to go back and develop new appreciation for the musicians I missed along the way.

joe farrell

12/16/37
Chicago Heights,
Illinois
saxophones
(tenor, soprano)
all reeds except bassoon
composer and arranger

Joe began playing the clarinet at age ten and became acquainted with the tenor saxophone in high school. He studied the tenor with Joe Sirolla at Roy Knapp Music School in Chicago in 1953. He went on to major in flute at the University of Illinois, where he received his B.S. in music education. While living in Chicago, he played with many of the local musicians, among them Ira Sullivan, Nicky Hill, and others. He came to New York in 1960. During the sixties he played with many artists, including Maynard Ferguson, Slide Hampton, Tito Rodriguez, the George Russell Sextet, Jaki Byard, Thad Jones-Mel Lewis, and also Elvin Jones. In the early seventies, he recorded with Chick Corea and the original Return to Forever, touring with Chick in Europe, Japan, and the United States. Since 1974 he has had his own quartet. In 1977 Joe once again recorded and toured extensively with Return to Forever. Joe is a very active studio musician who has appeared on albums by James Brown, the Young Rascals, Santana, Aretha Franklin, and many others.

J: From zero to five, I used to listen to Italian music. My people are Italian, and they played the radio all the time. I would sit with my ear next to the radio, and my mother told me I had all the tunes memorized with all the Italian words. I used to sing along with all the songs. That was until I was about five years. Then my sister married a musician. He played tenor sax and clarinet. We visited them in Chicago once or twice a month, and I always bugged him to play me some tunes. My father played very simple guitar, and my brother, the mandolin. At gatherings, they would play Italian songs and real simple stuff. When I was ten, my brother-in-law bought me a clarinet. That was in 1948. I would go and stay with them for two, three months, and he gave me lessons. He gave me a lot of Benny Goodman records—he had stacks of seventy-eights—and I would play them all the time. When I was in sixth and seventh grade, I played clarinet in the school band. I really wanted to play tenor, but in those days you had to learn clarinet first. Five years later, when I was in high school, my father got me a tenor sax. There was a piano player in school who knew a lot about jazz and the big bands, like Stan Kenton and Woody Herman. I'd go to his pad and he'd play me these records. I didn't know what was going on, but at school, before band rehearsals, we'd be in the back room having a ten-minute jam session Dixieland-style. The band director would play trumpet, and I'd get my clarinet out and try to play with him. Then, when I got my tenor, I really wanted to impress my friends by playing and improvising a lot.

In 1953, I started studying in Chicago. I'd get on the train after school, go in and have my lesson, have dinner, hang out a jam session till about ten. That's when I first heard musicians play live. I was sixteen at the time. After the sessions, I would go home and practice and try to incorporate all the things I had just heard. By then, I had started to listen to records of Stan Getz and really tried to imitate him. But I was really more influenced by the live players in Chicago, like Johnny Griffin. So I had the two things going—live, which was very impressive, and records, like Getz, Stan Kenton, and George Shearing. Later on, when I was a senior, I heard Bird [Charlie Parker]. He died in March of that year, and I'll never forget it because I always wanted to see him. I was working dance-band gigs around schools, and listening to as much music as I could—live and recorded. In the mid-fifties I went to the University of Illinois, and all vacations I would come back to Chicago and try to sit in at jam sessions.

JC: How did the college academia compare to the real world? What did you learn there?

J: I learned how to play and write arrangements, and so on. I learned how to play in the saxophone section, in orchestras, and concerts. But the best thing I did was sit in and play jam sessions.

JC: What was your major?

J: My major actually was music education, but I was also a flute major. I had all these instruments—tenor, curve soprano, flute, and clarinet. I played tenor in dance bands on weekends and some at jam sessions at college and in Chicago. During the week, I practiced flute, played in the orchestras and concert bands, and did my studies. I didn't start working professionally until I graduated in 1959. From that summer until New Year's Eve I worked with a dance band in Chicago. I had saved about five bills, and on New Year's Day, I packed my bags, got in my car, and drove to New

York. I didn't know anybody, so I began doing the same thing—going around to clubs and sitting in. I knew that was a way to get heard. A month after I had been in town, I met a drummer, Stew Martin, who had just gotten a gig with Maynard Ferguson. He said, "Hey, man, Maynard is auditioning tenor players. Why don't you come on down to the audition?" I went, and there were two or three cats there, and I got the gig. That's when I first started to earn bread playing professionally. It was 1960 and we opened at Birdland. And I made my first album—all within two months after I got there.

JC: What was the music scene like in New York in the early sixties?

J: Great! First of all, you had a dozen clubs with two bands each—a regular act and another act. Everywhere you went had two groups. There was a lot more playing going on in lofts than there is now. After I made my album, I continued to play with small groups—always sitting in; I was a professional jammer. After a year and a half with Maynard, I got my own band together, and finally started getting Monday nights at Birdland and other clubs. But I really couldn't keep it going, so I continued to work with other bands.

JC: During the late sixties, when Miles Davis made *Bitches' Brew,* he proved that money could be made from music. He began to incorporate electronic devices. How did this whole movement affect you?

J: I was still playing acoustic, and I was working with a group with no electronics except for a microphone. I was really playing straight-ahead jazz and didn't get into electronics until a few years later in the seventies, when I went with Chick [Corea]. I wasn't really electric until I got my own group together after that.

JC: Did you do it because you wanted to, or because you felt that you had to?

J: Oh, I liked it. I also needed it to blend in electric instruments. It was really hard to play the flute, for instance, when you had a loud drummer, a guitar player, and an electric bass behind you. I dug electronics because I could get a lot of different sounds. At first I was a hard person to convert, because I thought it wasn't the purest, but now I see what's happening in music. It changes, and you just go along with it. You have to, because you want to stay in this business. Also, it would be ridiculous if I played now the way I was playing in the late fifties and sixties.

JC: Was playing and recording with Chick a turning point for you in some way?

J: Well, that brought us to what's happening in the seventies. When we made that record* with Flora Purim, Airto, Stanley Clarke, and me, and we played those Latin rhythms Chick began writing in

---

* *Light as a Feather,* 1973, Polydor, PD 5525.

tunes, it changed the whole picture of the music scene. It seemed like after we made that record, everybody and their brother started playing sambas and songs with melodies. It became very popular, and that leads us to what's happening now.

JC: How do you compare the role of active studio player—which you are—to that of a leader on your own dates?

J: My approach is that I try to do the best job I can do, no matter what kind of music I'm playing—even if it is the worst. And, in terms of my really loving all the dates I have done, I have been into just the technical part of it—trying to get a good sound—you know, different things that I would be concerned with. Whereas, if it were *my* date, I would be interested in playing a good solo or being more inventive.

JC: Have you always handled your own business?

J: For years I was doing everything—I was a bandleader, father, landlord, and attorney. It had gotten to the point where I was mainly concerned with business, and playing very little. Now I have a manager and an attorney, and that leaves a lot more time for playing and writing.

JC: You said you had changed with the times, that it was necessary. Jazz musicians are enjoying a commercial success they haven't had to such a degree in the past, and a certain kind of music is being played that is making the kind of money I'm talking about. What are your feelings about "commercially oriented music"?

J: Here's what it amounts to…Most people don't realize that, essentially, we're playing the same way we basically always played—at least I am. But what has changed is the set. Now, instead of the piano, bass, and drums with no amplifiers, you have a guitar—maybe two guitars—a synthesizer, and maybe some electronic hookups. But when it comes to playing a solo, I am still trying to play as inventively as ever, and I'm just in a different setting. It's the same thing with all these records we're making. Instead of making them quartet, now it's with strings and a synthesizer background. This is aimed at reaching a wider audience. For some reason, they can relate to this more than to a small group just blowing, so you get a better return on that. You're still playing the same way, but instead of playing to thirty people in a club, you're reaching thirty-five hundred.

JC: So the doors have been opened in a way for more creative freedom?

F: It seems that way. If music has gotten to these audiences by different settings, the musician is able to go ahead and play acoustic if he wants to, and be appreciated. I see it happening now.

john
klemmer

7/3/46

Chicago, Illinois

saxophones

(tenor, soprano)

clarinet

piano

composer and arranger

producer

John began playing the guitar at age five, alto at eleven, and tenor in his teens. He led concert and stage bands while still in school, and studied theory, arranging, and jazz, and classical approaches to the tenor sax, clarinet, and flute. He studied at the Stan Kenton Clinics from 1960 to 1965, and privately with Joe Daley from 1962 to 1969. John learned film scoring from Albert Harris from 1970 to 1974. In the mid-seventies he appeared and recorded with Don Ellis's orchestra, providing some of the arrangements. It was around this time that Klemmer became interested in electronic devices, especially the Echoplex. He also played with the later Oliver Nelson in a State Department-sponsored tour of French West Africa in late 1968. Since the early seventies, he has been recording and, as a leader, touring extensively across the Untied States and Europe.

J: I started playing guitar at the age of five. After that, I wanted to be a cartoonist, a painter, a tap dancer, and a writer. Then, at age eleven, I started playing the alto saxophone. I'm really not sure what the motivation was. I think I saw someone play a saxophone on a television show when I was a child, and I loved the way it sounded, I loved the way it looked, and I asked my parents to buy me one. My parents were very cooperative; they furnished me with musical instruments and paid for any music lessons that I wanted. They didn't encourage me so much from an artistic point of view, but they supported my own desires to want to play music and learn. Being involved in music provided a great emotional release for me, an opportunity to get out of the middle-class suburbia that I was brought up in and move me into another kind of world. I studied a little bit of piano, clarinet, flute, and legitimate saxophone, as well as "jazz saxophone" or improvising. I made the transition from alto saxophone to tenor, because tenor was more in demand for bands, and I could play with bands and work more, so I switched over to the tenor.

JC: Who influenced you musically in your youth?

J: Primarily, Sonny Rollins and then John Coltrane, but I listened to everyone I possibly could— Miles Davis, Bill Evans—and I listened to musicians who played instruments other than saxophone. I just listened to everybody, but I tried to have them influence me spiritually rather than to take down any of their lines or their riffs, or anything like that. I was more inspired and influenced by their dedication and motivation in what they were doing, and they encouraged me to get into myself and get into my own thing as much as I could.

JC: Has your music gone through any major transitions?

J: My music has changed only in the way that it kept evolving and maturing. I don't think it drastically changes that much. I may change the surroundings around me drastically as far as rhythm sections and styles of rhythm sections are concerned. Basically, I believe it's been my same essence of playing that has continued to grow and evolve and mature as I have as a person.

JC: How important are electronic devices to your music?

J: I started incorporating electronic devices into my music in 1969. Predominantly the Echoplex, and sometimes a phase shifter, but I only used those electronic devices that do not distort the original sound of the saxophone, but only add an additional effect to it. For instance, I briefly used the ring modulator, but it distorted the original sound of the saxophone too much. Because of the depth of my involvement and commitment to music, electronics has become an integral part of my sound, and they're something that I continue to work with and find new ways to use. It's like anything else—it's how it's used. Some people are abusing them, some people are not. I only use it when I hear it.

JC: How did you develop your writing and arranging skills?

J: Just by years and years of constant writing and experimenting. I predominantly compose on the piano and sing the melodies, or at various times compose exclusively on the saxophone, or a combination of both.

JC: How did you achieve the commercial success you now enjoy?

J: By being, I feel, sincere and finding something that I really believed in completely, and that sincerity, I think, is the link with the public. I seem to have a very melodic sense of writing and playing, and people seem to pick up on that. I don't believe there's a formula; there might be procedures that each individual artist can find for himself that work to make him commercially successful, but I don't believe that there's any one formula for all. It's an individual thing. When I make records, I'm only consciously attempting to please myself. I'm aware, when I do the records, of what I feel will have more accessibility, and what won't, but if I believe in it and want to do it—no matter what it is, that's my primary concern.

JC: How much control do you have over your career, insofar as the "business" is concerned?

J: As an artist, I'm very aware of the music business, I've studied it very carefully, I'm very knowledgeable about it, I've run a lot of my own business most of my life. I discovered early in life that it is crucial that I protect myself and my art. I'm basically totally and completely in control of my own business, even through I have managers and agents and attorneys who work for me, but all final decisions are mine.

JC: How do you relate to the word "exploitation"?

J: I feel that, at times, there are people who are trying to exploit you on all levels all the time—not only in music, but in daily life. It's only if you allow yourself to be exploited. Exploitation—the word seems to have a negative connotation. For the most part, seemingly in this society, it is negative, but I feel that also, from a positive point of view, you can find ways to exploit your own talents and your own opportunities; but there are a lot of people out there who are trying to exploit artists, and it's only a matter of allowing them to, if you are naïve enough, or not knowledgeable enough to protect yourself from being exploited.

ronnie
laws

10/3/50,
Houston, Texas
saxophones
(tenor, soprano)
flutes
composer and arranger
producer

Ronnie was raised in Houston, where he was surrounded by music from an early age—his older brother Hubert is a well-known flautist, and his older sister Eloise is a singer and actress. Ronnie grew up with the people who would form the Crusaders, and began to work as early as high school with a local group called the Lightmen. Ronnie attended Stephen F. Austin State University, where he majored in flute. Laws remained at school for two years before moving to Los Angeles, where he began to get work almost immediately. One of his first appearances was with the rock R & B group called Von Ryan's Express; shortly thereafter, Ronnie played with Quincy Jones and Walter Bishop. He then joined Earth, Wind and Fire, appearing on the group's first record on Columbia. Moving on, Laws worked with Hugh Masekela for a time, then free lanced around town, playing with the Los Angeles band, Ujima, and working with his brother Hubert. When Ronnie finally began recording under his own name, he was produced by his friend, Crusader Wayne Henderson. His first album, *Pressure Sensitive*, became the largest-selling debut record in the thirty-seven-year history of Blue Note Records.

R: I began to play at age twelve. My motivation was just the inbred desire to want to perform and to want to play. I suppose that the motivation outside of that was feeling the family inspiration and encouragement in music—having brothers and sisters, and, basically, the whole family involved in a musical sense. My parents encouraged me to play, particularly my mother, because she had always expressed a love for music. She was a piano player herself. She played in the local church organization when I was a small kid, and it always fascinated me to see her play. In respect to the other family members, such as Hubert [Laws, the flautist] and my sisters, all participated in some musical endeavor, and this stimulated me and also encouraged me to want to take part.

JC: Who influenced you musically?

R: I would have to say it was mixed company, because being from Texas—Houston—I'm sure you know there is a heavy blues influence, as well as other exposures to jazz and classical music. This is really hard to pinpoint from all those categories what influenced me the most. I've always loved blues. I think blues is a very raw, very primitive way of expression—very genuine—not to say that the other forms are not. Blues has basically always had a common appeal to the majority of the people.

JC: Are there any composers in particular who have exerted a major influence on you?

R: I have always been impressed with composers such as Miles Davis, and more contemporary composers, like Herbie Hancock. They have always fascinated me and have influenced me to a degree.

JC: How do you account for your rapid ascent to the top in such a commercially oriented and competitive medium?

R: It seems that success has come to me very rapidly. As to how to account for this, I'll have to say that it really hasn't been a rapid career rise in the sense of it being an overnight thing from age twelve, when I started playing. I've been playing professionally for at least seven or eight years, maybe ten. The point is that, during that time, I was gaining experience and knowledge in my craft, paying dues just like other musicians and artists have to. A lot of it has to do with having a well-balanced view of life in general—putting things in their proper perspective and not letting one thing override the other. Being married at an early age—at twenty—I don't feel that I was mature. I have matured in the sense of responsibility—recognizing what life really is and not wasting time, which is characteristic of youth.

JC: Is there a formula for creating "hit records"?

R: Whatever appeals to the masses at the time will contribute to a hit record. Of course that means that an artist would really have to be aware of what's happening at the present—not necessarily the past, but the present—you know, what is widely accepted at the moment, what is the concept of the listening audience today. That, to me, constitutes whether a record will be popular or hit material. My brother, of course, was a major influence in my career. He has always been very encouraging, always been in my corner in respect to what's happening musically. I've gotten good instruction, and he has helped me to build a good foundation and start off basically on the right foot.

JC: Do you consider yourself to be a continuation of a certain tradition of reed players?

R: I would like to think so. Saxophone players, like John Coltrane, Sonny Rollins, Charlie Parker, and so on—artists whom I admired from the time I started to play the sax—I would feel very honored to think that I could be an offshoot from players of that caliber. I feel that it's also important, along with admiration for these musicians, to sort of approach the instrument at the same time with your own concept—that is, drawing experience and knowledge from what these musicians have contributed in a musical sense and taking what they have done and molding it into your own. Of course this is not the easiest thing to do, as is evident in many players today. But to me, it's always been imperative and important to establish my own musical identity.

JC: How do you feel about the wide-spread use of electronic devices that is now so prevalent among the present generation of musicians?

R: I feel that, in respect to electronic devices, I've often referred to them as toys, because they are. But nevertheless, they do add to the music a certain dimension. I think they have their place in music. It's really up to the individual artists to be able to exercise the usage of these types of devices in a very discreet manner, not overusing nor undermining the use of them. With respect to these technological advances, they have advanced the music field—the music itself and the development of the music. I think it's made it more interesting, brought about an extension, sort of a future approach to a more modern style of playing.

JC: What is your overall view of contemporary jazz-rock fusion?

R: I think in respect to contemporary music today, we are still in a period of transition. Yet, at the same time, I think it is innovative. Artists are crossing the board, so to speak—the borderlines of jazz, rock, rhythm and blues, country and western, and what have you. I feel the culmination of all these musical forms is being incorporated by individual artists into their music. I think there's a big transition from what it used to be, because years ago, labels meant exactly what they represented, in the sense that if you went to hear a jazz player, that's exactly what you heard, period. Of course, this would be the case with other musical forms. When you went to hear a symphonic concert, that's exactly what you would hear. But I think that in this day and age, there is a searching and also a merging together of all these musical forms. And I think that because of this, we are living in a period of transition in music that is innovative.

JC: Have you ever felt any unusual pressure to be commercial, or are you pretty much in control of your directions and goals?

R: I have never really felt that my music, in particular, is commercial in any sense. Of course, anything that's salable is commercial—like it or not. But the point is that I've always felt that I've had relative freedom to express myself musically, and I would really like to maintain that freedom— being able to express whatever I feel emotionally and to be able to convey that to persons of the musical listening audience. I feel that it is dangerous for an artist to feel restricted or inhibited in any way, as far as the industry and the listening public go. When any one artist is put into one cat- egory and tries to expand or go beyond that, he's usually highly criticized for wanting to explore other fields. I think this can cause a great disadvantage, not only to the artist, but to the musical listeners, because they are being deprived of growth in the music itself. The music I create is not "commercial" to me, because I feel that it represents me—my background and everything I stand for. It really has never fazed me, because to me it's just music that appeals to me, music I've grown up with, and music that I'm expressing through my instrument and through my writing. Because I'm doing what I want to do, I'm very happy and very into my music.

david
liebman

9/6/46

Brooklyn, New York

saxophones

(tenor, soprano)

flutes

composer and arranger

producer

David's professional career began at fourteen in the New York area. He attended Queens College, majoring in music, but transferred to New York University, from which he graduated with a B.A. in American history and a substitute teacher's license in 1968. While studying privately with Joe Allard and Charles Lloyd in 1970, David joined the fusion band Ten Wheel Drive. At the same time, he co-founded Free Life Communications, a musicians' cooperative funded by the New York State Council on the Arts, an offshoot of which was Open Sky Trio with Bob Moses and Frank Tusa. In 1972 David formed the band Sawbuck, the nucleus of which was later to become the Ellis/Liebman band. Around that time David worked with drummer Pete LaRocca and recorded *My Goal's Beyond* with John McLaughlin. He joined Elvin Jones in late 1972, and played with Miles Davis from 1973 to 1975. In 1974, while still playing with Miles, he formed Lookout Farm with Richie Beirach, Frank Tusa, Jeff Williams, Eleana Steinberg, John Abercrombie, Badal Roy, and Don Alias. Lookout Farm was the first American contemporary music group to tour India, sponsored by a federal government grant. In 1977 Liebman and Pee Wee Ellis formed the Ellis/Liebman Band with Link Chamberland, Jimmy Strassburg, Tony Saunders, and Eleana Steinberg.

In late 1977, he and Julian Priester toured with the Eddie Henderson quintet. David has worked as a clinician for both the Summer Jazz Camps and H. Couf Saxophons, and is a member of the National Association of Jazz Educators. With members of Lookout Farm he co-authored a book, *Small Group Improvisation—A Case Study.* In March of 1978 David joined Chick Corea for a world tour.

D: I began on the piano. I was nine years old. I studied classical music because my mother had played piano when she was young and she wanted me to take at least two years of piano before I decided what instrument I wanted to play. This is the true way to teach a student, a kid, to get into music. When you're a student you learn how to do things automatically. When you get older you become reflective about what you do and you are not really as disciplined as you used to be. So when you're young, you just kind of do the four pages the teacher said had to be written, if you're that kind of student, and you finish it, and by the time you're twelve or fifteen years old you know it even though you didn't know how you got it.

I always wanted to play saxophone because I liked the sound and also I was into middle and late fifties rock and roll and I really liked the saxophone players. People like Duane Eddy and Billy Haley and the Comets had great R & B sax players. I never really wanted to play classical music. I wanted to be a rock and roll singer and I wanted to be a ballplayer. You know, all those things you go through when you're young—you want to go through all those dreams.

By the time I got into public school, music became involved in my life with shows and little musicals and things. So as soon as that started happening, it just became the main thing in my life. It was never a thing like I'll become a musician, or I'll be a this or that. I was actually going to be a doctor and I was really interested in medicine until I really started getting into music. When I was about sixteen or seventeen, the whole thing changed. When I was going to Hebrew school I wanted to be a rabbi. Everybody was into being Jewish.

JC: Are you still into being Jewish?

D: I feel I'm returning to a certain part of it again. I think it's going to come out in me. It's something that comes out in the later part of your life.

JC: What about Coltrane; was he a major influence then?

D: Well, hearing Coltrane, live, was the biggest influence in my life. It's the central factor in my life. I heard him play about twenty-five or thirty times and I said, That's what I've got to do. I didn't know what it was when I first heard it; I didn't know who Coltrane was. I was just getting into Dave Brubeck and Horace Silver, that kind of stuff. The first time I heard him play was at Birdland. When he came on, I didn't know what the hell he was doing. I said, This guy sounds like he's missing notes. He played "My Favorite Things," and I said, This couldn't be, he'd never play a song like that. It was very inspiring. It made me want to play jazz.

After school I took off and I went away for a while, took a little cabin upstate and just stayed there for about six months and practiced. I started getting into all kinds of music: classical, Indian, world music, and other countries.

JC: Were you listening to mainly horn players?

D: No, I started taking solos off of other instruments, piano and trumpet solos, especially trumpet solos because the range of a trumpet is a little more limited. It's not all that easy to get around, so trumpet players tend to play in a bebop fashion. They play very close knit lines, melodic lines, which is really the essence of music. It's not going around the instrument like crazy; it's playing a line within an octave is what's happening. You should be able to play a whole tune, a whole solo, tell a whole story in a fifth, if you're really there. So trumpet players were very good for that and they tongue slower.

JC: How do you compose?

D: I use piano, saxophone, and drums. Sometimes tunes come from the saxophone. For a rock tune, they usually come on the drums first. I usually take the writing of a tune as a natural event, make it an improvisation, capture that moment, unless it's something I've been thinking about. Most of the time my tunes are inspired by the moment, by a mood, or I just happen to sit down and something comes out. Most of my tunes are named after either moods or a person that it reminds me of.

JC: How would you differentiate, say, between Charlie Parker's horizontal approach and, let's say, John Coltrane's vertical approach to the improvised line?

D: Well, the point is that Bird played, it's not more melodically, but he played through the chords in the sense that Trane played up and down the chords. It's a matter of the emphasis. I mean everybody plays every direction in order to be a great improviser because you have to go everywhere; but the emphasis of Bird's playing was melodic, a melody that worked through the chords, whereas with Trane it was an ongoing, scalier kind of thing that worked through the chord also, but a more up-and-down type of thing, so the notes sounded that way also, from the very motion of it.

JC: What are your feelings about jazz-rock?

D: You always like the music best that you grew up on, that inspired you. So bebop, of course, to me is the heavy music, that's artistic. I think what's going on now I identify with and feel a part of and feel like I've contributed to and so forth, so I'm more in a way objective about it, or maybe I'm more subjective about it, but something's different. I'm less involved emotionally. It doesn't really kill me. When I hear Trane play a ballad, I get chills. I hardly get chills from any music I've heard in the last five years. Very rarely. So that's one thing. Musically, I think it's a style, a period of time that we're going through. I like some of it and some of it I don't like. I think that what's happening is that the emphasis is on certain aspects of the music; for example, rhythm has kind of negated the influence of melody. If you think about most of the bands now, you think of the strongest thing being the rhythm, and in the case of Weather Report, the strongest thing would be the color. But you don't really think of melodies, per se, or telling a story, and the harmony is very limited. So, therefore, the music is a little one-sided. But it has captured something, and that is the rhythm of the day, and it really does capture that. It really is a statement of the time.

JC: When you're on the stage do you play mainly for yourself and the band or do you feel a definite attempt to communicate?

D: A definite attempt to communicate, there's no question about it, but I expect that the audience that is there have come to see me communicate with the other musicians and then they will be pleased. So, therefore, it's a beautiful function, going about communicating with the other musicians, which has really got to be your main thing, provides the contact with the audience.

JC: Could you extrapolate a bit on your earlier references to your Jewish roots?

D: It's getting to be a little, I don't want to say, mystical, or get into like a thing, but definitely, I'm getting to a point in my life where certain things are happening to me. You know, I'm reaching a maturity, I think.

tom scott

5/19/48

Los Angeles, California

saxophones (tenor and
all others)

flutes

miscellaneous woodwinds

lyricon

composer and arranger

producer

Tom grew up in Los Angeles, where his composer-father and pianist-mother provided early musical inspiration. Beginning on the clarinet, he eventually discovered the soprano, tenor, and alto saxes. Before graduating from high school, he led award-winning groups at the Lighthouse Intercollegiate Jazz Festival and the Hollywood Bowl Battle of the Bands. At sixteen, he composed his first score for an educational film. He attended San Fernando Valley State College, and later USC, but did not finish. While at USC, he played with a number of jazz bands—the Don Ellis Band, the Howard Roberts Quintet, Oliver Nelson, and the Roger Kellaway Quartet. Tom first recorded his own material with his own group, the Tom Scott Quartet, a band that featured John Guerin, Chuck Domanico, and Mike Wofford; this band later evolved into the L.A. Express. During the mid seventies, Tom contributed arrangements to Joni Mitchell's *For the Roses* and *Court and Spark*. Later, Tom and the rest of the L.A. Express toured with Mitchell and can be heard on the live recording *Miles of Aisles*. The L.A. Express underwent several changes in personnel and finally disbanded. Since the late seventies, Tom has again been recording under his own name as a leader. In 1977, he toured and recorded with the CBS All Stars—Alphonso Johnson, Mark Soskin, Steve Kahn, and Billy Cobham.

An active composer for both television and films, some of Tom's credits in this area include: *Baretta*, *Three for the Road*,

Cannon, Dan August, Barnaby Jones, Streets of San Francisco, Conquest of the Planet of the Apes, Uptown Saturday Night, and *The Nine Lives of Fritz the Cat.* More recently, he contributed arrangements and his skills as a player to Steely Dan's *Aja.*

T: My father, Nathan Scott, has been a composer most of his life. He works in television and motion pictures. My mother was a pianist; she accompanied Nelson Eddy once on tour and taught piano students. So there was a lot of music happening, but not too much modern jazz 'cause they were mostly into classical music.

They never really pushed me into music; it was really mostly my own doing. When I was in fourth grade, I started on the clarinet. By the time I got to junior high school, I was into Benny Goodman and Buddy DeFranco. In seventh grade there was one opening in a dance band for a baritone player. More than anything else, I wanted to get into that dance band, so I took over the school baritone sax and played it a lot. I didn't practice a lot of scales, but I would just play it for hours and hours; and then I discovered Gerry Mulligan and kind of got on the way toward some knowledge of modern jazz. By ninth grade, I had my first alto sax and started taking flute lessons. There was a lot of continuity in my studying because I was taking private lessons on one instrument or another continuously from age eight till about sixteen or seventeen. I was fortunate to have a very "liberated" junior-high school music teacher, Mr. David Winseman. We had a regular stage band, a Dixieland band, and a group with four flutes and a rhythm section—like a modern jazz combo with trumpet, tenor, and rhythm section.

JC: Were you composing then?

T: I didn't compose that much. What I started doing was transcribing solos: Gerry Mulligan and Coltrane, and later on, entire big-band arrangements.

JC: Were you listening to big-band recordings much?

T: Yes. The voicing and the harmony fascinated me. I wanted to find out what was going on, not just with the lead lines and the melodies, but with all those inside voices. That really fascinated me— all the second and fourth tenor parts.

JC: Where did your music go from there?

T: By that time I was firmly rooted in modern jazz and was listening a lot to Coltrane, Miles Davis, and Cannonball Adderley. I was drawn much more to so-called East Coast jazz than the West Coast. There was something about the style and the kind of tone the players were getting—that attracted me more, and I'd listen to that music all my waking hours. I used to wake up before school to Miles's "My Funny Valentine." I'd even wake up early to hear the whole track. I didn't care much about rock 'n' roll in those days. I took a class with Don Ellis at UCLA—the university extension class—and he invited me to play in his big band which was working at the Havana Club downtown. We were only making about five bucks apiece by splitting the take at the door, but it was a tremendous opportunity to work with those odd time signatures which fascinated me. I saw that as a new area of jazz that hadn't been explored too heavily. The other thing was the electronic saxophone. About that time the Conn Corporation hired an amplifier maker to design an octave coupler for the saxophone. Selmer had just come out with one, so I became the playing musician/consultant for Conn.

JC: You were probably one of the few people at that point?

T: Oh, yeah—there were very few people who had them and hardly anyone knew what they were. So I began to attract a little attention playing in Don Ellis's band because as a soloist I was fluent in the odd time signatures, plus I had an electric saxophone with an Echoplex which hadn't been used too much before.

JC: In retrospect, what role would you say electronic devices have played in contemporary and in your music?

T: Well, I think there is still a lot to be done to transform all the electronic advances into music. You've got to pass the gimmick stage and get on to the music stage; and the justification for using any of that stuff is not just that it's there, but that it has a music role—it's called for in context with the music. There's always a temptation that, when new things are invented and there are new gimmicks coming out every month, you should use them. I'm not as anxious to just use them for their own sake as I was in those days, because they were really exciting and new to me. Now I'm using them less than I was, but the idea is to use them at the right time.

JC: How did you break into films and television?

T: The electronic saxophone was of interest to a few composers of television—Dave Grusin and others who were coming into Dontes jazz club and hearing me play. I remember Dave especially getting me on dates of his very early, like eighteen or something, and how thrilled I was just to be there at all; but the electronic saxophone and the fact that I could read music in seven-four and nine-eight time signatures, for example, helped me get in the door. You know, being a success in anything is a two-step process: it's the timing of getting asked to be somewhere—getting that first foot in the door—and of maintaining a career—being able to perform what's asked of you. I got very lucky because I was there at the right time, and I guess was able to do it. But in any case, I started doing an awful lot of woodwind playing for TV shows and records.

JC: How would you describe composing for media as compared to composing for your own group?

T: You have to be the best kind of composer you can be. You have to sublimate your own personal taste because your job becomes being able to provide whatever will best enhance that scene. If you take pride in doing the best you possibly can, then your personal taste becomes whatever is called for.

JC: What long-term goals do you foresee for yourself for the future?

T: One of my ideas it to put together some kind of book about the contemporary rhythm section. I think there's no question that the rhythm section is where today's music is based; that's the most important aspect. There is very little, if any, published material that really deals with the rhythm section and the kind of rhythmic interplay that goes on between the drums and the piano and the bass and guitar, primarily on a record. When I was involved with the L.A. Express as the horn player and arranger/composer, I knew relatively little about the rhythm section. We just kind of left the rhythm guys to work out their own stuff. But now as I'm studying and listening very carefully to all the rhythmic subtleties that go on, I'm realizing that it's knowing those things that can put me way out in front in terms of my ability to create contemporary, lasting horn music. I guess I'd call it the liberation of the rhythm section. In the forties and fifties, the rhythm section was merely a tool for accompanying a soloist. Now it's as if I look at myself as the lead voice or the top voice in the rhythm section, rather than a horn soloist with a rhythm accompaniment.

JC: How about the road for you?

T: I definitely have plans to go on the road. I think there's no experience like the experience of live performance. It keeps me on my toes. I find that in the studio there is a real danger of getting involved in studio techniques, and it tends to make you not play as well if you know that you can always do it over again. That's the major difference between live performance and recording. You've got to keep yourself at optimum level—you've got to think of every performance as your best one. I do see the recording studio as kind of a music lab. I'm fascinated by the prospect of new explorations inside within the context of making a record. And with multitracking how joyous it is to be able to compose and orchestrate and perform an entire piece for eight or nine or ten instruments and play all the parts. How challenging and different it is to match the vibrato and pitch and timbre and dynamics when you're playing a part along with something you've just recorded. The recording studio for me has really been an "earn-while-you-learn" kind of situation, because I've learned a lot and discovered many things in hearing myself back that I needed to improve upon. It has just opened up a whole new world, and I feel that that's a major part of my future.

wayne shorter

8/25/33

Newark, New Jersey

saxophones

(tenor, soprano)

composer and arranger

producer

Wayne attended the High School of Music and Art in Newark, New Jersey, where he majored in art and minored in music. His instrument at that time was the clarinet. When he was seventeen, Wayne received his first tenor saxophone. Wayne attended New York University, where he received a B.A. in music education. Graduating from college in 1956, Wayne began to gain recognition when he became a member of Art Blakey's band, where he remained from 1959 to 1963. In 1964, he joined the Miles Davis band, and gradually began to incorporate the soprano saxophone into his music. While playing with Miles, Wayne contributed many compositions, among them "E.S.P.," "Iris," "Orbits," "Footprints," "Dolores," "Limbo," "Vonetta," "Prince of Darkness," "Masqualero," "Nefertiti," "Fall," "Pinocchio," "Paraphernalia," "Sanctuary." In 1970, Wayne, along with Joe Zawinul, created Weather Report, one of the most important and commercially successful groups to emerge in the seventies. In 1976 and 1977, Wayne toured with the V.S.O.P. band, the old Miles Davis quintet (Herbie Hancock, Tony Williams, Ron Carter, with the addition of Freddie Hubbard in place of Miles). Wayne, who records as a leader, has also contributed to the records of Joni Mitchell and Steely Dan.

W: When I was six or seven years old, we lived in Newark. We had neighborhood street parties where all the different cultures would get together in the evening. They had those gaily colored lanterns and all kinds of food, and always music going on—"Roll Out the Barrel"—that's one of the things I remember hearing—and street dancing. I must have been quite, quite young, because I can remember that I was very close to the ground—looking up at everything, and the older people seemed like giants dancing around. Anyway, the connection between life and music began then. And there was always the radio—my father would habitually come home from work and just sit down and put on the same radio station.

When I was about sixteen, I got a clarinet, because hearing all that music on the radio made me want to play, and I was attracted to the clarinet because it looked slick. I got a good start on it and then got into the whole reed family. When I was seventeen, my grandmother got me a saxophone.

JC: Did you go to college?

W: Yeah, I went to NYU and majored in art, minored in music, and took a lot of electives. I played hooky a lot and hung out at the theater around the corner. They had all the bands there—Dizzy Gillespie, Charlie Parker, Stan Kenton, Woody Herman, Duke Ellington—and the whole bebop thing was coming in. I heard Martin Block on the radio one night saying, "I want to play something a little bit different—kind of a new music—they call it 'bop.'" I was checking out bebop and was surprised when he announced it. My last year of high school, we had formed a band which we called the Bebop Band, which we later called The Group.

JC: When did you start composing music?

W: That year when we started The Group. We played for dances and I was writing things that I heard—mambos, cha-chas. I even wrote an arrangement on something that Beethoven wrote. I wrote twenty-three arrangements that year. Also, when we had those bands, there were very few trumpet players around, so I was playing the clarinet and reading the trumpet parts. Between the ages of fifteen and twenty-one, I did a lot of writing and drawing. I was going on an adventure, and I said, "Hey, this is something else—this feels funny; it feels good." After NYU I used to go up to Birdland, the Open Door and Café Bohemia in the Village. The Open Door is the place I started—that's where I first saw Charlie Parker.

After I graduated, one week I was hanging out at the Café Bohemia. Everybody was in the joint—Kenny Clark, Donald Byrd, Max Roach, Jimmy Smith had just come to town, and Cannonball [Adderley] had come from Florida—all in that same week. I was standing at the bar, and Donald Byrd said, "Hey, Wayne, come on up." We'd already gotten to know each other through playing together at jam sessions. So I went up on the bandstand and we played, and I said, "Hey, I'm playing with these guys," and it felt real good. I didn't know that they were deciding to leave the U.S. and go to Europe. They decided you couldn't make any money playing bebop here because the people weren't ready for it; they didn't know about jazz being the greatest art that America had;

they didn't even dig it. Meanwhile, I'm standing with a draft notice in my pocket. And that was that—I went into the Army for two years, 1956-1958. When I got out, I went to New York to work, and I met a lot more people, and some of the same people I had known before I got drafted. Before I got out of the Army, there was a place up the street from where I lived called Sugar Hill, where we used to work before I got drafted. We had another small group then called the Jazz Informers. That was the last thing I was involved with in Newark. During my last month there, I would go to Washington and check out Miles and Coltrane.

JC: But you didn't know Miles then?

W: No, but I had been checking him out since I was sixteen—checking him and Bird together. My friends and I would have meetings at our houses and discuss the future of bebop—the music and the lifestyle—thinking that you were hip if your clothes were wrinkled and you looked sloppy on the bandstand. It was after that that I met Coltrane at Birdland. He had heard me play somewhere and he said, "Hey, you're playing that funny stuff, like me. Come on over to my house." I used to go over, and he'd play the piano for me while I played the tenor. Then we would take turns—I'd play the piano for him, and he'd play tenor. He'd say, "Play anything you want to play—go anywhere…" And he would just go to different places and meet me around the corner, as it were. I noticed that what he was playing consistently was the thing that led him to "Giant Steps"—those chords (we called them augmented thirds) kept going round and round. We were in on the birth of that thing. I knew it was new, and I said, "I'm not going to touch it, that's Trane's—and he's going to go that way. If there is anything new that I am going to do, I'm going to have to do it all by myself." Then he called me to work with him one night at Birdland. We had a rehearsal at his house, and that night we were playing. Opposite us was Cannonball and his brother Nat. Cannonball and Trane were working with Miles then but they had time off and they split up and got different bands. Elvin Jones was on drums that night. It was historic; everybody realized it— we tore that place up. Ten years later, when I went to California, people were still talking about it—"Yeah, we heard about it out here—that memorable Monday night at Birdland." That's when Trane started playing all the new stuff he had written. It was a new wave. After that, Trane had to go back to work with Miles and Cannonball. That was when I first started hanging out with Joe Zawinul—there at Birdland. One night Trane came in there on his night off and told me he was deciding to leave Miles and get his own thing together. He said, "You want to be with Miles? You got it. I'm finished doing the Miles gig." It was during that time that I had worked for four weeks with Maynard Ferguson, and Trane and Lee Morgan were very cognizant of my life. They had come to Newark one time when they were co-leading a group, and I was standing there and Lee saw me. He said, "Hey, I heard about you—you're Wayne Shorter, aren't you?" He asked me to come up and play with them. Now, dig this—here I was with Maynard and we were in Canada, and Art

Blakey was up there with the Jazz Messengers. Hank Mobley did not show up, so Lee Morgan comes running across the street and says, "You want to join the Messengers?" And I say, "Yeah!" So I went with Art and stayed for five years. During the last year, Miles would call my house 'cause we would be playing in different places, and he would walk in and check me out. Then he wanted me to join his band, but I didn't want to just up and leave the Messengers unless I could do it in the right way, because I was musical director. I didn't go immediately to join Miles—I took a whole summer off, just checking some things out about possibly starting my own group. But I saw that it meant a lot of work and growing old fast—a hard way to go. George Coleman had left the Miles group, and Miles's manager called me and said Miles didn't have a saxophone player. And Herbie Hancock and Tony Williams were calling me at the same time, saying, "Hey, man, we've got the opening—wouldn't it be nice if you were with the band." And then I got on the phone with Miles, while he was in California and I was in New York. It was me on the phone with Miles, Tony, and Herbie. I flew on out there—no rehearsals.

JC: You're such a prodigious composer. It must be something that is just second nature to you. Does it just flow from you?

W: Not now—it doesn't flow right now. It's kind of easy when it does flow and you're thinking about yourself, and something comes through you. But it's lonely, solitary—it's to the point of selfishness. Now it's not; it doesn't flow just like that. This thing called inspiration doesn't manifest itself like that. Something else is manifesting itself in its place, and I'm allowing it to. A lot of people don't. They say, "I must do the thing I know best, and keep it up to this level." And at the same time, other aspects of their lives deteriorate and they say, "I wonder why—what kind of Karma is this?"

JC: Having embraced Buddhism, how would you relate it to life?

W: Music, or whatever a person does, is only one aspect of their life, a fragmented aspect. Buddhism means human beings—humanity—life. Buddhism means your whole life—that's what it means.

grover washington, jr.

12/12/43

Buffalo, New York

saxophones (tenor, soprano, and baritone)

clarinet

electric bass

piano

composer and arranger

producer

Grover started on the saxophone at age ten, taking lessons at the Wurlitzer School of Music. He studied chord progressions with Elvin Shepherd and began playing professionally at sixteen with the Columbus, Ohio, based band, the Four Clefs, with whom he traveled extensively. When the group broke up in 1963, Grover joined organist Keith McAllister for two years. He spent two years at Trenton State College where he majored in music. He was stationed at Fort Dix during his two years in the Army, and worked local gigs in Philadelphia, playing with organ trios and rock groups, in addition to working with drummer Billy Cobham in New York City for Jazz Interactions. After the service, Grover played with Don Gardner's Sonotones in Philadelphia, 1967-1968. From 1969 to 1970, he worked for a local record distributor—the first full-time job he had ever held: "I was totally immersed in jazz at the time, and this taught me another side of music. I got to check out people like Jimi Hendrix, Jethro Tull, and John Mayall." In 1971, he became a full-time member of Charles Earland's band, with whom he remained until he became a leader in the seventies, recording, traveling, and enjoying major commercial success from 1975 on after his record, *Mr. Magic*, written by Ralph MacDonald and William Salter, and arranged and conducted by Bob James.

G: I started playing at around age ten, and my first love was really classical music, but even then I had to listen to all kinds of music because I just couldn't figure out where all the chords came from. I didn't know about chords and improvisation, and I stayed in the classical field for a long time doing concerts, small quartet things, saxophone and woodwind ensembles. My early lessons were on the saxophone, then it was the piano, the drum and percussion family, and the bass guitar.

JC: How did you manage to find the time and energy, not to mention the knowledge, for learning all these instruments? I mean, usually it takes a hell of a lot just to master one.

G: It was basically what I wanted to do at a very early age, so I had the time. I could really get into all of them on the basic level, and just worked myself up to things I could read. Some things with some of the instruments could apply to the others.

JC: What about composing?

G: Composing? That's something that is just coming out. I guess I've been writing tunes in the last four years, but just in the last couple of years I'm really starting to get more confident of my composing.

JC: You have enjoyed tremendous commercial success since the mid-seventies. Do you have any feelings on simply why it happened then and not before?

G: What it basically comes down to is that everybody is looking for something just right in the middle. They don't want to get too far out; they don't want to get too far in. But at the same time, they want something that sounds a little challenging, for example, the *Mr. Music* album. That was my first gold album, and there were only four tunes on the album, but they were all different. I tried to tell a different story with each one because I felt that that was the way it really ought to be done. Each song should have a story and a mood and a character all its own.

JC: How has electronics contributed to your music?

G: Well, it opened my ears up to a lot of things that I had been unknowingly prejudiced about just because of the fact that it was electric. It really has to do with taste—the way a musician makes use of an electronic device.

JC: You've worked with a lot of great composers and arrangers, like Don Sebesky, Bob James, and Andy West—how have their influences shaped your music?

G: It just hit me like a spark and it's still there. It's the kind of thing that you really want to share with everybody, and it's all music, whether it's acoustic or electric, contemporary or rock, or folk and country—it should all say something.

selected **discographies**

These discographies were compiled and edited with Dan Pickering (except where noted) from sources supplied by the artists and their managers. The albums included chart the musicians' recording careers and the development of their music over time; the sections of the discographies devoted to the musicians' work as session players on other artists' albums give an idea of the rich climate of cooperation and shared creativity that characterizes the world of jazz-rock music. Every attempt has been made to provide complete information for each album. However, some of the albums listed have gone out of print and will be available only through dealers specializing in used and/or rare albums. These have been indicated where possible.

—J. C.

JOHN ABERCROMBIE

AS LEADER:	TITLE	LABEL & NO.
John Abercrombie with Jack DeJohnette/Jan Hammer	**Timeless**	ECM 1047
John Abercrombie/ Jack DeJohnette/Dave Holland	**Gateway**	ECM 1061 ST
John Abercrombie/ Collin Walcott/Jack DeJohnette/Dave Holland	**Cloud Dance**	ECM 1062
John Abercrombie/ Enrico Rava/Palle Danielson/Jon Christenson	**Pilgrim and the Stars**	ECM 1063 ST
John Abercrombie/ Jack DeJohnette/Alex Foster/Mike Richmond/Warren Bernhardt	**Untitled**	ECM I-1074
John Abercrombie/ Jack DeJohnette	**Pictures**	ECM I 1079
John Abercrombie/ Ralph Towner	**Sargasso Sea**	ECM 1080

AS SIDEMAN WITH:		
Johnny "Hammond" Smith	**Nasty**	Prestige (*out of print*)
Brecker Brothers/ Billy Cobham	**Dreams**	Columbia C 30225
Billy Cobham	**Crosswinds**	Atlantic SD 7300
Billy Cobham	**Total Eclipse**	Atlantic SD 18121
Billy Cobham	**Shabazz**	Atlantic SD 18139
Jack DeJohnette	**Cosmic Chicken**	Fantasy/Prestige P 10094
Michal Urbaniak	**Fusion III**	Columbia PC 33542
Dave Liebman	**Lookout Farm**	ECM 1039 ST
Dave Liebman	**Drum Ode**	ECM 1046
Dave Liebman	**Sweet Hands**	Horizon SP 702
Gato Barbieri	**Under Fire**	Flying Dutchman 10156
Gato Barbieri	**Bolivia**	Flying Dutchman 10158

AIRTO

AS LEADER:	TITLE	LABEL & NO.
Airto	**Essential**	Buddha 5668
Airto	**Identity**	Arista 4068
Airto	**I'm Fine, How Are You**	Warner Bros. B 3084
Airto	**In Concert**	CTI 6041
Airto	**Promises of the Sun**	Arista 4116
Airto	**Seeds on the Ground**	Buddha 5085
Airto	**Natural Feelings**	Sky Buddha (*out of print*)
Airto	**Free**	CTI 6020
Airto	**Fingers**	CTI 6028 (*out of print*)
Airto	**Virgin Land**	CTI/Salvation SAL 701

AS SIDEMAN WITH:		
Miles Davis	**Big Fun**	Columbia PG 32866
Miles Davis	**Bitches' Brew**	Columbia PG 26
Miles Davis	**Miles at the Fillmore**	Columbia CG 30038
Miles Davis	**On the Corner**	Columbia PC 31906
Miles Davis	**Live-Evil**	Columbia G 30954

George Benson	**White Rabbit**	CTI 6015
George Benson	**Bad Benson**	CTI 6045
Stan Getz	**Captain Marvel**	Columbia KC 32706
John McLaughlin	**My Goal's Beyond**	Douglas AD 6003
Weather Report	**Weather Report**	Columbia PC 30661
Cannonball Adderley	**Happy People**	Capitol ST 11121
Wayne Shorter	**Super Nova**	Blue Note 84332
Wayne Shorter	**Native Dancer**	Columbia 33418
Joe Zawinul	**Zawinul**	Atlantic 1579
Return to Forever	**Return to Forever**	ECM 1022
Return to Forever	**Light as a Feather**	Polydor PD 5525
Santana	**Welcome**	Columbia PC 32445
Santana	**Borboletta**	Columbia PC 33135
Flora Purim	**Butterfly Dreams**	Milestone M 9052
Flora Purim	**Stories to Tell**	Milestone M 9058
Flora Purim	**Open Your Eyes You Can Fly**	Milestone M 9065
Flora Purim	**500 Miles High in Montreux**	Milestone 9070
Flora Purim	**Encounter**	Milestone 9077
Flora Purim	**Nothing Will Be as It Was...Tomorrow**	Warner Bros. 2985
Norman Connors	**Dance of Magic**	Cobblestone 9024
Paul Simon	**Paul Simon**	Columbia PC 30750
Paul Simon	**Paul Simon's Greatest Hits**	Columbia JC 35032
Paul Desmond	**Summertime**	A&M SP 3015

BRIAN AUGER

AS LEADER:	TITLE	LABEL & NO.
Brian Auger & The Trinity/Julie Driscoll	**Open**	ATCO SD 33-258
Brian Auger & The Trinity	**Definitely What!**	ATCO SD 33-273
Brian Auger & The Trinity/Julie Driscoll	**Street Noise**	ATCO SD 2-701
Brian Auger & The Trinity	**Befour**	RCA LSP 4372
Brian Auger's Oblivion Express	**Oblivion Express**	RCA LSP 4462
Brian Auger's Oblivion Express	**A Better Land**	RCA LSP 4540
Brian Auger's Oblivion Express	**Second Wind**	RCA LSP 4703

Brian Auger's Oblivion Express	**Closer to It**	RCA APL 1-0140
Brian Auger's Oblivion Express	**Straight Ahead**	RCA APL 1-0454
Brian Auger's Oblivion Express	**Live Oblivion, Vol. I**	RCA CPL 1-0645
Brian Auger's Oblivion Express	**Reinforcements**	RCA CAP 1-1210
Brian Auger's Oblivion Express	**Live Oblivion, Vol. 2**	RCA CPL 2-1230
Brian Auger's Oblivion Express	**Happiness Heartaches**	Warner Bros. B 2981
Brian Auger/Julie Tippetts	**Encore**	Warner Bros. BSK 3153

AS SIDEMAN WITH:

Sonny Boy Williamson	**Don't Send Me No Flowers**	Marmalade/Polydor 608004
Rod Stewart	**Shake/I Just Got Some**	Columbia DB 7892
Yardbirds	**For Your Love/Got to Hurry**	Columbia DB 7499
Mogul Thrash	**Mogul Thrash**	RCA 2030

ROY AYERS

AS LEADER:	TITLE	LABEL & NO.
Roy Ayers	**Daddy Bug & Friends**	Atlantic 1692
Roy Ayers	**Everybody Loves the Sunshine**	Polydor 6070
Roy Ayers	**Lifeline**	Polydor 6108
Roy Ayers	**Mystic Voyage**	Polydor 6057
Roy Ayers	**Red, Black, and Green**	Polydor 6078 PD 5045
Roy Ayers	**Tear to a Smile**	Polydor 6046
Roy Ayers	**Vibrations**	Polydor 6091
Roy Ayers	**Stoned Soul Picnic**	Atlantic SD 1415
Roy Ayers	**Daddy Bug**	Atlantic SD 1538
Roy Ayers	**Virgo Vibes**	Atlantic SD 1488
Roy Ayers	**West Coast Vibes**	United Artists UAL 3325
Roy Ayers	**Bird Call**	United Artists S 6325
Roy Ayers	**Ubiquity**	Polydor (out of print)
Roy Ayers	**He's Coming**	Polydor PD 5022
Roy Ayers	**Virgo Red**	Polydor PD 6016
Roy Ayers	**Roy Ayers Live at Montreux**	Polydor (in Japan & Europe)
Roy Ayers	**Comin' Home Baby**	Columbia (out of print)
Roy Ayers	**All Blues**	Columbia (out of print)
Roy Ayers	**Change Up the Groove**	Polydor PD 6032

AS SIDEMAN WITH:

Curtis Amy	**Way Down**	Pacific Jazz (*out of print*)
Curtis Amy	**Tippin' on Through**	Pacific Jazz (*out of print*)
Gerald Wilson	**On Stage**	Pacific Jazz (*out of print*)
Jack Wilson Quartet featuring Roy Ayers	**Brazilian Mancini**	Atlantic 1406
Leroy Vinnegar	**Leroy Walks**	Contemporary CTP 7003
Herbie Mann	**Muscle Shoals Nitty Gritty**	Atlantic 526
Herbie Mann	**Impressions of the Middle East**	Atlantic 1475

PRODUCED:

Ubiquity	**Star Booty**	Electra 6E120
Ramp	**Come into Knowledge**	Blue Thumb 6028
Merry Clayton	**Keep Your Eye on the Sparrow**	Ode PE 34957

GATO BARBIERI

AS LEADER:	TITLE	LABEL & NO.
Gato Barbieri	**Gato Barbieri**	ESP/Disk 1049
Gato Barbieri	**The Third World**	Flying Dutchman 10177
Gato Barbieri	**Fenix**	Flying Dutchman 10144
Gato Barbieri	**El Pompero**	Flying Dutchman 10151
Gato Barbieri	**Bolivia**	Flying Dutchman 10158
Gato Barbieri	**Under Fire**	Flying Dutchman 10156
Gato Barbieri	**Yesterdays**	Flying Dutchman 0550
Gato Barbieri	**Legend of Gato Barbieri**	Flying Dutchman 10165
Gato Barbieri	**El Gato**	Flying Dutchman 1147
Gato Barbieri	**Chapter 1—Latin America**	Impulse 9248
Gato Barbieri	**Chapter 2—Hasta Siempre**	Impulse 9263
Gato Barbieri	**Chapter 3—Viva Emiliano Zapata**	Impulse 9279
Gato Barbieri	**Chapter 4—Alive in New York**	Impulse 9303
Gato Barbieri	**Confluence**	Arista 1003
Gato Barbieri	**Impulse Artists on Tour**	Impulse 9264
Gato Barbieri	**Impulsively**	Impulse 9266
Gato Barbieri	**Last Tango in Paris**	United Artists LA 045-G
Gato Barbieri	**Caliente**	A&M 4597
Gato Barbieri	**Ruby Ruby**	A&M 4655
Gato Barbieri/ Various Artists	**Leonard Feather's Encyclopedia of Jazz in the Seventies**	Victor 1984

AS SIDEMAN WITH:

Don Cherry	**Symphony for Improvisors**	Blue Note 84247
Gary Burton	**Genuine Tong Funeral**	RCA LSP 3988
Carla Bley/Mike Mantler	**Tropic Appetites**	Watt 1
Mike Mantler/Carla Bley	**Jazz Composer's Orchestra**	JCOA 1001/2
Carla Bley	**Escalator over the Hill**	JCOA 3LP-EOTH
Carla Bley/Charlie Hayden	**Liberation Music Orchestra**	ABC/Impulse AS 9183
Don Cherry	**Togetherness**	Durium MSA 77127
Oliver Nelson	**Success Suite**	Flying Dutchmen 10149

JOE BECK

AS LEADER:	TITLE	LABEL & NO.
Joe Beck	**Carioca Blues**	Polydor (*forthcoming*)
Joe Beck	**Beck**	Kudu 21
Joe Beck	**Watch the Time**	Polydor 6092
Joe Beck/Various Artists	**The Guitar Album**	Columbia 31045
Joe Beck	**Nature Boy**	Verve/Forecast 3081
Joe Beck	**Rock Encounter**	Polydor 24-4026

AS SIDEMAN WITH:

Paul Simon	**Still Crazy After All These Years**	Columbia PC 33540
Paul Simon	**Paul Simon's Greatest Hits**	Columbia JC 35032
Joe Farrell	**Penny Arcade**	CTI Q 6034
Joe Farrell	**Upon This Rock**	CTI 6042
Joe Farrell	**Canned Funk**	CTI 6053
Larry Coryell	**Lion and the Ram**	Arista 4108
Bobby Timmons	**Got to Get It**	Milestone 9011
Esther Phillips	**For All We Know**	Kudu KU 28
Esther Phillips	**Esther Phillips/Joe Beck**	Kudu KU 23
Michel Legrand	**Michel Legrand & Friends**	Gryfon/RCA BGL 1-1392A
Don Sebesky	**Giant Box**	CTI X-6031-32
Don Sebesky	**The Rape of El Morro**	CTI 6061
Gene Ammons	**Got My Own**	Prestige 10058
Dave Sanborn	**Taking Off**	Warner Bros. 2873
Frank Sinatra	**Round No. 1**	SABB 11357
Grover Washington, Jr.	**Mr. Magic**	Kudu 20
Bill Watrous	**Wild Life**	Columbia KC 33090
Idris Muhammad	**The Power of Soul**	Kudu 17
Gato Barbieri	**Caliente**	A&M 4597
Duke Ellington/ Theresa Brewer	**It Don't Mean a Thing**	Flying Dutchman 10112

GEORGE BENSON

AS LEADER:	TITLE	LABEL & NO.
George Benson	**Bad Benson**	CTI 6045
George Benson/Joe Farrell	**Benson & Farrell**	CTI 6069
George Benson	**Benson Burner**	Columbia 33569
George Benson	**George Benson Cookbook**	Columbia 9413
George Benson	**George Benson/Jack McDuff**	Prestige 24072
George Benson	**Beyond the Blue Horizon**	CTI 6009
George Benson	**Blue Benson**	Polydor 6084
George Benson	**Body Talk**	CTI 6033
George Benson	**Breezin'**	Warner Bros. 2919
George Benson	**California Concert**	CTI X-2-2
George Benson	**50 Years of Jazz Guitar**	Columbia 33566
George Benson	**Good King Bad**	CTI 6062
George Benson	**The Greatest**	Arista 7000
George Benson	**In Concert/Carnegie Hall**	CTI 6072
George Benson	**In Flight**	Warner Bros. BK 2983
George Benson	**It's Uptown**	Columbia CS 9325
George Benson	**Nadia's Theme**	A&M 3412
George Benson	**New Boss Guitar of George Benson**	Prestige 9310
George Benson	**Other Side of Abbey Road**	A&M 3028
George Benson	**Shape of Things to Come**	A&M 3014
George Benson	**Spirituals to Swing** (John Hammond's 30th Anniversary Concert)	Columbia CG 30776
George Benson	**Tell It Like It Is**	A&M 3020
George Benson	**White Rabbit**	CTI 6015
George Benson	**Weekend in L.A.**	Warner Bros. 2WB 3139
George Benson	**Giblet Gravy**	Verve V6-8749

AS SIDEMAN WITH:

Miles Davis	**Miles in the Sky**	Columbia PC 9628
Don Sebesky	**Giant Box**	CTI X-6031-32
Freddie Hubbard	**First Light**	CTI 6013
Freddie Hubbard	**Sky Dive**	CTI 6018
Freddie Hubbard	**Straight Life**	CTI 6007
Stanley Turrentine	**Sugar**	CTI 6005
Helen Humes	**The Talk of the Town**	Columbia PC 33488
Ronnie Foster	**On the Avenue**	Blue Note LA 261-6
Stevie Wonder	**Songs in the Key of Life**	Tamla TB 34062

CARLA BLEY

AS LEADER:	TITLE	LABEL & NO.
Carla Bley	**Tropic Appetites**	Watt 1
Carla Bley/Michael Mantler	**Michael Mantler & Carla Bley**	Watt 3
Carla Bley	**Dinner Music**	Watt 6
Jazz Composer's Orchestra	**Escalator over the Hill**	JCOA 3LP-EOTH
Jazz Composer's Orchestra	**Communication**	Fontana (out of print)
Jazz Composer's Orchestra	**Jazz Composer's Orchestra**	JCOA 1001/2
Liberation Music Orchestra	**Liberation Music Orchestra**	ABC/Impulse AS-9183

AS SIDEWOMAN WITH:

Jazz Realities	**Jazz Realities**	Fontana (out of print)
Gary Burton Quartet & Orchestra	**A Genuine Tong Funeral**	RCA LSP 3988
Michael Mantler	**No Answer**	Watt 2
Michael Mantler	**The Hapless Child**	Watt 4
Michael Mantler	**Silence**	Watt 5
Michael Mantler	**Movies**	Watt 7
John Greaves/ Peter Blegvad	**Kew. Rhone.**	Virgin V 2082
Don Cherry & Jazz Composer's Orchestra	**Relativity Suite**	JCOA 1006
Clifford Thornton & Jazz Composer's Orchestra	**Gardens of Harlem**	JCOA 1008
Grachan Moncur III & Jazz Composer's Orchestra	**Echoes of Prayer**	JCOA 1009
Jan Steele/John Cage	**Voices and Instruments**	Obscure No. 5
Pastorius/Metheny/ Ditmas/Bley	**Pastorius/Metheny/ Ditmas/Bley**	Improvising Artists 373846

MIKE BRECKER

AS LEADER:	TITLE	LABEL & NO.
Brecker Brothers	**Brecker Brothers**	Arista AL 4037
Brecker Brothers	**Back to Back**	Arista AL 4061
Brecker Brothers	**Don't Stop the Music**	Arista AL 4122
Dreams	**Dreams**	Columbia C 30225
Dreams	**Imagine My Surprise**	Columbia C 30960

AS SIDEMAN WITH:

Tony Camillos Bazuka	**Bazuka**	A&M SP 3411
Randy Brecker	**Score**	Solid State SS 18051
Ron Carter	**Anything Goes**	Kudu KU 25S1
Billy Cobham	**Crosswinds**	Atlantic SD 7300
Billy Cobham	**Total Eclipse**	Atlantic SD 18121

Billy Cobham	**A Funky Thide of Sings**	Atlantic SD 18149
Billy Cobham	**Shabazz**	Atlantic SD 18139
Charles Earland	**Revelation**	Mercury SRM1-1149
Hal Galper	**The Guerilla Band**	Mainstream MRL 337
Hal Galper	**Wild Bird**	Mainstream MRL 354
Hal Galper	**Hal Galper**	Inner City
Mike Gibbs/Gary Burton	**In the Public Interest**	Polydor PD 6503
Garland Jeffreys	**Ghost Writer**	A&M SP 4629
Steve Khan	**Tightrope**	Tappan Zee/Columbia JC 34857
Herbert Laws	**Chicago Theme**	CTI 6058 S-1
John Lee/Gerry Brown	**Still Can't Say Enough**	Blue Note BN LA 701G
Jimmy McGriff	**Red Beans**	Groove Merchant GM3314
Arif Mardin	**Journey**	Atlantic SD 1661
Idris Muhammad	**Turn This Mutha' Out**	Kudu KU 84
Mark Murphy	**Mark Murphy Sings**	Muse MR 5078
Mark Murphy	**Bridging a Gap**	Muse MR 5009
Laura Nyro	**Smile**	Columbia PC 33912
Esther Phillips	**For All We Know**	Kudu KU 28
Esther Phillips	**What a Difference a Day Makes**	Kudu KU 23
David Sanborn	**Taking Off**	Warner Bros. BS 2873
Don Sebesky	**The Rape of El Morro**	CTI 6061
Horace Silver	**In Pursuit of the 27th Man**	Blue Note BN LA 054-F
Phoebe Snow	**Never Letting Go**	Columbia JC 34875
James Taylor	**One Man Dog**	Warner Bros. BS 2660
James Taylor	**Walking Man**	Warner Bros. W 2794
Dominic Troiano	**Burnin' at the Stake**	Capitol ST 11665
White Elephant	**White Elephant**	Just Sunshine JSS 3000
William Eaton	**Struggle Bunny**	Marlin 2211
Patti Austin	**End of a Rainbow**	CTI 5001
Larry Coryell & The Eleventh House	**Aspects**	Arista AL 4077
Weldon Irvine	**Sinbad**	RCA APL 1-1363
The Manhattan Transfer	**Coming Out**	Atlantic SD 18193
Patti Austin	**Havana Candy**	CTI 75006
Chet Baker	**You Can't Go Home Again**	Horizon SP 726
Joe Beck	**Watch the Time**	Polydor PD 16092
Darius Brubeck	**Chaplin's Back**	Paramount PAS 6026
Michael Franks	**Sleeping Gypsy**	Warner Bros. BS 3004
Lorraine Frisaura	**Be Happy for Me**	ATV PYE 12141
John Lennon	**Mind Games**	Apple SW 3114
Mel Lewis	**Mel Lewis & Friends**	Horizon SP 716
Mike Mainieri	**Love Play**	Arista AB 4113
Robert Mason	**Stardrive**	Elektra EKS 75058B
Claus Ogerman	**Gate of Dreams**	Warner Bros. BS 3006
Yoko Ono	**Feeling the Space**	Apple EW 3412
Esther Phillips	**Performance**	Kudu KU 18
The Section	**The Section**	Warner Bros. BS 2661
Carly Simon	**Hotcakes**	Elektra 7E-1002-B
Paul Simon	**Still Crazy After All These Years**	Columbia PC 33540
Joe Thomas	**Feelings from Within**	Groove Merchant GM 3315
Michael Franks	**The Art of Tea**	Reprise MS 2230
Grant Green	**The Main Attraction**	Kudu KU 29
Freddie Hubbard	**Windjammer**	Columbia PC 34166
Orleans	**Waking & Dreaming**	Asylum 7E-1070-B-SP
Pavlov's Dog	**At the Sound of the Bell**	Columbia PC 33964
The Players Association	**Born to Dance**	Vanguard 79398
James Taylor	**In the Pocket**	Warner Bros. BS 2912
Aerosmith	**Get Your Wings**	Columbia PC 32847
Air	**Air**	Embryo SD 733
Average White Band	**Average White Band**	Atlantic SD 7308
Average White Band	**Average White Band & Ben E. King**	Atlantic SD 19105
Bootsy's Rubber Band	**Bootsy's Rubber Band**	Warner Bros. BS 2972
Hank Crawford	**Tico Rico**	Kudu KU 35 S1
Kiki Dee	**Kiki Dee (Elton John)**	MCA 1188
Joe Farrell	**La Catedral y el Toro**	Warner Bros. BS 3121
Bruce Fisher	**Red Hot**	Mercury SRM1-1158
Funkadelic	**Tales of Kid Funkadelic**	Westbound W 227
Geils	**Geils**	Atlantic SD 19103
Nick Holmes	**Soulful Crooner**	Just Sunshine JSS 3
Fred Wesley & the Horny Horns	**The Horny Horns**	Atlantic SD 18214
Elton John	**Blue Moves**	MCA 2-11004
Martee Lebous	**The Lady Wants to Be a Star**	Image IM 301B
Webster Lewis	**On the Town**	Epic PE 34186
David Matthews	**Shoogie Wanna Boogie**	Kudu KU 30
Bette Midler	**Divine Miss M**	Atlantic SD 7238
Bette Midler	**Songs for the New Depression**	Atlantic SD 18155

Barry Miles	**Silver Light**	London PS 661
Russell Morris	**Russell Morris**	RCA APL 1-1073B
Idris Mohammad	**House of the Rising Sun**	Kudu KU 27
Odyssey	**Odyssey**	RCA APL 1-2204A
Parliament	**Mother Ship Connection**	Casablanca NBLP 7022
Parliament	**Cloves of Dr. Funkenstein**	Casablanca NBLP 7034
Esther Phillips	**Capricorn Princess**	Kudu KU 31
Andy Pratt	**Shiver in the Night**	Nemperor NE 3443
Lou Reed	**Berlin**	RCA APL 1-9297
Ringo Starr	**Ringo's Rotogravure**	Atlantic SD 18193
Todd Rundgren	**Something—Anything**	Warner Bros. 2 BX 2066
Zbigniew Seifert	**Zbigniew Seifert**	Capitol ST 11618
John Simon	**Journey**	Warner Bros. BS 2663
Bruce Springsteen	**Born to Run**	Columbia PC 33795
Tornader	**Hit It Again**	Polydor PD 1-6098
John Tropea	**Short Trip to Space**	Marlin 2204
Luther Allison	**Night Life**	Gordy G6-974-S1
Average White Band	**Soul Searching**	Atlantic SD 18179
George Benson	**Good King Bad**	CTI 6062
Blue Oyster Cult	**Agents of Fortune**	Columbia PC 34164
Jaco Pastorius	**Jaco Pastorius**	Epic PE 33949
Ben Sidran	**Free in America**	Arista AL 4081
Ralph MacDonald	**The Path**	Marlin 2210

RANDY BRECKER

AS LEADER:	TITLE	LABEL & NO.
Randy Brecker	**Score**	Solid State SS 18051
Brecker Brothers	**Brecker Brothers**	Arista AL 4037
Brecker Brothers	**Back to Back**	Arista AL 4061
Brecker Brothers	**Don't Stop the Music**	Arista AL 4122
Dreams	**Dreams**	Columbia C 30225
Dreams	**Imagine My Surprise**	Columbia C 30960

AS SIDEMAN WITH:

Tony Camillos Bazuka	**Bazuka**	A&M SP 3411
Ron Carter	**Anything Goes**	Kudu KU 25S1
Billy Cobham	**Crosswinds**	Atlantic SD 7300
Billy Cobham	**Total Eclipse**	Atlantic SD 18121
Billy Cobham	**A Funky Thide of Sings**	Atlantic SD 18149
Billy Cobham	**Shabazz**	Atlantic SD 18139

Charles Earland	**Revelation**	Mercury SRM1-1149
Hal Galper	**The Guerilla Band**	Mainstream MRL 337
Hal Galper	**Wild Bird**	Mainstream MRL 354
Hal Galper	**Hal Galper**	Inner City
Mike Gibbs/Gary Burton	**In the Public Interest**	Polydor PD 6503
Garland Jeffreys	**Ghost Writer**	A&M SP 4629
Steve Khan	**Tightrope**	Tappan Zee/Columbia JC 34857
Herbert Laws	**Chicago Theme**	CTI 6058 S-1
John Lee/Gerry Brown	**Still Can't Say Enough**	Blue Note BN LA 701G
Jimmy McGriff	**Red Beans**	Groove Merchant GM 3314
Arif Mardin	**Journey**	Atlantic SD 1661
Idris Muhammad	**Turn This Mutha' Out**	Kudu KU 84
Mark Murphy	**Mark Murphy Sings**	Muse MR 5078
Mark Murphy	**Bridging a Gap**	Muse MR 5009
Laura Nyro	**Smile**	Columbia PC 33912
Esther Phillips	**For All We Know**	Kudu KU 28
Esther Phillips	**What a Difference a Day Makes**	Kudu KU 23
David Sanborn	**Taking Off**	Warner Bros. BS 2873
Don Sebesky	**The Rape of El Morro**	CTI 6061
Phoebe Snow	**Never Letting Go**	Columbia JC 34875
James Taylor	**One Man Dog**	Warner Bros. BS 2660
James Taylor	**Walking Man**	Warner Bros. W 2794
Dominic Troiano	**Burnin' at the Stake**	Capitol ST 11665
White Elephant	**White Elephant**	Just Sunshine JSS 3000
William Eaton	**Struggle Bunny**	Marlin 2211
Patti Austin	**End of a Rainbow**	CTI 5001
Larry Coryell & The Eleventh House	**Aspects**	Arista AL 4077
Weldon Irvine	**Sinbad**	RCA APL 1-1363
The Manhattan Transfer	**Coming Out**	Atlantic SD 18193
Joe Beck	**Nature Boy**	MGM MGS 2044
Walter Bishop, Jr.	**Soul Village**	Muse MR 5142
Susan Carter	**Wonderful Deeds & Adventures**	Epic BN 26510
Children of All Ages	**Children of All Ages**	Different Drummer DD 1005
Children of All Ages	**Just Might Turn Out to Be Sages**	Adama ADS 9500
Larry Coryell	**Introducing The Eleventh House**	Vanguard VSD 79342
Hank Crawford	**Don't You Worry 'Bout a Thing**	Kudu KU 19 S1
Donato Deodato	**Donato Deodato**	Muse 5017

Peter Duchin	**Come Home Baby**	Bell 6041
Charles Earland	**The Great Pyramid**	Mercury SRM1-1113
Charles Earland	**Odyssey**	Mercury SRM1-1049
Johnny Hodges	**3 Shades of the Blues**	Flying Duthman FDS120
Mike Longo	**900 Shares of the Blues**	Groove Merchant GM 3304-B
James Moody	**Sun Journey**	Vanguard VSD 7931
Alphonse Mouzon	**Funky Snakefoot**	Blue Note BN LA 222-G
Idris Muhammad	**Power of Soul**	Kudu KU 17
Bob Moses	**Bittersweet in the Ozone**	Mozown MZ 001
Duke Pearson	**Introducing Duke Pearson's Big Band**	Blue Note BST 84276
David Pomerantz	**Time to Fly**	MCA DL 7-5329
Don Pullen	**Tomorrow's Promises**	Atlantic SD 1699
Horace Silver	**You Gotta Take a Little Love**	Blue Note BST 84309
Horace Silver	**That Healin' Feelin'**	Blue Note BST 84352
Horace Silver	**In Pursuit of the 27th Man**	Blue Note BN LA 054-F
Jack Wilkins	**Jack Wilkins Quartet (Merge)**	Chiaroscuro CR 156
Gato Barbieri	**Caliente**	A&M SP 4597
Judy Collins	**Judith**	Elektra 70 1032-BSP
Dan Hartman	**Images**	Blue Sky PZ 34322
Michel Legrand	**Michel Legrand & Friends**	Gryfon/RCA BGL 1-1392A
Roland Prince	**Color Visions**	Vanguard VSD 79371
Aerosmith	**Get Your Wings**	Columbia PC 32847
Air	**Air**	Embryo SD 733
Average White Band	**Average White Band**	Atlantic SD 7308
Average White Band	**Average White Band & Ben E. King**	Atlantic SD 19105
Gato Barbieri	**Chapter 3—Viva Emiliano Zapata**	Impulse 9279
Bootsy's Rubber Band	**Bootsy's Rubber Band**	Warner Bros.BS 2972
Hank Crawford	**Tico Rico**	Kudu KU 35 S1
Kiki Dee	**Kiki Dee (Elton John)**	MCA 1188
Joe Farrell	**La Catedral y el Toro**	Warner Bros. BS 3121
Maynard Ferguson	**Conquistador**	Columbia 34457
Bruce Fisher	**Red Hot**	Mercury SRM1-1158
Funkadelic	**Tales of Kid Funkadelic**	Westbound W 227
Eric Gale	**Forecast**	Kudu KU 11
Eric Gale	**Ginseng Woman**	Columbia 34421
Eric Gale	**Multiplication**	Columbia 34938
Geils	**Geils**	Atlantic SD 19103
Ralph Graham	**Wisdom**	RCA APL 1-1918
Nick Holmes	**Soulful Crooner**	Just Sunshine JSS 3
Fred Wesley & the Horny Horns	**The Horny Horns**	Atlantic SD 19214
Bob James	**Two**	CTI 6057 S-1
Elton John	**Blue Moves**	MCA 2-11004
Hubert Laws	**Romeo & Juliet**	Columbia 34330
Martee Lebous	**The Lady Wants to Be a Star**	Image IM 301B
Webster Lewis	**On the Town**	Epic PE 34186
Infinite McCoys	**Infinite McCoys**	Mercury SR 61 163
Gary McFarland	**America the Beautiful**	Skye SK 8
David Matthews	**Shoogie Wanna Boogie**	Kudu KU 30
Bette Midler	**Divine Miss M**	Atlantic SD 7238
Bette Midler	**Songs for the New Depression**	Atlantic SD 18155
Barry Miles	**Silver Light**	London PS 661
Barry Miles	**Sky Train**	RAC BGL 1-2200-B
Russell Morris	**Russell Morris**	RCA APL 1-1073B
Odyssey	**Odyssey**	RCA APL 1-2204A
Parliament	**Mother Ship Connection**	Casablanca NBLP 7022
Parliament	**Cloves of Dr. Funkenstein**	Casablanca NBLP 7034
Duke Pearson	**Now Hear This**	Blue Note BST 84308
Esther Phillips	**Capricorn Princess**	Kudu KU 31
Andy Pratt	**Shiver in the Night**	Nemperor NE 3443
Lou Reed	**Berlin**	RCA APL 1-0207
Ringo Starr	**Ringo's Rotogravure**	Atlantic SD 18193
Todd Rundgren	**Something—Anything**	Warner Bros. 2 BX 2066
Don Sebesky	**Jazz Rock Syndrome**	Verve V6-8756
John Simon	**Journey**	Warner Bros. BS 2663
Bruce Springsteen	**Born to Run**	Columbia PC 33795
Tornader	**Hit It Again**	Polydor PD 1-6098
John Tropea	**Short Trip to Space**	Marlin 2204
Stanley Turrentine	**Don't Mess with Mr. T**	CTI 6030
Vitamin E	**Sharing**	Buddha BDS 5690
Grover Washington, Jr.	**Soul Box, Vols. I & II**	2-Kudu KU 12/13
Grover Washington, Jr.	**Feels So Good**	Kudu KU 24-sl
Phil Woods	**New Phil Woods Album**	RCA BGL 1-1391-A
Luther Allison	**Night Life**	Gordy G6-974-S1
Average White Band	**Soul Searching**	Atlantic SD 18179

George Benson	**Good King Bad**	CTI 6062
Blue Oyster Cult	**Agents of Fortune**	Columbia PC 34164
Jaco Pastorius	**Jaco Pastorius**	Epic PE 33949
Ben Sidran	**Free in America**	Arista AL 4081
Ralph MacDonald	**The Path**	Marlin 2210

GERRY BROWN

AS LEADER:	TITLE	LABEL & NO.
John Lee/Gerry Brown	**Mango Sunrise**	Blue Note LA 541
John Lee/Gerry Brown	**Still Can't Say Enough**	Blue Note LA 701
John Lee/Gerry Brown	**Infinite Jones**	Keytone KT 444056
John Lee/Gerry Brown and Various Artists	**Blue Note Live at the Roxy**	Blue Note LA 663-2

AS SIDEMAN WITH:

Larry Coryell	**Aspects**	Arista AL 4077
Stanley Clarke	**School Days**	Nemperor NE 439
Return to Forever	**Musicmagic**	Columbia PC 34682
Chris Hinze	**Sister Slick**	Columbia 80271
Michal Urbaniak	**Fusion III**	Columbia PC 33542
Michal Urbaniak	**Funk Factory**	Atlantic (*out of print*)

GARY BURTON

AS LEADER:	TITLE	LABEL & NO.
Gary Burton	**Time Machine**	RCA LSP 3642
Gary Burton	**Tennesse Firebird**	RCA LSP 3719
Gary Burton	**Duster**	RCA LSP 3835
Gary Burton	**Lofty Fake Anagram**	RCA LSP 3901
Gary Burton	**Genuine Tong Funeral**	RCA LSP 3988
Gary Burton	**In Concert**	RCA LSP 3985
Gary Burton	**Country Roads**	RCA LSP 4098
Gary Burton	**Throb**	Atlantic SD 1531
Gary Burton	**Alone at Last**	Atlantic 1560
Gary Burton	**Paris Encounter**	Atlantic 1598
Gary Burton/Chick Corea	**Crystal Silence**	ECM 1024
Gary Burton	**New Quartet**	ECM 1030
Gary Burton	**Seven Songs**	ECM 1040
Gary Burton	**Ring**	ECM 1051
Gary Burton/Ralph Towner	**Matchbook**	ECM 1056
Gary Burton	**Hotel Hello**	ECM 1055
Gary Burton	**Dreams So Real**	ECM 1072

Gary Burton	**Passengers**	ECM 1092
Gary Burton/Keith Jarrett	**Gary Burton & Keith Jarrett**	Atlantic 1577
Gary Burton	**Percussive Jazz**	Ovation 1714
Gary Burton	**Turn of the Century**	Atlantic 2-321
Gary Burton/Larry Coryell	**Gary Burton/Larry Coryell**	RCA 7XL1-7101

RON CARTER

AS LEADER:	TITLE	LABEL & NO.
Ron Carter	**All Blues**	CTI 6037
Ron Carter/Jim Hall	**Alone Together**	Milestone 9045
Ron Carter	**Anything Goes**	Kudu KU 25S1
Ron Carter	**Blues Farm**	CTI 6027
Ron Carter	**Magic**	Prestige 24053
Ron Carter	**Out Front**	Prestige 7377
Ron Carter	**Piccolo**	Milestone 55004
Ron Carter	**Spanish Blues**	CTI 6051
Ron Carter	**Uptown Conversation**	Embryo SD 521
Ron Carter	**Yellow & Green**	CTI 6064
Ron Carter	**Where**	New Jazz 8265
V.S.O.P.	**V.S.O.P.**	Columbia PC 34688
V.S.O.P.	**The Quintet/V.S.O.P. Live**	Columbia C-2-34976

AS SIDEMAN WITH:

Miles Davis	**Seven Steps to Heaven**	Columbia CS 8851
Miles Davis	**Miles Davis In Europe**	Columbia CS 8983
Miles Davis	**ESP**	Columbia CS 9150
Miles Davis	**Miles Smiles**	Columbia CS 9401
Miles Davis	**Sorcerer**	Columbia CS 9532
Miles Davis	**Nefertiti**	Columbia CS 9594
Miles Davis	**Miles in the Sky**	Columbia CS 9628
Miles Davis	**My Funny Valentine**	Columbia CS 9106
Miles Davis	**Four and More**	Columbia CS 9253
Miles Davis	**Miles in Tokyo**	CBS/Sony SOPL-162
Miles Davis	**Miles in Berlin**	German CBS BPG-629765
Miles Davis	**Filles de Kilimanjaro**	Columbia CS 9750
Miles Davis	**Big Fun**	Columbia PG 32866
Miles Davis	**Quiet Nights**	CBS C 58906; SONP 50163
Miles Davis	**Live-Evil**	Columbia G 30954
Miles Davis	**Miles Davis' Greatest Hits**	Columbia CS 9808
Michel Legrand	**Michel Legrand & Friends**	Gryfon/RCA BGL 1-1392A

Michel Legrand	**Recorded Live at Jimmy's**	RCA BGL1 0850
Eric Dolphy	**Eric Dophy**	Prestige 24008
Eric Dolphy	**Out There**	New Jazz 8252
Eric Dolphy	**Far Cry**	New Jazz 8270
Roberta Flack	**First Take**	Atlantic S-8234
Roberta Flack	**Quiet Fire**	Atlantic SD 1594
Arethra Franklin	**Soul '69**	Atlantic SD 8212
Freddie Hubbard	**Sky Dive**	CTI 6018
Freddie Hubbard	**First Light**	CTI 6013
Freddie Hubbard	**Red Clay**	CTI 6001
Freddie Hubbard	**Keep Your Soul Together**	CTI 6036
Freddie Hubbard	**Straight Life**	CTI 6007
Herbie Hancock/ Freddie Hubbard	**In Concert, Vols. I & II**	CTI 6044, CTI 6049
Herbie Hancock	**Empyrean Isles**	Blue Note 84175
Herbie Hancock	**Maiden Voyage**	Blue Note 84195
Herbie Hancock	**Blow-Up (sound track)**	MGM E-4447
Herbie Hancock	**Speak Like a Child**	Blue Note 84279
Milt Jackson	**Big Band Bags**	Milestone 47006
Milt Jackson	**Olinga**	CTI 6046
Milt Jackson	**Sunflower**	CTI 6024
Milt Jackson	**Big Bags**	Riverside RS 9429
Milt Jackson	**Milt Jackson & the Hip String Quartet**	Verve V6-8761
Milt Jackson	**Goodbye**	CTI 6038
Milt Jackson	**Invitation**	Riverside RS 9446
Milt Jackson	**Milt Jackson at the Museum of Modern Art**	Limelight LS 86024
Hubert Laws	**Rite of Spring**	CTI 6012
Hubert Laws	**Crying Song**	CTI 6000
Hubert Laws	**Afro-Classic**	CTI 6006
Hubert Laws	**Morning Star**	CTI 6022
Hubert Laws	**Law's Cause**	Atlantic SD 1509
Hubert Laws	**Carnegie Hall**	CTI 6025
Wes Montgomery	**A Day in the Life**	A&M 3001
Wes Montgomery	**Down Here on the Ground**	A&M SP 3006
Wes Montgomery	**While We're Young**	Verve 68653
Wes Montgomery	**Tequila**	Verve 831671
Wes Montgomery	**So Much Guitar**	Riverside RLP 9382
Yusef Lateef	**Many Faces of Yusef Lateef**	Milestone 47009

Yusef Lateef	**3 Faces**	Riverside RS 9325
Sonny Rollins	**Now's the Time**	RCA LSP 2927
Stan Getz	**Sweet Rain**	Verve V6-8693
Stan Getz	**Voices**	Verve V6-8707
Stan Getz/ Bob Brookmeyer	**Stan Getz/ Bob Brookmeyer '65**	Columbia CS 9037
Stan Getz/Bill Evans	**Stan Getz & Bill Evans**	Verve V6-8833
Bill Evans/George Russell	**Living Time**	CBS-KC, 31490; CBS/Sony SOPL-114
Donald Byrd	**Up**	Verve V6-8609
Donald Byrd	**Electric Byrd**	Blue Note BST 84349
Wayne Shorter	**Speak No Evil**	Blue Note BST 84194
Wayne Shorter	**All Seeing Eye**	Blue Note BST 84219
Wayne Shorter	**Schizophrenia**	Blue Note BST 84297
Wayne Shorter	**Odyssey of Iska**	Blue Note BST 84363
Wayne Shorter	**Motto Grosso Feio**	Blue Note LA 014-G
Sam Rivers	**Contours**	Blue Note BST 84206
Sam Rivers	**Fuschia Swing Song**	Blue Note BST 84184
Roy Ayers	**Stoned Soul Picnic**	Atlantic SD 1514
Bobby Hutcherson	**Components**	Blue Note BST 84213
Bobby Hutcherson	**Natural Illusions**	Blue Note BST 84416
George Benson	**Giblet Gravy**	Verve V6-8749
George Benson	**White Rabbit**	CTI 6015
George Benson	**Other Side of Abbey Road**	A&M 3028
George Benson	**Beyond the Blue Horizon**	CTI 6009
George Benson	**Body Talk**	CTI 6033
Gene Ammons	**The Black Cat**	Prestige PR 10006
Hank Crawford	**It's a Funky Thing to Do**	Cotillion SD 18003
Kai Winding/J. J. Johnson	**Israel K. & J.J.**	A&M MSP 3008
Charles Tolliver	**Charles Tolliver & His All Stars**	Black Lyon BLP 30117
Paul Desmond	**Skylark**	CTI 6039
Paul Desmond	**Summertime**	A&M SP 3015
Paul Desmond	**The Bridge over Troubled Water**	A&M SP 3082
Joe Henderson	**Power to the People**	Milestone MSP 9024
Joe Henderson	**Tetragon**	Milestone MSP 9017
Flora Purim	**Stories to Tell**	Milestone M 9058
Grover Washington, Jr.	**Soul Box, Vols. I & II**	2-Kudu 12/13
Booker Little	**Out Front**	Candid 9027
Jazz Composer's Orchestra	**Jazz Composer's Orchestra**	JCOA 1001/2
McCoy Tyner	**Super Trios**	Milestone 55003

McCoy Tyner	Fly with the Wind	Milestone 9067
McCoy Tyner	Trident	Milestone 9063
McCoy Tyner	Real McCoy	Blue Note 84264
McCoy Tyner	Expansions	Blue Note 84338
McCoy Tyner	Extensions	Blue Note LA 006F
Larry Coryell	Real Great Escape	Vanguard 6509
Ernie Wilkins	Big New Band '60	Everest SDBR-1104
Randy Weston	Randy Weston	Roulette SR 65001
Randy Weston	Blue Moses	CTI 6016
Coleman Hawkins	Night Hawk	Swingville 2016, Prestige 7671
Coleman Hawkins	The Hawk Relaxes	Moodsville 15
Jaki Byard	Out Front	Prestige PR 7397
Jaki Byard	Here's Jaki	New Jazz 8256
Jaki Byard	Hi-Fly	New Jazz 8273
Jaki Byard	Jaki Bard with Strings	Prestige LP 7573
Johnny Griffin	Johnny Griffin with Strings White Gardenia	Riverside RS 9387
Johnny Griffin	The Kerry Dancers	Riverside RS 9420
Pony Poindexter	Pony's Express	Epic BA 17035
Tadd Dameron	Magic Touch	Riverside RS 9419
Charles Bell	Dimension	Atlantic SD 1400
Dizzy Reece	Asia Minor	New Jazz 8274
Sam Jones	Down Home	Riverside RS 9432
Benny Golson	Pop + Swing = Jazz	Audio Fidelity AFL 1978
Benny Golson	Free	Argo LP-716
Bobby Timmons	Born to Be Blue	Riverside RS 9468
Bobby Timmons	Got to Get It	Milestone 9011
Bobby Timmons Trio	Bobby Timmons Trio in Person	Riverside RS 9391
Bobby Timmons	Soul Man	Prestige 7465
Chico Hamilton	Further Adventures of Chico Hamilton	Impulse A-9114
Oliver Nelson	Sound Pieces	Impulse S-9129
Steve Kuhn	Steve Kuhn	Buddha 5098
Steve Kuhn	3 Compositions of McFarland	Impulse A-9136
Hank Jones	Happenings	Impulse A-9132
J. J. Johnson	The Total	RCA LSP 3833
Edlin "Buddy" Terry	Electric Soul!!!	Prestige PR 7525
Joe Jones	Psychedelic Soul Jazz	Prestige PR 7557
Soul Flutes	Trust in Me	A&M SP 3009
Pepper Adams/Zoot Sims	Encounter	Prestige PR 7677
Thad Jones/Pepper Adams	Thad Jones/ Pepper Adams Quintet	Milestone MSP 9001
Bobbi Humphrey	Dig This	Blue Note BST 84421
Astrud Gilberto with Turrentine	Astrud Gilberto with Turrentine	CTI 6008
Stanley Turrentine	Salt Song	CTI 6010
Stanley Turrentine	Cherry	CTI 6017
Stanley Turrentine	Don't Mess with Mr. T	CTI 6030
Stanley Turrentine	The Sugar Man	CTI 6052
Stanley Turrentine	Sugar	CTI 6005
Deodato	Prelude	CTI 6021
Gabor Szabo	Mizrab	CTI 6026
Gabor Szabo	Rambler	CTI 6035
Don Ellis	How Time Passes	Candid LS 9004
Don Ellis	New Ideas	New Jazz 8257
Rocky Boyd	Ease It	Jazztime JT 001
Gil Evans	The Individualism of Gil Evans	Verve V6-8555
Kenny Burrell	Guitar Forms	Verve V6-8612
Kenny Burrell	Night Song	Verve V6-8751
Kenny Burrell	God Bless the Child	CTI 6011
Art Farmer	The Many Faces of Art Farmer	Scepter LP 521
Eddie Harris	In Sound	Atlantic SD 1448
Eddie Harris	Mean Greens	Atlantic SD 1453
Eddie Harris	Tender Storm	Atlantic SD 1478
Friedrich Gulda	Music for 4 Soloists and Band No. 1	MPS 15097
Charles Lloyd	Nirvana	CBS CS 9609
Charles Lloyd	Of Course	CBS CS 9212
Mal Waldron	The Quest	New Jazz LP 8269
Riverside All Stars	A Jazz Version of "Kean"	Riverside RS 9397
Cecil Payne	Cecil Payne Performing Charlie Parker Music	Charlie Parker PLP 801
Cecil Payne	The Connection	Charlie Parker PLP 806
Leo Wright	Suddenly the Blues	Atlantic SD 1393
Archie Shepp	The Way Ahead	Impulse A-9170
Les McCann	Comment	Atlantic S 1547
Gato Barbieri	Fenix	Flying Dutchman 10144
Gato Barbieri	Chapter 3—Viva Emiliano Zapata	Impulse 9279
Airto (Moreira)	Seeds on the Ground	Buddha 5085
Airto (Moreira)	Free	CTI 6020
Gene Harris	Gene Harris of the Three Sounds	Blue Note BST 84423

Mark Murphy	**Bridging a Gap**	Muse 5009
Toshiko Akiyoshi	**Toshiko at Top of the Gate**	SL 5108
Andrew Hill	**Gass Roots**	Blue Note BST 84303
Ray Bryant	**Up Above the Rock**	Cadet S-818
Barry Harris	**Magnificent**	Prestige 7733
Woody Shaw	**Blackstone Legacy**	Contemporary S-7627/28
Nancy Wilson	**But Beautiful**	Capital ST 798
Chet Baker	**She Was Good to Me**	CTI 6050
Gerry Mulligan/ Chet Baker	**Carnegie Hall Concert, Vols. 1 & 2**	CTI 6054, CTI 6055
Various Artists	**Gretsch Drum Night at Birdland**	Roulette R-52049
Various Artists	**California Concert**	CTI X-22
Various Artists	**Twenty Songs of the Century**	Bell, CBS
Various Artists	**The Sound of Feeling**	Verve V6-8743
Various Artists	**25 Years of Prestige**	Prestige P 24046

PHILIP CATHERINE

AS LEADER:	TITLE	LABEL & NO.
Philip Catherine	**September Man**	Atlantic 40562
Philip Catherine	**Guitars**	Atlantic 50193
Philip Catherine	**Nairam**	Warner Bros. BS 2950
Philip Catherine with Larry Coryell	**Twin House**	Atlantic 50342
Philip Catherine	**Toots Thielman/ Philip Catherine and Friends**	Keystone KT 444057

AS SIDEMAN WITH:

John Lee/Jerry Brown	**Mango Sunrise**	Blue Note LA 541-6
Niels Henning/ Osted Pedersen	**Jay Walkin'**	Steeplechase SCS 1041
Jean-Luc Ponty	**Open Strings**	MPS 21 21288-2
Charles Mingus	**3 or 4 Shades of Blues**	Atlantic SD 1700
Sunbirds	**Sunbirds**	MPS 2121110-2
Mike Gibs	**The Only Chrome Waterfall Orchestra**	Bronze ILPS 9353
Charlie Mariano	**Cascade**	Keystone KT 444054
Marc Moulin	**Placebo**	EMI C064-95378
Kenny Drew Trio	**Morning**	Steeplechase SCS 1048
Jack Sels	**The Complete Jack Sels, Vol. I**	Vogel 101 HA
Jack Sels	**The Complete Jack Sels, Vol. II**	Vogel 102 HA
Peter Herbolzheimer	**Wide Open**	BASF/MPS 2121948-8
Chris Hinze	**Sister Slick**	CBS 80271

Michel Legrand	**You Must Believe in Spring**	Polydor 2382-044
Herb Geller	**An American in Hamburg**	Nova 6-28332 DX
Coryell/Mouzon	**Back Together Again**	Atlantic SD 18220
Jean-Luc Ponty/ Stephane Grapelli	**Jean-Luc Ponty/ Stephane Grappelli**	Festival 30AM6139
Pork Pie	**Transitory**	MPS 2122099-0
Pork Pie	**The Door Is Open**	MPS DC 228754

STANLEY CLARKE

AS LEADER:	TITLE	LABEL & NO.
Stanley Clarke	**Children of Forever**	Polydor PD 5531
Stanley Clarke	**Stanley Clarke**	Nemperor NE 431
Stanley Clarke	**Journey to Love**	Nemperor NE 433
Stanley Clarke	**School Days**	Nemperor NE 439

AS SIDEMAN WITH:

Return to Forever	**Return to Forever**	ECM 1022
Return to Forever	**Light as a Feather**	Polydor PD 5525
Return to Forever	**Hymn of the Seventh Galaxy**	Polydor PD 5536
Return to Forever	**Where Have I Known You Before**	Polydor PD 6509
Return to Forever	**No Mystery**	Polydor PD 6512
Return to Forever	**Romantic Warrior**	CBS PC 34076
Return to Forever	**Musicmagic**	CBS PC 34682
Chick Corea	**My Spanish Heart**	Polydor PD 29003
Quincy Jones	**I Heard That**	A&M 3705
Arethra Franklin	**Let Me in Your Life**	Atlantic 7292
Roy Buchanan	**Loading Zone**	Atlantic 18219
Dee Dee Bridgewater	**Just Family**	Elektra/Asylum GE-119
Flora Purim	**Butterfly Dreams**	Milestone M 9052
Airto	**Free**	CTI 6020
Eumir Deodato	**Deodato II**	CTI 6029
Joe Farrell	**Moon Germs**	CTI 6023
Pharoah Sanders	**Live at the East**	Impulse Q 9227
Pharoah Sanders	**Village of the Pharoahs**	Impulse 9254
Curtis Fuller	**Crankin'**	Mainstream 333
Joe Henderson	**In Pursuit of Blackness**	Milestone 9034
Luis Gasca	**For Those Who Chant**	Blue Thumb (out of print)
Donny Hathaway	**Extensions of a Man**	Atco 7092
Norman Connors	**Dance of Magic**	Buddha 5674
Norman Connors	**Dark of Light**	Buddha 5675

Stan Getz	**Captain Marvel**	Columbia KC 32706
Santana	**Borboletta**	Columbia PC 33135
Stanley Cowell	**Illusion Suite**	ECM 1026
Paul Jeffrey	**Family**	Mainstream 376
Frank Foster	**The Loud Minority**	Mainstream 349
Various Artists	**The Bass**	Impulse 4284
Lenny White	**Venusian Summer**	Nemperor NE 435
Al DiMeola	**Land of the Midnight Sun**	Columbia 34074
John McLaughlin	**Johnny McLaughlin/ Electric Guitarist**	Columbia JC 35326

BILLY COBHAM

AS LEADER:	TITLE	LABEL & NO.
Dreams	**Dreams**	Columbia C 30225
Dreams	**Imagine My Surprise**	Columbia C 30960
Billy Cobham	**Crosswinds**	Atlantic 7300
Billy Cobham	**A Funky Thide of Sings**	Atlantic 18149
Billy Cobham	**Life & Times**	Atlantic 18166
Billy Cobham	**Shabazz**	Atlantic 18139
George Duke/ Billy Cobham Band	**Live on Tour in Europe**	Atlantic SD 18194
Billy Cobham	**Spectrum**	Atlantic 7268
Billy Cobham	**Total Eclipse**	Atlantic 18121
Billy Cobham	**Magic**	Columbia JC 34939
Billy Cobham	**Inner Conflicts**	Atlantic SD 19174

AS SIDEMAN WITH:		
Don Sebesky	**Giant Box**	CTI X-6031-32
Quincy Jones/ Various Artists	**Montreux Summit, Vol. I**	Columbia JG 35005
Larry Coryell	**Spaces**	Vanguard 6558
John McLaughlin	**Inner Mounting Flame**	Columbia PC 31067
John McLaughlin	**Birds of Fire**	Columbia PCQ 31996
John McLaughlin	**My Goal's Beyond**	Douglas AD 6003
John McLaughlin	**Between Nothingness and Eternity**	Columbia C 32766
John McLaughlin	**Johnny McLaughlin/ Electric Guitarist**	Columbia JC 35326
Miles Davis	**Jack Johnson**	Columbia PC 30455
Miles Davis	**Big Fun**	Columbia PG 32866
Miles Davis	**1st Great Rock Festival of the Seventies**	Columbia G3X 30805

Miles Davis	**Live-Evil**	Columbia G 30954
Miles Davis	**Get Up with It**	Columbia PC 33236
McCoy Tyner	**Fly with the Wind**	Milestone 9067
Mose Allison	**Western Man**	Atlantic SD 1584
Stanley Turrentine	**Salt Song**	CTI 6010
Stanley Clarke	**School Days**	Nemperor NE 439
Ron Carter	**Uptown Conversation**	Embryo SD 521
Ron Carter	**Spanish Blues**	CTI 6051
Ron Carter	**Blues Farm**	CTI 6027
Ron Carter	**All Blues**	CTI 6037
Ron Carter	**Yellow & Green**	CTI 6064
George Benson	**White Rabbit**	CTI 6015
David Sancious	**Forest of Feeling**	Epic KE 33441
Airto (Moreira)	**Virgin Island**	CTI/Salvation SAL 701
Pete & Sheila Escovito	**Solo Two**	Fantasy F 9524
Purple	**Purple**	CBS/Sony SOPM-157
Jackie & Roy	**To the Heart**	ABC ABCD 945
Jackie & Roy	**Time and Love**	CTI 6019
Hubert Laws	**Carnegie Hall**	CTI 6025
Carly Simon	**Hot Cakes**	Electric 701002
Randy Weston	**Blue Moses**	CTI 6016
Kenny Burrell	**God Bless the Child**	CTI 6011
Freddie Hubbard	**Sky Dive**	CTI 6018
Horace Silver	**Serenade to a Soul Sister**	Blue Note BST 84277
Nimmuy Owens	**No Escaping It**	Polydor 24 4031
Gene Ammons	**Big Band Jug**	Prestige 10070
Roy Barretto	**The Other Road**	Fania SLP 00448
The Starland Vocal Band	**The Starland Vocal Band**	Sindsong/RCA BHL 11351
Steve Kuhn	**Steve Kuhn**	Buddha BDS 5098
Milt Jackson	**Goodbye**	CTI 6038
Santana/McLaughlin	**Love Devotion Surrender**	Columbia KC 32034
Gabor Szabo	**Mizrab**	CTI 6026
Milt Jackson	**Sunflower**	CTI 6024
Deodato	**Deodato II**	CTI 6029
David Pomeranz	**Time to Fly**	Decca DL 75329
Johnny Hammond	**The Prophet**	Kudu KU 10
Johnny Hammond	**Breakout**	Kudu KU 1
Johnny Hammond	**Wild Horses Rock Steady**	Kudu KU 4

Les McCann	**Comment**	Atlantic SD 1547
Jim Pepper	**Pepper's Pow Wow**	Embryo SD 731
Deodato	**Whirlwinds**	MCA 410
Roberta Flack & Donny Hathaway	**Roberta Flack and Donny Hathaway**	Atlantic SD 7216
Deodato	**Prelude**	CTI 6021
George Benson	**Giblet Gravy**	Verve V6-8749
Kenny Burrell	**Nite Song**	Verve V6-8751
Roy Ayers	**Ubiquity**	Polydor (*out of print*)
Roy Ayers	**He's Coming**	Polydor PD 5022

CHICK COREA

AS LEADER:	TITLE	LABEL & NO.
Chick Corea	**Tones for Joan's Bones**	Vortex 2004
Chick Corea	**Now He Sings, Now He Sobs**	Solid State SS 18039
Chick Corea	**Song of Singing**	Blue Note LA 472-H2
Chick Corea	**Piano Improvisations, Vol. 1**	Polydor ECM 1014 ST
Chick Corea	**Piano Improvisations, Vol. 2**	Polydor ECM 1020 ST
Chick Corea	**Circling In**	Blue Note BST 84353
Chick Corea	**A.R.C.**	ECM 1009 ST
Chick Corea	**Circle, Paris Concert**	ECM 1018/19 ST
Chick Corea	**Inner Space**	Atlantic SD 2-305
Chick Corea	**Crystal Silence**	ECM 1024
Return to Forever	**Return to Forever**	ECM 1022
Return to Forever	**Light as a Feather**	Polydor PD 5525
Return to Forever	**Hymn of the Seventh Galaxy**	Polydor PD 5536
Return to Forever	**Where Have I Known You Before**	Polydor PD 6509
Chick Corea	**Chick Corea**	Blue Note LA 395-H2-0798
Return to Forever	**No Mystery**	Polydor PD 6512
Return to Forever	**The Romantic Warrior**	CBS PC 34076
Chick Corea	**The Leprechaun**	Polydor PD 6062
Chick Corea	**My Spanish Heart**	Polydor PD 29003
Return to Forever	**Musicmagic**	Columbia PC 34682
Chick Corea	**Bliss**	Muse 5011
Chick Corea	**Mad Hatter**	Polydor PD 16130
Chick Corea/Bill Evans	**Corea/Evans**	Verve 2510

AS SIDEMAN WITH:

Miles Davis	**Filles de Kilimanjaro**	Columbia CS 9750
Miles Davis	**In a Silent Way**	Columbia CS 9875

Miles Davis	**On the Corner**	Columbia PC 31906
Miles Davis	**Water Babies**	Columbia 34396
Miles Davis	**Bitches' Brew**	Columbia PG 26
Miles Davis	**Miles Davis at the Fillmore**	Columbia CG 30038
Miles Davis	**Live-Evil**	Columbia G 30954
Miles Davis	**Big Fun**	Columbia PG 32866
Anthony Braxton	**The Complete Braxton**	Freedom FLP 40112/113 (*import*)
Stanley Clarke	**Children of Forever**	Polydor PD 5531
Joe Farrell	**Joe Farrell Quartet**	CTI 6003
Stan Getz	**Captain Marvel**	Columbia KC 32706
Eric Kloss	**To Hear Is to See**	Prestige 7689
Eric Kloss	**Consciousness**	Prestige 7793
Hubert Laws	**Law's Cause**	Atlantic SD 1509
John McLaughlin	**Johnny McLaughlin/ Electric Guitarist**	Columbia JC 35326
Wayne Shorter	**Super Nova**	Blue Note 84332
Wayne Shorter	**Motto Grosso Feio**	Blue Note LA 014-G
The Trio	**Conflagration**	Dawn DNLS 3022 (*import*)
Peter Warren	**Bass Is**	Enja 2018 (*import*)
Bobby Hutcherson	**Total Eclipse**	Blue Note 84291
Sadao Watanabe	**Round Trip**	Vanguard VSP 79344
Larry Coryell	**Spaces**	Vanguard 79345
Elvin Jones	**Live at Town Hall**	P.M. 004

LARRY CORYELL

AS LEADER:	TITLE	LABEL & NO.
Larry Coryell	**Barefoot Boy**	Flying Dutchman 10139
Larry Coryell	**Basics**	Vanguard 79375
Larry Coryell	**Coryell**	Vanguard 6547
Larry Coryell	**At the Village Gate**	Vanguard 6573
Larry Coryell	**Introducing The Eleventh House**	Vanguard VSD 79342
Eleventh House	**Level One**	Arista AL 4052
Eleventh House	**Aspects**	Arista AL 4077
Larry Coryell	**Essential**	Vanguard VSD 75/76
Larry Coryell	**Fairyland**	Zodiac 5003
Larry Coryell	**Guitar Player**	MCA 6002
Larry Coryell	**Lady Coryell**	Vanguard 6509
Larry Coryell	**Lion and the Ram**	Arista 4108

Larry Coryell	**Offering**	Vanguard 79319
Larry Coryell	**Real Great Escape**	Vanguard 79329
Larry Coryell	**Restful Mind**	Vanguard 79359
Larry Coryell	**Spaces**	Vanguard 6558
Larry Coryell/ Alphonse Mouzon	**Back Together Again**	Atlantic SD 18220
Free Spirits	**Out of Sight and Sound**	ABC 593

AS SIDEMAN WITH:

Chico Hamilton	**The Dealer**	Impulse 9130
Gary Burton	**Genuine Tong Funeral**	RCA LSP 3988
Gary Burton	**Gary Burton/Larry Coryell**	RCA 7XL1-7101
Gary Burton	**Duster**	RCA LSP 3835
Gary Burton	**Lofty Fake Anagram**	RCA LSP 3901
Gary Burton	**In Concert**	RCA LSP 3985
Jazz Composer's Orchestra	**The Jazz Composer's Orchestra**	JCOA 1001/2
Mike Mantler	**Movies**	Watt 7
Leon Thomas	**Blues and the Soulful Truth**	Flying Dutchman FD 10155
Charles Mingus	**3 or 4 Shades of Blues**	Atlantic SD 1700
Philip Catherine	**Twin House**	Atlantic 50342
Steve Khan	**Two for the Road**	Arista AB 4156
Herbie Mann	**Memphis Underground**	Atlantic 1522
Lenny White	**Venusian Summer**	Nemperor NE 435
Michal Urbaniak	**Fusion III**	Columbia PC 33542
Bob Thiel	**Mysterious Flying Orchestra**	Flying Dutchman (out ofprint)
Eddie "Cleanhead" Vinson	**Live from Montreux**	Flying Dutchman (out of print)
5th Dimension	**Earthbound**	ABC ABCD 897
Jimmy Webb	**And So: On**	Reprise S-6448

MILES DAVIS (since 1951)

AS LEADER:	TITLE	LABEL & NO.
Miles Davis	**Agartha**	Columbia 33967
Miles Davis	**Basic Miles**	Columbia 32025
Miles Davis	**Big Fun**	Columbia PG 32866
Miles Davis	**Bitches' Brew**	Columbia PG 33402 (GQ 30997)
Miles Davis	**Black Giants**	Columbia PG 33402
Miles Davis	**Blue Moods**	Fantasy 86001
Miles Davis	**Capitol Jazz Classics Vol. 2**	Capitol 11026
Miles Davis	**Collectors Items**	Prestige 24022

Miles Davis	**Conception**	Prestige 7744
Miles Davis	**Dark Magus**	CBS/Sony (Japan)
Miles Davis	**Miles Davis**	Blue Note 81501-81502
Miles Davis	**Miles Davis at Carnegie Hall**	Columbia PC 8612
Miles Davis	**Miles Davis at the Fillmore**	Columbia CG 30038
Miles Davis	**Miles Davis' Greatest Hits**	Columbia PC 9808
Miles Davis	**Miles Davis' Greatest Hits**	Prestige 7457
Miles Davis	**Miles Davis in Concert**	Columbia PG 32092
Miles Davis	**Miles Davis In Europe**	Columbia CS 8983
Miles Davis	**Miles Davis in Person**	Columbia C2S-820
Miles Davis	**Miles Davis Plays for Lovers**	Prestige 7352
Miles Davis	**Miles Davis Plays Jazz Classics**	Prestige 7373
Miles Davis	**Decade of Jazz, Vol. 2**	Blue Note LA 159-62
Miles Davis	**Dig**	Prestige 24054
Miles Davis	**ESP**	Columbia PC 9150
Miles Davis	**Early Miles**	Prestige 7674
Miles Davis	**Ezz-Ethic**	Prestige 7827
Miles Davis	**Filles de Kilimanjaro**	Columbia CS 9750
Miles Davis	**Four and More**	Columbia PC 9253
Miles Davis	**Get Up with It**	Columbia PG 33236
Miles Davis	**Green Haze**	Prestige 24064
Miles Davis	**In a Silent Way**	Columbia CS 9875
Miles Davis	**Jack Johnson**	Columbia PC 30455
Miles Davis	**Jazz at the Plaza, Vol. 1**	Columbia PC 32470
Miles Davis	**Kind of Blue**	Columbia PC 8163
Miles Davis	**Lenny**	United Artists LA 359-11
Miles Davis	**Live-Evil**	Columbia G 30954
Miles Davis	**Miles Ahead**	Columbia PC 8633
Miles Davis	**Miles**	Prestige 7822
Miles Davis	**Miles & Monk at Newport**	Columbia PC 8978
Miles Davis	**Miles in the Sky**	Columbia CS 9628
Miles Davis	**Miles Smiles**	Columbia CS 9401
Miles Davis	**Milestones**	Columbia PC 9428
Miles Davis	**My Funny Valentine**	Columbia PC 9106
Miles Davis	**My Old Flame**	Up Front 171
Miles Davis	**Nefertiti**	Columbia CS 9594
Miles Davis	**Odyssey**	Prestige 7540
Miles Davis	**Oleo**	Prestige 7847
Miles Davis	**On the Corner**	Columbia PC 31906

Miles Davis	**Porgy & Bess**	Columbia PC 8085
Miles Davis	**Twofer Giants, Vols. 1 & 2**	Prestige PRP 1-2
Miles Davis	**Quiet Nights**	CBS C 58906; SONP 50163
Miles Davis	**Roots of Modern Jazz**	Olympic 7135
Miles Davis	**'Round Midnight**	Columbia PC 8649
Miles Davis	**Seven Steps to Heaven**	Columbia CS 8851
Miles Davis	**Sketches of Spain**	Columbia PC 8271
Miles Davis	**Someday My Prince Will Come**	Columbia PC 8456
Miles Davis	**Something Else**	Blue Note LA 169-G
Miles Davis	**Sorcerer**	Columbia CS 9532
Miles Davis	**Steamin'**	Prestige 7580
Miles Davis	**Tallest Trees**	Prestige 24012
Miles Davis	**25 Years of Prestige**	Prestige 24046
Miles Davis	**Walkin'**	Prestige 7608
Miles Davis	**Water Babies**	Columbia PC 34396
Miles Davis	**Workin' & Steamin'**	Prestige 24034
Miles Davis	**Tune Up**	Prestige P 24077
Miles Davis	**Miles Davis in Tokyo**	CBS/Sony SOPL-162
Miles Davis	**Miles Davis in Berlin**	German CBS BPG-629765

AL DiMEOLA

AS LEADER:	TITLE	LABEL & NO.
Al DiMeola	**Casino**	Columbia JC 35277
Al DiMeola	**Elegant Gypsy**	Columbia 34461
Al DiMeola	**Land of the Midnight Sun**	Columbia 34074

AS SIDEMAN WITH:

Return to Forever	**Where Have I Known You Before**	Polydor PD 6509
Return to Forever	**No Mystery**	Polydor PD 6512
Return to Forever	**The Romantic Warrior**	Columbia PC 34076
Lenny White	**Venusian Summer**	Nemperor NE 435
Stomu Yamashta	**Go**	Island 9387
Stomu Yamashta	**Go Too**	Arista 4138

GEORGE DUKE

AS LEADER:	TITLE	LABEL & NO.
George Duke	**Reach for It**	Epic E 34883
George Duke	**From Me to You**	Epic PE 34469
George Duke	**Liberated Fantasies**	MPS/BASF G 22835
George Duke	**I Love the Blues, She Heard Me Cry**	MPS/BASF MC 25671
George Duke	**The Aura Will Prevail**	MPS/BASF MC 25613
George Duke	**Feel**	MPS/BASF MC 25355
George Duke	**Faces in Reflection**	MPS/BASF MC 22018
George Duke	**Save the Country**	Liberty LST 11004
George Duke	**The Inner Source**	MPS/BASF 29-20912-1
George Duke	**The George Duke Quartet**	Saba 15-074
George Duke/ Billy Cobham Band	**Billy Cobham/George Duke Band Live on Tour**	Atlantic SD 18194
George Duke	**Don't Let Go**	Epic JE 35366

AS SIDEMAN WITH:

Flora Purim	**Open Your Eyes You Can Fly**	Milestone M 9065
Flora Purim	**Stories to Tell**	Milestone M 9058
Flora Purim	**Butterfly Dreams**	Milestone M 9052
Frank Zappa	**Bongo Fury**	DiscReet DS 2234
Frank Zappa	**One Size Fits All**	DiscReet DS 2216
Frank Zappa	**Roxy and Elsewhere**	DiscReet 2DS 2202
Frank Zappa	**Apostrophe**	DiscReet DS 2175
Frank Zappa	**Overnight Sensation**	DiscReet MS 2149
Frank Zappa	**Waka/Jawaka**	Bizarre/Reprise 2094
Frank Zappa	**The Grand Wazoo**	Bizarre/Reprise MS 2093
Airto (Moreira)	**Virgin Land**	CTI/Salvation SAL 701
Nat Adderley	**Double Exposure**	Prestige P 10090
David Axelrod	**Heavy Axe**	Fantasy F 9450
Joe Williams	**Joe Williams 'Live'**	Fantasy F 9441
Gene Ammons	**Brasswind**	Prestige P 10080
Cal Tjader	**Amazones**	Fantasy F 9502
Alphonse Mouzon	**The Man Incognito**	Blue Note LA 584-G
Nancy Wilson	**This Mother's Daughter**	Capitol ST 11518
Sonny Rollins	**Nucleus**	Milestone M 9064
Gerald Wilson	**Eternal Equinox**	World Pacific ST 20160
Eddie Henderson	**Sunburst**	Blue Note LA 464-G
Luis Gasca	**Born to Love You**	Fantasy F 9461
John Klemmer	**Touch**	ABC ABCO-922
Alphonso Johnson	**Moonshadows**	Epic PE 34118
Ruben and the Jets	**For Real**	Mercury SRM1-659
The Third Wave	**Here and Now**	MPS 14-263
Peter Magadini	**Polyrhythm**	Briko BR 1000
Newport Jazz Festival Artists	**Newport in New York '72— The Jam Sessions, Vols. 3 and 4**	Cobblestone CST 9026

Gladys Knight & the Pips	**Second Anniversary**	Buddha BDS 5639
Suggie Otis	**Freedom Flight**	Epic E 30752
Raul De Souza	**Sweet Lucy**	Capitol ST 11648
Lee Ritenour	**Captain Fingers**	Epic PE 34426

JOE FARRELL

AS LEADER:	TITLE	LABEL & NO.
George Benson/Joe Farrell	**Benson & Farrell**	CTI 6069
Joe Farrell	**Canned Funk**	CTI 6053
Joe Farrell	**Moon Germs**	CTI 6023
Joe Farrell	**Out Back**	CTI 6014
Joe Farrell	**Penny Arcade**	CTI 6034
Joe Farrell	**Song of the Wind**	CTI 6067
Joe Farrell	**Upon This Rock**	CTI 6042
Joe Farrell	**La Catedral y el Toro**	Warner Bros. BS 3121
Joe Farrell	**Joe Farrell Quartet**	CTI 6003

AS SIDEMAN WITH:		
Thad Jones/Mel Lewis	**Presenting Thad Jones**	Solid State (UA)
Thad Jones/Mel Lewis	**Live at the Village Vanguard**	Solid State 18016
Thad Jones/Mel Lewis	**Monday Night**	Solid State 18048
Thad Jones/Mel Lewis	**Presenting Joe Williams**	Solid State 18008
Thad Jones/Mel Lewis	**Presenting Ruth Brown with Thad Jones/Mel Lewis**	Solid State (out of print)
Thad Jones/Mel Lewis	**Central Park North**	Solid State 18051
Return to Forever	**Return to Forever**	ECM 1022
Return to Forever	**Light as a Feather**	Polydor PD 5525
Return to Forever	**Musicmagic**	Columbia PC 34682
Chick Corea	**Tones for Joan's Bones**	Vortex 2004
Chick Corea	**Inner Space**	Atlantic SD 2-305
Chick Corea	**The Leprechaun**	Polydor PD 6062
Chick Corea	**Mad Hatter**	Polydor PD 16130
Elvin Jones	**Puttin It Together**	Blue Note 84282
Elvin Jones	**The Ultimate**	Blue Note 84305
Charles Mingus	**Mingus Revisited**	Trip 5513
Maynard Ferguson	**Newport Suite**	Roulette RE 116 (out of print)
Maynard Ferguson	**Maynard '61**	Roulette RE 122 (out of print)
Maynard Ferguson	**Let's Face the Music and Dance**	Roulette (out of print)
Pate Martino	**Strings**	Prestige 7547
George Benson	**Good King Bad**	CTI 6062

Don Sebesky	**Giant Box**	CTI X 6031-32
Elvin Jones (& Chick Corea)	**Merry-Go-Round**	Blue Note 84414 (out of print)

STEVE GADD

AS SIDEMAN WITH:		
Patti Austin	**End of a Rainbow**	CTI 5001
Ashford & Simpson	**Come As You Are**	Warner Bros. BS 2858
Ashford & Simpson	**So So Satisfied**	Warner Bros. BS 2992
Chet Baker	**She Was Too Good to Me**	CTI 6050-sl
Gato Barbieri	**Ruby Ruby**	A&M 4655
George Benson	**Bad Benson**	CTI 6045
John Blair	**We Belong Together**	CTI 75004
Brecker Brothers	**Don't Stop the Music**	Arista AL 4122
Tony Camillo Bazuka	**Bazuka**	A&M SP 3411
Ron Carter	**Anything Goes**	Kudu KU 25-sl
Merry Clayton	**Keep Your Eye on the Sparrow**	ODE SP 77030
Judy Collins	**Bread and Roses**	Elktra F1076
Judy Collins	**Judith**	Elktra 7E1032
Chick Corea	**The Leprechaun**	Polydor PD 6062
Chick Corea	**Mad Hatter**	Polydor PD 16130
Chick Corea	**My Spanish Heart**	Polydor PD 29003
Hank Crawford	**Hank Crawford's Back**	Kudu KU 33-sl
Hank Crawford	**I Hear a Symphony**	Kudu KU 26-sl
Hank Crawford	**Tico Rico**	Kudu KU 35-sl
Jim Croce	**I Got a Name**	ABC X 797
Al DiMeola	**Elegant Gypsy**	Columbia PC 34461
Art Farmer	**Crawl Space**	CTI 7073
Joe Farrell	**La Catedral y el Toro**	Warner Bros. BS 3121
Joe Farrell	**Penny Arcade**	CTI 6034
Maynard Ferguson	**Primal Scream**	Columbia PC 33953
Aretha Franklin	**With Everything I Feel in Me**	Atlantic SD 181116
Michael Franks	**Birchfield 9**	Warner Bros. BSK 3167
Eric Gale	**Ginseng Woman**	Columbia PC 34421
Eric Gale	**Multiplication**	Columbia PC 34938
Art Garfunkel	**Watermark**	Columbia 34975
Henry Gross	**Henry Gross**	A&M SP 4416
Jim Hall	**Concierto**	CTI 6060-sl
Milt Jackson	**Goodbye with Hubert Laws**	CTI 6038
Bob James	**Four**	CTI 7074

Bob James	**Heads**	Columbia JC 34896
Garland Jeffreys	**Ghost Writer**	A&M SP 4629
Steve Khan	**Tightrope**	Tappan Zee/Columbia JC 34857
Earl Klugh	**Finger Paintings**	Blue Note BN LA 737-H
Earl Klugh	**Living Inside Your Love**	Blue Note BN LA 667-G
Gladys Knight	**I Feel a Song**	Buddha BDS 5612
Hubert Laws	**The Chicago Theme**	CTI 6058-sl
Hubert Laws	**Romeo and Juliet**	Columbia PC 34330
Kenny Loggins	**Celebrate Me Home**	Columbia PC 34655
Jon Lucien	**Premonition**	Columbia PC 34255
Van McCoy	**Rhythms of the World**	H & L 69014
Ralph MacDonald	**The Path**	Marlin 2210
Michael Mainieri	**Love Play**	Arista AL 4133
Melissa Manchester	**Singin'**	Arista 4136
Chuck Mangione	**Alive!**	Mercury 0592
Chuck Mangione	**Main Squeeze**	A&M SP 4612
Herbie Mann	**Waterbed**	Atlantic SD 1676
Sergio Mendez	**The New Brasil 77**	Elektra 7E1102
Melba Moore	**Peach Melba**	Buddha BDS 5629
Melba Moore	**This Is It**	Buddha BDS 5657
New York Community Choir	**The New York Community Choir**	RCA APL 1-2293
Noel Pointer	**Hold On**	UA LA 848H
Noel Pointer	**Phantasia**	Blue Note BN LAB 60H
David Sanborn	**Taking Off**	Warner Bros. BS 2873
Leo Sayer	**Endless Flight**	Warner Bros. BS 2962
Don Sebesky	**Rape of El Morro**	CTI 6061
Paul Simon	**Still Crazy After All These Years**	Columbia PC 33540
Paul Simon	**There Goes Rhymin' Simon**	Columbia KC 32280
Phoebe Snow	**Never Letting Go**	Columbia JC 34875
Phoebe Snow	**Second Childhood**	Columbia PC 33952
Ringo Starr	**Ringo the 4th**	Atlantic SD 19108
Steely Dan	**Aja**	ABC AB 1006
Jeremy Steig	**Firefly**	CTI 7075
Stuff	**Stuff**	Warner Bros. BS 2968
Stuff	**More Stuff**	Warner Bros. BS 3061
Stylistics	**Sun and Soul**	H & L 69019
John Tropea	**Tropea**	Marlin 2200
John Tropea	**Short Trip to Space**	Marlin 2204

Michal Urbaniak	**Fusion III**	Columbia PC 33542
Frankie Valli	**Lady Put the Light Out**	Private Stock PS 7002
Cedar Walton	**Moebius**	RCA APL 1-1009
Grover Washington, Jr.	**Feels So Good**	Kudu KU 24-sl

MICHAEL GIBBS

AS LEADER:	TITLE	LABEL & NO.
Michael Gibbs	**Michael Gibbs**	Deram SML 1063
Michael Gibbs	**Tanglewood '63**	Deram SML 1087
Michael Gibbs	**Just a Head**	Polydor 2683 011
Michael Gibbs	**In the Public Interest**	Polydor 2383 252
Michael Gibbs	**Seven Songs for Orchestra Quartet & Chamber**	ECM 1040 ST
Michael Gibbs	**Will Power**	Argo 2DA 164/5
Michael Gibbs	**The Only Chrome— Waterfall Orchestra**	Bronze 1LPS 9353

ORCHESTRATIONS:

Jaco Pastorius	**Jaco Pastorius**	Columbia PE 33949
Narada Michael Walden	**Garden of Love Light**	Atlantic SD 18199
Narada Michael Walden	**I Cry, I Smile**	Atlantic SD 19141
Peter Gabriel	**Peter Gabriel**	Atco SD 36147
Mahavishnu/ John McLaughlin	**Apocalypse**	Columbia KC 32957
Stanley Clarke	**Stanley Clarke**	Nemperor NE 431
Lenny White	**Big City**	Nemperor NE 441
Joni Mitchell	**Don Juan's Reckless Daughter**	Asylum BB 701

JAN HAMMER

AS LEADER:	TITLE	LABEL & NO.
Jan Hammer	**First Seven Days**	Nemperor NE 432
Jan Hammer	**Oh Yeah**	Nemperor NE 437
Jan Hammer with Jack DeJohnette/John Abercrombie	**Timeless**	ECM 1047
Jan Hammer	**Melodies**	Nemperor NE 35003
Jan Hammer	**Make Love**	MSP /BASF 20688
Jan Hammer with Jerry Goodman	**Like Children**	Nemperor NE 430
Jan Hammer with Jeff Beck	**Jeff Beck with the Jan Hammer Group Live**	Epic PE 34433

AS SIDEMAN WITH:		
John McLaughlin	**Inner Mounting Flame**	Columbia PC 31067

John McLaughlin	**Birds of Fire**	Columbia KC 31996
John McLaughlin	**Between Nothingness and Eternity**	Columbia C 32766
John McLaughlin/ Carlos Santana	**Love Devotion Surrender**	Columbia C 32034
Jeff Beck	**Wired**	Epic PE 33849
David Earl Johnson	**Time Is Free**	Vanguard VSU 79401
Lenny White	**Big City**	Nemperor NE 441
Al DiMeola	**Elegant Gypsy**	Columbia 31461
Roy Buchanan	**Loading Zone**	Atlatnic 18219
Billy Cobham	**Spectrum**	Atlantic 7268
Stanley Clarke	**Stanley Clarke**	Nemperor NE 431
Tommy Bolin	**Teaser**	Nemperor NE 436
Elvin Jones	**On the Mountain**	PM 005 (*out of print*)
Elvin Jones (&Chick Corea)	**Merry-Go-Round**	Blue Note 84414 (*out of print*)

HERBIE HANCOCK

AS LEADER:	TITLE	LABEL & NO.
Herbie Hancock	**Blow-Up** (*sound track*)	MGM E 4447
Herbie Hancock	**Death Wish** (*sound track*)	Columbia 33169
Herbie Hancock	**Adam's Apple**	Blue Note 84232
Herbie Hancock	**Best of Herbie Hancock, Vol. I**	Blue Note 89907
Herbie Hancock	**Contours**	Blue Note 84206
Herbie Hancock (Chick Corea, Keith Jarrett, McCoy Tyner)	**Chick Corea,Herbie Hancock, Keith Jarrett, McCoy Tyner**	Atlantic 1696
Herbie Hancock	**Crossings**	Warner Bros. 2617
Herbie Hancock	**Empyrean Isles**	Blue Note 84175
Herbie Hancock	**Fat Albert Rotunda**	Warner Bros. 1834
Herbie Hancock	**Free Form**	Blue Note 84118
Herbie Hancock	**Happenings**	Blue Note 84231
Herbie Hancock	**Herbie Hancock**	Blue Note LA 399-H2
Herbie Hancock	**Head Hunter**	Columbia PC Q 32731
Herbie Hancock	**In Concert, Vol. II**	CTI 6049
Herbie Hancock	**Love Me by Name**	A&M 4564
Herbie Hancock	**Maiden Voyage**	Blue Note 84195
Herbie Hancock	**Man-Child**	Columbia 33812
Herbie Hancock	**Mwandishi**	Warner Bros. 1898
Herbie Hancock	**My Point of View**	Blue Note 84126
Herbie Hancock	**Piano Giants**	Prestige 24052
Herbie Hancock	**Prisoner**	Blue Note 84312

Herbie Hancock	**Secrets**	Columbia 34820
Herbie Hancock	**Sextant**	Columbia 32212
Herbie Hancock	**Speak Like a Child**	Blue Note 84279
Herbie Hancock	**Succotash**	Blue Note LA 152-G
Herbie Hancock	**Takin' Off**	Blue Note 84109
Herbie Hancock	**Thrust**	Columbia 32965
Herbie Hancock	**Traces**	Up Front/Springboard 194
Herbie Hancock	**Treasure Chest**	Warner Bros. 2W S 2807
Herbie Hancock	**Una Mas**	Blue Note 84127
Herbie Hancock	**Inventions and Dimensions**	Blue Note 84147
Herbie Hancock	**Dedication**	CBS/Sony (*Japan*)
Herbie Hancock	**Flood**	CBS/Sony
V.S.O.P.	**V.S.O.P.**	Columbia PC 34688
V.S.O.P.	**The Quintet/V.S.O.P. Live**	Columbia C 2-34976

AS SIDEMAN WITH:

Miles Davis	**Seven Steps to Heaven**	Columbia CS 8851
Miles Davis	**Miles Davis in Europe**	Columbia CS 8983
Miles Davis	**My Funny Valentine**	Columbia CS 9106
Miles Davis	**Four and More**	Columbia CS 9253
Miles Davis	**Miles in Tokyo**	CBS/Sony SOPL 162
Miles Davis	**Miles in Berlin**	German CBS BPG 629765
Miles Davis	**ESP**	Columbia CS 9150
Miles Davis	**Miles Smiles**	Columbia CS 9401
Miles Davis	**Sorcerer**	Columbia CS 9532
Miles Davis	**Nefertiti**	Columbia CS 9594
Miles Davis	**Miles in the Sky**	Columbia CS 9628
Miles Davis	**Filles de Kilimanjaro**	Columbia CS 9750
Miles Davis	**In a Silent Way**	Columbia CS 9875
Miles Davis	**Big Fun**	Columbia PG 32866
Miles Davis	**Jack Johnson**	Columbia S 30455
Miles Davis	**Live-Evil**	Columbia G 30954
Miles Davis	**On the Corner**	Columbia KC 31906
Miles Davis	**Get Up with It**	Columbia PC 33236
Miles Davis	**Water Babies**	Columbia PC 34396
Pepper Adams/ Donald Byrd Quintet	**Out of This World**	Warwick W 2041
Donald Byrd	**Royal Flush**	Blue Note 84101
Donald Byrd	**Free Form**	Blue Note 84118
Donald Byrd	**A New Perspective**	Blue Note 84124
Donald Byrd	**Up**	Verve V6-8609

Freddie Hubbard	**Hubtones**	Blue Note 84115
Freddie Hubbard	**Straight Life**	CTI 6007
Freddie Hubbard/ Stanley Turrentine	**In Concert, Vol. I**	CTI 6044
Grant Green	**Feelin' the Spirit**	Blue Note 84312
Hank Mobley	**No Room for Squares**	Blue Note 84149
Sony Rollins	**Now's the Time**	RCA LSP 2927
Grant Green	**Goin' West**	Blue Note 84310
Freddie Hubbard	**Red Clay**	CTI 6001
Lee Morgan	**Search for the New Land**	Blue Note 84169
Stan Getz/ Bob Brookmeyer	**Stan Getz/ Bob Brookmeyer '65**	Columbia CS 9037
Grachan Moncur III	**Some Other Stuff**	Blue Note 84177
Lee Morgan	**Cornbread**	Blue Note 84222
Jackie McLean	**It's Time**	Blue Note 84179
Anthony Williams	**Lifetime**	Blue Note 84180
Anthony Williams	**Spring**	Blue Note 84126
Wayne Shorter	**Speak No Evil**	Blue Note BST 84194
Wayne Shorter	**All Seeing Eye**	Blue Note BST 84219
Wayne Shorter	**Schizophrenia**	Blue Note BST 84297
Wayne Shorter	**Native Dancer**	Columbia 33418
Bobby Hutcherson	**Components**	Blue Note 84213
George Benson	**Giblet Gravy**	Verve V6-8749
George Benson	**Shape of Things to Come**	A&M SP 3014
George Benson	**White Rabbit**	CTI 6015
Wes Montgomery	**California Dreaming**	Verve V6-8672
Wes Montgomery	**A Day in the Life**	A&M SP 3001
Wes Montgomery	**Down Here on the Ground**	A&M SP 3006
Wes Montgomery	**Road Song**	A&M SP 3012
Kenny Burrell	**Blues—The Common Ground**	Verve V6-8746
K & J.J.	**Israel**	A&M SP 3008
Charles Tolliver	**Charles Tolliver & His All Stars**	Black Lyon BLP 30117
Paul Desmond	**Summertime**	A&M SP 3015
Roy Ayers	**Stoned Soul Picnic**	Milestone SD 1514
Roy Ayers	**Daddy Bug**	Atlantic SD 1538
Joe Henderson	**Power to the People**	Milestone MSP 9024
Ron Carter	**Uptown Conversation**	Embryo SD 521
Attila Zoller	**Gypsy Cry**	Embryo SD 523
Phil Woods	**Round Trip**	Verve V6-8791

Miroslav Vitous	**Infinite Search**	Embryo SD 524
Kawaida	**Kawaida**	O'be OB 301
Quincy Jones	**Gula Matari**	A&M SP 3030
Quincy Jones	**Body Heat**	A&M SP 3617
Norman Connors	**Dance of Magic**	Cobblestone CST 9024
Norman Connors	**Love from the Sun**	Buddha BDS 5142
Norman Connors	**Dark of Light**	Cobblestone CST 9035
Joe Farrell	**Moon Germs**	CTI 6023
Joe Farrell	**Penny Arcade**	CTI Q 6034
Milt Jackson	**Sunflower**	CTI 6024
Eddie Henderson	**Realization**	Capricorn CP 0118
Eddie Henderson	**Inside Out**	Capricorn CP 0122
The Pointer Sisters	**That's a Plenty**	Blue Thumb BTS 6009
The Pointer Sisters	**Steppin'**	Blue Thumb BTS 6021
Victoria	**Victoria**	San Francisco Records 206
Airto (Moreira)	**Identity**	Arista 4068
Miroslav Vitous	**Magical Shepherd**	Warner Bros. B 2925
Bobby Womack	**Safety Zone**	United Artists LA 544-G
Jaco Pastorius	**Jaco Pastorius**	Epic OE 33949
Jon Lucien	**Premonition**	Columbia PC 34255
Wah Wah Watson	**Elementary**	Columbia PC 34328

FREDDIE HUBBARD

AS LEADER:	TITLE	LABEL & NO.
Freddie Hubbard	**Artistry of Freddie Hubbard**	Impulse 27
Freddie Hubbard	**Backlash**	Atlantic 1477
Freddie Hubbard	**Baddest Hubbard**	CTI 6047
Freddie Hubbard	**Blue Spirits**	Blue Note 84196
Freddie Hubbard	**Blues & the Abstract Truth**	Impulse 5
Freddie Hubbard	**Breaking Point**	Blue Note 84172
Freddie Hubbard	**California Concert**	CTI X 2-2
Freddie Hubbard	**Compulsion**	Blue Note 84217
Freddie Hubbard	**Contours**	Blue Note 84206
Freddie Hubbard	**The Drums**	Impulse 9272
Freddie Hubbard	**Echoes of Blues**	Atlantic 1687
Freddie Hubbard	**First Light**	CTI 6013
Freddie Hubbard	**Goin' Up**	Blue Note 84056
Freddie Hubbard	**Here to Stay**	Blue Note LA 496-H2
Freddie Hubbard	**High Energy**	Columbia KC 33048

Freddie Hubbard	Hubtones	Blue Note 84115
Freddie Hubbard	Freddie Hubbard	Blue Note LA 356-H2
Freddie Hubbard	In Concert, Vol. I	Blue CTI 6044
Freddie Hubbard	In Concert, Vol. II	Blue CTI 6049
Freddie Hubbard	Jazz Years	Atlantic 2-316
Freddie Hubbard	Keep Your Soul Together	CTI 6036
Freddie Hubbard	Liquid Love	Columbia PC 33556
Freddie Hubbard	Night of the Cookers, Vol. I	Blue Note 84207
Freddie Hubbard	Night of the Cookers, Vol. II	Blue Note 84208
Freddie Hubbard	Polar A C	CTI 6056
Freddie Hubbard	Ready for Freddie	Blue Note 84045
Freddie Hubbard	Red Clay	CTI 6001
Freddie Hubbard	Sky Dive	CTI 6018
Freddie Hubbard	Straight Life	CTI 6007
Freddie Hubbard	Takin' Off	Blue Note 84109
Freddie Hubbard	Windjammer	Columbia PC 34166
Freddie Hubbard	Bundle of Joy	Columbia JO 34902
V.S.O.P.	V.S.O.P.	Columbia PC 34688
V.S.O.P.	The Quintet/V.S.O.P. Live	Columbia C 2-34976
Freddie Hubbard	Body and Soul	Impulse S 38
Freddie Hubbard	The Black Angel	Atlantic S 1549
Freddie Hubbard	Sing Me a Song of Songmy	Atlantic SD 1576
Freddie Hubbard	High Blues Pressure	Atlantic 1501
Freddie Hubbard	A Soul Experiment	Atlantic SD 1526
Freddie Hubbard	The Hub of Hubbard	BASF 20726
Freddie Hubbard	Reevaluation: The Impulse Years	Impulse 9237
Freddie Hubbard	Art of Freddie Hubard:	Atlantic SD 2-314
Herbie Hancock/ Freddie Hubbard	In Concert, Vols. I & II	CTI 6044, CTI 6049
Freddie Hubbard/ Stanley Turrentine	In Concert, Vol. I	CTI 6044

AS SIDEMAN WITH:

Art Blakey	Mosaic	Blue Note 84090
Art Blakey	Free for All	Blue Note 84170
Art Blakey	Thermo	Milestone 47008
Art Blakey	Buhaina's Delight	Blue Note 84104
Dexter Gordon	Doin' All Right	Blue Note 84077
Herbie Hancock	Empyrean Isles	Blue Note 84175
Herbie Hancock	Maiden Voyage	Blue Note 84195
Randy Weston	Blue Moses	CTI 6016

John Coltrane	Olea	Atlantic 1373
John Coltrane	Ascension	Impulse S 95
Quincy Jones	Walking in Space	A&M SP 3023
Wayne Shorter	All Seeing Eye	Blue Note BST 84219
Wayne Shorter	Speak No Evil	Blue Note BST 84194
Art Blakey	Kyoto	Riverside 493
Art Blakey	Three Blind Mice	U.S. 5633
Jackie McLean	Bluesnik	Blue Note 84067
Ornette Coleman	Free Jazz	Atlantic S 1364

BOB JAMES

AS LEADER:	TITLE	LABEL & NO.
Bob James	One * †	CTI 6043
Bob James	Two * †	CTI 6057
Bob James	Three * †	CTI 6063
Bob James	BJ 4 * †	CTI 6074
Bob James	Heads * †	Tappan Zee/Columbia JC 34896

AS SIDEMAN WITH:

Hubert Laws	The Chicago Theme *	CTI 6058
Hubert Laws	The S. F. Concert *	CTI 7071
Grover Washington, Jr.	Soul Box, Vols. I & II *	2-Kudu KU 12/13
Grover Washington, Jr.	Mister Magic	Kudu KU 20
Grover Washington, Jr.	Feels So Good *	Kudu KU 24-sl
Idris Muhammad	Power of Soul *	Kudu KU 17
Gabor Szabo	Macho †	Salvation (CTI) SAL 704
Hubert Laws	Romeo & Juliet †	Columbia 34330
Eric Gale	Ginseng Woman †	Columbia PC 34421
Eric Gale	Multiplication †	Columbia PC 34938
Freddie Hubbard	Windjammer †	Columbia PC 34166
Kenny Loggins	Celebrate Me Home †	Columbia PC 34655
Blood, Sweat & Tears	More Than Ever †	Columbia PC 34233
George Duke, Billy Cobham, Steve Khan, Stan Getz, et al.	Montreux Summit, Vol. I	Columbia JG 35005
Steve Khan	Tightrope †	Tappan Zee/Columbia JC 34857
Chet Baker	She Was Too Good to Me	CTI 6050

[key: * = Arranger , † = Producer]

AL JARREAU

AS LEADER:	TITLE	LABEL & NO.
Al Jarreau	We Got By	Warner Bros. MS 2224

| Al Jarreau | Glow | Warner Bros. MS 2248 |
| Al Jarreau | Look to the Rainbow/
Al Jarreau in Europe | Warner Bros. 2BZ 3052 |

KEITH JARRETT

AS LEADER:	TITLE	LABEL & NO.
Keith Jarrett	The Survivors Suite	ECM 1-1085
Keith Jarrett	Byablue	ABC AS 9331
Keith Jarrett	Arbour Zena	ECM 1070
Keith Jarrett	Backhand	Impulse 9305
Keith Jarrett	Belonging	ECM 1050
Keith Jarrett	Birth	Atlantic 1612
Keith Jarrett	Gary Burton/Keith Jarrett	Atlantic 1577
Keith Jarrett	Herbie Hancock, Chick Corea, Keith Jarrett, McCoy Tyner	Atlantic 1696
Keith Jarrett	Death and the Flower	Impulse 9301
Keith Jarrett	The Drums	Impulse 9272
Keith Jarrett	Expectations	Columbia PG 31580
Keith Jarrett	Facing You	ECM 1017
Keith Jarrett	Fort Yawuh	Impulse Q 9240
Keith Jarrett	Hymns—Spheres	ECM 1086
Keith Jarrett	Impulse Artists on Tour	Impulse Q 9264
Keith Jarrett	Impulsively	Impulse Q 9266
Keith Jarrett	In the Light	ECM 1033-34
Keith Jarrett	El Juicio	Atlantic 1673
Keith Jarrett	Koln Concert	ECM 1064-65
Keith Jarrett	Luminescence	ECM 1049
Keith Jarrett	Mourning of a Star	Atlantic 1596
Keith Jarrett	Mysteries	Impulse 9315
Keith Jarrett	Piano Giants	Prestige 24052
Keith Jarrett	The Progressives	Columbia CG 31574
Keith Jarrett	Ruta & Daity	ECM 1021
Keith Jarrett	Shades	Impulse 9322
Keith Jarrett	Solo Concerts	ECM 1035-37
Keith Jarrett	Treasure Island	Impulse Q 9274

AS SIDEMAN WITH:

Miles Davis	Miles Davis at the Fillmore	Columbia (2) CG 30038
Miles Davis	Live-Evil	Columbia (2) G 30954
Miles Davis	Get Up with It	Columbia 2 KG 33236
Charles Lloyd	Dream Weaver	Atlantic SD 1459

Charles Lloyd	Forest Flower	Atlantic SD 1473
Charles Lloyd	Journey Within	Atlantic SD 1493 (out of print)
Charles Lloyd	Soundtrack	Atlantic SD 1519 (out of print)
Charles Lloyd	Best of Charles Lloyd	Atlantic SD 1556
Kenny Wheeler	Gnu Hi	ECM 1069
Paul Motian	Conception Vessel	ECM 1028

ALPHONSO JOHNSON

AS LEADER:	TITLE	LABEL & NO.
Alphonso Johnson	Moonshadows	Epic PE 34118
Alphonso Johnson	Yesterday's Dreams	Epic PE 34364
Alphonso Johnson	Spellbound	Epic JE 34869

AS SIDEMAN WITH:

Cannonball Adderley	Lovers	Fantasy F 9505
Angelle Troslain	Angelle	Epic PE 34836
Chet Baker	You Can't Go Home Again	Horizon SP 726
Norman Connors	You Are My Starship	Buddha 06-98
George Duke	The Aura Will Prevail	MPS/BASF MC 25613
George Duke	Liberated Fantasies	MPS/BASF G 22835
Cobham/Duke Band	Live on Tour in Europe	Atlantic SD 18194
Eddie Henderson	Sunburst	Blue Note LA 464
Allan Holdsworth	Velvet Darkness	CTI 6068
Quincy Jones	I Heard That	A&MM SP 3705
Chuck Mangione	Land of Make Believe	Mercury SRM 1-684
Lee Ritenour	Captain Fingers	Epic PE 34426
Weather Report	Mysterious Traveler	Columbia KC 32494
Weather Report	Tale Spinnin'	Columbia PC 33417
Weather Report	Black Market	Columbia PC 34099
John McLaughlin	Johnny McLaughlin/ Electric Guitarist	Columbia JC 35326

STEVE KHAN

AS LEADER:	TITLE	LABEL & NO.
Steve Khan	Tightrope	Tappan Zee/Columbia JC 34857
Steve Khan with Larry Coryell	Two for the Road	Arista AB 4156

AS SIDEMAN WITH:

Larry Coryell	Level One	Arista AL 4052
Larry Coryell	Aspects	Arista AL 4077
Brecker Brothers	Back to Back	Arista AL 4061

Brecker Brothers	**Don't Stop the Music**	Arista AL 4122
David Sanborn	**Taking Off**	Warner Bros. BS 2873
Steve Marcus	**Sometime Other Than Now**	Flying Dutchman 1461
Grover Washington, Jr.	**A Secret Place**	Kudu 32
George Benson/Joe Farrell	**Benson & Farrell**	CTI 6069
Joe Beck	**Beck**	Kudu 21
Maynard Ferguson	**New Vintage**	Columbia JC 34971
Freddie Hubbard	**Windjammer**	Columbia PC 34166
Hubert Laws	**Romeo & Juliet**	Columbia 34330
Various Artists	**Montreux Summit, Vol. I**	Columbia PC 35005
Various Artists	**Montreux Summit, Vol. II**	Columbia JG 35090
Mark Colby	**Mark Colby**	Columbia JC 35298
Walter Bishop, Jr.	**Soul Village**	Muse 5142
Bob James	**Heads**	Tappan Zee/ Columbia JC 34896
Michal Urbaniak	**Fusion**	Columbia KC 32852
Buddy Rich	**Plays, and Plays**	RCA 2273
David Matthews	**Shoogie Wanna Boogie**	Kudu 30
Clive Stevens	**Atmospheres**	Capitol 11263
Wilton Felder	**Bulitt**	Pacific Jazz 20152
Phil Moore, Jr.	**Right On**	Atlantic 1530
Steely Dan	**Aja**	ABC AB 1006
Phoebe Snow	**Never Letting Go**	Columbia JC 34875
Kenny Loggins	**Celebrate Me Home**	Columbia PC 34655
Billy Joel	**The Stranger**	Columbia JC 34987
Ashford & Simpson	**So So Satisfied**	Warner Bros. BS 2992
Ashford & Simpson	**Send It**	Warner Bros. BS 3008
Esther Phillips	**What a Difference a Day Makes**	Kudu KU 23
Esther Phillips	**For All We Know**	Kudu KU 28
Esther Phillips	**Capricorn Princess**	Kudu 31
James Brown	**Hot**	Polydor 6059
Luther Allison	**Night Life**	Gordy 974
Phillipe Wynne	**Starting All Over**	Cotillion 9920
Felix Cavaliere	**Destiny**	Bearsville 6958
Blood, Sweat & Tears	**Live**	CBS 22006
Blood, Sweat & Tears	**More Than Ever**	Columbia PC 34233
Martin Mull	**I'm Everyone I've Ever Loved**	ABC 997
D. C. Larue	**The Tea Dance**	Pyramid 9006
Tim Buckley	**Blue Afternoon**	Straight 1060
Patti Austin	**End of a Rainbow**	CTI 5001

Patti Austin	**Havana Candy**	CTI 75006

JOHN KLEMMER

AS LEADER:	TITLE	LABEL & NO.
John Klemmer	**Involvement**	Cadet LP/LPS 797
John Klemmer	**And We Were Lovers**	Cadet LPS 808
John Klemmer	**Blowin' Gold**	Cadet Concept LPS 321
John Klemmer	**All the Children Cried**	Cadet Concept LPS 326
John Klemmer	**Eruptions**	Cadet Concept LPS 330
John Klemmer	**Constant Throb**	Impulse AS 9214
John Klemmer	**Waterfalls**	Impulse AS 9220
John Klemmer	**Intensity**	Impulse AS 9244
John Klemmer	**Magic and Movement**	Impulse AS 9269
John Klemmer	**Fresh Feathers**	ABCD 836
John Klemmer	**Touch**	ABCD 922
John Klemmer	**Barefoot Ballet**	ABCD 950
John Klemmer	**Lifestyle**	AB 1007
John Klemmer	**Scorpion**	ABC (out of print)
John Klemmer	**Cry**	ABC Impulse (out of print)

AS SIDEMAN WITH:

Dave Remington/Big Band	**Chicago Shouts!**	Universal 76835 S
Oliver Nelson/Steve Allen	**Soulful Brass #2**	Flying Dutchman FDS 101
Oliver Nelson	**Black, Brown and Beautiful**	Flying Dutchman FDS 116
Don Ellis	**Autumn**	Columbia CS 9721
Don Ellis	**The Band Goes Underground**	Columbia CS 9889
Don Ellis	**Don Ellis at the Fillmore**	Columbia G 30243
John Lee Hooker	**Born in Mississippi, Raised Up In Tennessee**	ABCX 768
Ray Manzarek	**The Whole Thing Started with Rock & Roll and Now It's Out of Control**	Mercury SRM 1-1014
Various Artists	**The Drums**	ABC Impulse ASH 9272
Freda Payne	**Out of Payne Comes Love**	ABCD 901
Gloria Lynne	**I Don't Know How to Love Him**	ABC Impulse ASD 9311
Catherine M. Lord	**C. M. Lord**	Capitol ST 11514
Steely Dan	**The Royal Scam**	ABCD 931
Roy Haynes	**Thank You, Thank You**	Galaxy GXY 5103
Terence Boylan	**Terence Boylan**	Asylum 7E1091
Hal Gordon	**Inner Strength**	Pelican SE 1002-B
Bobby Bryant	**Swahili Strut**	Cadet CA 50011

EARL KLUGH

AS LEADER:	TITLE	LABEL & NO.
Earl Klugh	**Earl Klugh**	Blue Note LA 596-G
Earl Klugh	**Living Inside Your Love**	Blue Note BN LA 667-G
Earl Klugh	**Finger Paintings**	Blue Note LA 737-H
Earl Klugh	**Blue Note Live at the Roxy**	Blue Note LA 663-J2

AS SIDEMAN WITH:		
George Benson	**White Rabbit**	CTI 6015
George Benson	**Body Talk**	CTI 6033
Flora Purim	**Stories to Tell**	Milestone M 9058
Dramatics	**Drama V**	ABC D916
Noel Pointer	**Phantasia**	Blue Note LA 763-8
McCoy Tyner	**Inner Voices**	Milestone M 9079

RONNIE LAWS

AS LEADER:	TITLE	LABEL & NO.
Ronnie Laws/Various Artists	**Blue Note Live at the Roxy**	Blue Note LA 663-J2
Ronnie Laws	**Fever**	Blue Note LA 628-G
Ronnie Laws	**Friends & Strangers**	Blue Note LA 730-H
Ronnie Laws	**Pressure Sensitive**	Blue Note LA 452-G

AS SIDEMAN WITH:		
Earth, Wind & Fire	**Last Days in Time**	Columbia C 31702

JOHN LEE

AS LEADER:	TITLE	LABEL & NO.
John Lee/Gerry Brown	**Infinite Jones**	Keytone KT 444056
John Lee/Gerry Brown	**Mango Sunrise**	Blue Note LA 541G
John Lee/Gerry Brown	**Still Can't Say Enough**	Blue Note BN LA 701G
John Lee/Gerry Brown and Various Artists	**Blue Note Live at the Roxy**	Blue Note LA 663-J2

AS SIDEMAN WITH:		
Bruce Fisher	**Red Hot**	Mercury SRM 1-1168
Philip Catherine	**September Man**	Atlantic 40562
Philip Catherine	**Guitars**	Atlantic 50193
Philip Catherine	**Niram**	Warner Bros. BS 2950
Joachim Kuhn	**Cinemascope**	MPS/BASF 21-22270-5
Joachim Kuhn / Alphonse Mouzon	**Hip Elegy**	MPS/BASF G22794
Joachim Kuhn	**Spring Fever**	Atlantic ATL 50280
Eleventh House	**Level One**	Arista 4052
Eleventh House	**Aspects**	Arista AL 4077
Coryell/Mouzon	**Back Together Again**	Atlantic SD 18220
Charlie Mariano	**Cascade**	Keytone KT 444054
Chris Hinze	**Sister Slick**	Columbia CBS 80271
Art Webb	**Love Eyes**	Atlantic SD 18226
Jeremy Steig, James Moody, & Chris Hinze	**Flute Summit**	Atlantic 50 027
Piano Conclave	**Piano Conclave**	MPS/BASF 20 227863
Zbigniew Seifert	**Zbigniew Seifert**	Capitol ST 11618
Jasper Van't Hof	**Eyeball**	Keytone KT 444055
Chris Hinze	**Mission Suite**	MPS 21 29 177-4
Carlos Garnett	**New Love**	Muse 5133

WILL LEE

AS SIDEMAN WITH:		
Maynard Ferguson	**Conquistador**	Columbia 34457
Narada Michael Walden	**Garden of Love Light**	Atlantic SD 18199
Deodata	**First Cuckoo**	MCA 491
Deodata	**Very Together**	MCA 2219
Joe Beck	**Beck**	Kudu 21
Sonny Stitt	**Never Can Say Goodbye**	Cadet 60040 (out of print)
Dreams	**Imagine My Surprise**	Columbia C 30960
Art Farmer	**Crawl Space**	CTI 7073
Lalo Schifrin	**Towering Toccata**	CTI 5003
Barry Manilow	**Barry Manilow II**	Arista 7006
Barry Manilow	**This One's For You**	Arista 7008
Bob James	**Three**	CTI 6063
Bob James	**Heads**	Tappan Zee/Columbia JC 34896
Carole Bayer Sager	**Carole Bayer Sager**	Elektra 1100
Gloria Gaynor	**I've Got You**	Polydor 6063
Elliott Randall	**Elliott Randall's New York**	Kirshner 3435
Lonnie Smith	**Keep on Movin'**	Groove Merchant 3312
Pat Martino	**Starbright**	Warner Bros. BS 2921
Laura Nyro	**Smile**	Columbia PC 33912
Steve Satten	**Watcha Gonna Do for Me?**	Columbia PC 33478 (out of print)
Johnny Carson	**Magic Moments from Tonight Show**	Casa Blanca 1296 (out of print)
Weather Report	**I Sing the Body Electric**	Columbia 31352
Herbie Mann	**Waterbed**	Atlantic SD 1676

Mike Mainieri	**Love Play**	Arista AB 4113
Roy Buchanan	**A Street Called Straight**	Atlantic 18170
Roy Buchanan	**Loading Zone**	Atlantic 18219
Vickie Sue Robinson	**Half and Half**	RCA APL 1-2294
Patti Austin	**End of a Rainbow**	CTI 5001
Patti Austin	**Havana Candy**	CTI 7-5006
John Tropea	**Tropea**	Marlin 2200
John Tropea	**Short Trip to Space**	Marlin 2204
Odyssey	**Odyssey**	RCA APL 1-2204A
Burt Bacharach	**Futures**	A&M 4622
Tom Scott	**Blow It Out**	Ode (Epic) 34966
New York Community Choir	**The New York Community Choir**	RCA APL 1-2293
Libby Titus	**Libb Titus**	Columbia 34152
Steve Goodman	**Say It in Private**	Asylum 1118
Brecker Brothers	**Brecker Brothers**	Arista AL 4037
Brecker Brothers	**Back to Back**	Arista AL 4061
Brecker Brothers	**Don't Stop the Music**	Arista AL 4122
Phoebe Snow	**Second Childhood**	Columbia PC 33952
Phoebe Snow	**Never Letting Go**	Columbia JC 34875
Steve Marcus	**Sometime Other Than Now**	Flying Dutchman BDL 1-1461
Meco Star Wars	**And Other Galactic Funk**	Millennium 8001
R. B. Greaves	**R. B. Greaves**	Bareback 3333
Grant Green	**The Main Attraction**	CTI (out of print)
Mark Radice	**Intense**	Road Show LA 788-G (out of print)
Esther Phillips	**What a Difference a Day Makes**	Kudu KU 23
Esther Phillips	**For All We Know**	Kudu KU 28
Don Sebesky	**The Rape of El Morro**	CTI 6061
Buddy Rich	**Plays, and Plays**	RCA 1-2273
George Benson	**In Concert—Carnegie Hall**	CTI 6072
George Benson/Joe Farrell	**Benson & Farrell**	CTI 6069
Steve Khan	**Tightrope**	Tappan Zee/Columbia JC 34857
Grady Tate	**Master Grady Tate**	ABC 9390 (Impulse)
Earl Klugh	**Living Inside Your Love**	Blue Note BN LA 667-G
Noel Pointer	**Phantasia**	Blue Note (UA) LA 336
Ralph MacDonald	**The Path**	TK Marlin 2210

ON MOVIE SOUNDTRACKS:

	Carrie	United Artists LA 716-8
	Bobby Deerfield	Casablanca 7071

DAVID LIEBMAN

AS LEADER:	TITLE	LABEL & NO.
Dave Liebman	**Lookout Farm**	ECM 1039 ST
Dave Liebman	**Drum Ode**	ECM 1046
Dave Liebman	**Sweet Hands**	A&M 702
Dave Liebman	**Forgotten Fantasies**	A&M 709
Dave Liebman	**Light'n Up Please!**	A&M 721
Dave Liebman	**Night Scapes**	CBS Sony (Japan)
Dave Liebman	**First Visit**	Phonogram/Philips (Japan)

AS SIDEMAN WITH:		
Miles Davis	**On the Corner**	Columbia PC 31906
Miles Davis	**Get Up with It**	Columbia PC 33236
Miles Davis	**Dark Magus**	CBS/Sony (Japan)
Elvin Jones	**Genesis**	Blue Note 84369
Elvin Jones	**Live at the Lighthouse**	Blue Note LA 015-G-2
Elvin Jones (with Chick Corea)	**Merry-Go-Round**	Blue Note 84414 (out of print)
Elvin Jones	**Mr. Jones**	Blue Note LA 110-G
John McLaughlin	**My Goal's Beyond**	Douglas AD 6003
Lars Werner	**Och Hans Vanner**	Love (Sweden)
10 Wheel Drive	**Brief Replies**	Polydor 244024 (out of print)
10 Wheel Drive	**Peculiar Friends**	Polydor 244062 (out of print)
Terumasa Hino	**Hino's Journey to Air**	Love (Japan)
Esther Phillips	**From a Whisper to a Scream**	Kudu 05 (out of print)
Open Sky Trio	**Open Sky**	P.M. 001
Open Sky Trio	**Spirit in the Sky**	P.M. 003
Badal Roy	**Ashiribad**	Trio (Japan)
Badal Roy	**Passing Dreams**	Atmo Records
Link Chamberlain	**Link Chamberlain**	Muse MRS 064
Frank Tusa	**Father Time**	Enja (Germany)
Fred Thompkins	**Somesville**	Festival 9002
Bob Moses	**Bittersuite in the Ozone**	Mozown MZ 001
Prince Igor Yahilevich	**From Russia with Love**	Different Drummer DD 1002

RALPH MacDONALD

AS LEADER:	TITLE	LABEL & NO.
Ralph MacDonald	**Sound of a Drum**	Marlin 2202
Ralph MacDonald	**The Path**	TK Marlin 2210
Grover Washington, Jr.	**Mr. Magic**	Kudu 20

Grover Washington, Jr.	**All the King's Horses**	Kudu 07
Grover Washington, Jr.	**Feels So Good**	Kudu KU 24-sl
George Benson	**Breezin'**	Warner Bros. 2919
George Benson	**In Flight**	Warner Bros. BK 2983
George Benson	**Weekend in L.A.**	Warner Bros. 2WB 3139
Bob James	**One**	CTI 6043
Bob James	**Two**	CTI 6057
Bob James	**Three**	CTI 6063
Bob James	**BJ 4**	CTI 6074
Bob James	**Heads**	Tappan Zee/Columbia JC 34896
Tom Scott	**New York Connection**	Ode PE 34959
Tom Scott	**Blow It Out**	Ode PE 34966
Crusaders	**Free as the Wind**	ABC BT 6029
Average White Band	**Average White Band**	Atlantic SD 7308
Ashford & Simpson	**Come As You Are**	Warner Bros. BS 2858
Ashford & Simpson	**Gimme Something Real**	Warner Bros. BS 2739
Ashford & Simpson	**I Wanna Be Selfish**	Warner Bros. BS 2789
Ashford & Simpson	**Send It**	Warner Bros. BS 3008
Ashford & Simpson	**So So Satisfied**	Warner Bros. BS 2992
Chuck Mangione	**Main Squeeze**	A&M SP 4612
Brothers Johnson	**Look Out for #1**	A&M 4567
Brothers Johnson	**Right on Time**	A&M 4644
Quincy Jones	**Mellow Madness**	A&M 4526
Roberta Flack	**Killing Me Softly**	Atlantic 7271
Roberta Flack	**Quiet Fire**	Atlantic SD 1594
Roberta Flack	**Feel Like Makin' Love**	Atlantic 18131
Roberta Flack & Donny Hathaway	**Donny Hathaway & Roberta Flack**	Atlantic SD 7216
Paul Simon	**Still Crazy After All These Years**	Columbia PC 33540
Paul Simon	**Paul Simon's Greatest Hits**	Columbia JC 35032
Don Sebesky	**Giant Box**	CTI X 6031-32
Freddie Hubbard	**Windjammer**	Columbia PC 34166
Esther Phillips	**What a Difference a Day Makes**	Kudu KU 23
Eric Gale	**Multiplication**	Columbia JC 34938
Eric Gale	**Ginseng Woman**	Columbia PC 34421
Eric Gale	**Forecast**	Kudu KU 11
Joe Farrell	**La Catedral y el Toro**	Warner Bros. BS 3121
William Salter	**It's So Beautiful to Me**	Marlin 2205
John Tropea	**Short Trip to Space**	Marlin 2204

Roland Kirk	**Bright Moments**	Atlantic (*out of print*)

JOHN McLAUGHLIN

AS LEADER:	TITLE	LABEL & NO.
John McLaughlin	**Devotion**	Columbia C 32034
John McLaughlin	**My Goal's Beyond**	Douglas AD 6003
John McLaughlin	**Extrapolation**	Polydor PD 5510
Mahavishnu Orchestra	**Inner Mounting Flame**	Columbia KC 31067
Mahavishnu Orchestra	**Birds of Fire**	Columbia KC 31996
Mahavishnu Orchestra	**Between Nothingness and Eternity**	Columbia C 32766
Mahavishnu Orchestra	**Apocalypse**	Columbia KC 32957
Mahavishnu Orchestra	**Visions of the Emerald Beyond**	Columbia PC 33411
Mahavishnu Orchestra	**Inner Worlds**	Columbia PC 33908
John McLaughlin	**Shakti with John McLaughlin**	Columbia PC 34162
Shakti with John McLaughlin	**A Handful of Beauty**	Columbia PC 34372
Shakti with John McLaughlin	**Natural Elements**	Columbia JC 34980
John McLaughlin with Carlos Santana	**Love Devotion Surrender**	Columbia C 32034
John McLaughlin	**Johnny McLaughlin/ Electric Guitarist**	Columbia JC 35326

AS SIDEMAN WITH:		
Miles Davis	**In a Silent Way**	Columbia PC 9875
Miles Davis	**Bitches' Brew**	Columbia PG 26
Miles Davis	**Jack Johnson**	Columbia PC 30455
Miles Davis	**Live-Evil**	Columbia CG 30954
Tony Williams	**Emergency I**	Polydor 25-3001
Tony Williams	**Emergency II**	Polydor 24-4017
Stanley Clarke	**School Days**	Nemperor NE 439
Stanley Clarke	**Journey to Love**	Nemperor NE 433
Graham Bond	**Solid Bond**	Warner Bros. 2555
Jack Bruce	**Things We Like**	Atco SD 33349
John Surman	**Where Fortune Smiles**	Pye PYE 12103
Miroslav Vitous	**Mountain in the Clouds**	Atlantic 1622
Wayne Shorter	**Super Nova**	Blue Note 84332
Larry Coryell	**Spaces**	Vanguard 6558

MIKE MAINIERI

AS LEADER:	TITLE	LABEL & NO.
Mike Mainieri	**Insight**	Solid State SS 18029
Mike Mainieri	**Journey Through an Electric Tube**	Solid State SS 18049
Mike Mainieri	**Love Play**	Arista AL 4113
Mike Mainieri	**White Elephant**	Just Sunshine JSS 3000
Mike Mainieri	**Blues on the Other Side**	Argo (*out of print*)

AS SIDEMAN WITH:		
Bob James	**Heads**	Tappan Zee/Columbia JC 34896
Buddy Rich	**Playtime and Caravan were combined on the album: Both Sides**	Argo and Mercury Mercury EMS 2-402
Laura Nyro	**Season of Light**	Columbia 34786
Nick Holmes	**Soulful Crooner**	Just Sunshine JSS 3
Paul Desmond	**Sky Lark**	CTI 6039
Urbie Green	**Señor Blues**	CTI 7079
David Spinozza	**Spinozza**	A&M SP 4677
Art Farmer/Jim Hall	**Big Blues**	CTI 7083

CHUCK MANGIONE

AS LEADER:	TITLE	LABEL & NO.
Chuck Mangione	**Friends and Love**	Mercury SRM 2-800
Chuck Mangione	**Friends and Love Highlights**	Mercury SRM 1-681
Chuck Mangione	**Together**	Mercury SRM 2-7501
Chuck Mangione	**The Chuck Mangione Quartet**	Mercury SRM 1-631
Chuck Mangione	**Alive!**	Mercury SRM 1-650
Chuck Mangione	**Land of Make Believe**	Mercury SRM 1-684
Chuck Mangione	**Encore**	Mercury SRM 1-1050
Chuck Mangione	**Jazz Brothers**	Milestone M 47042
Chuck Mangione	**Chase the Clouds Away**	A&M SP 4518
Chuck Mangione	**Bellavia**	A&M SP 4557
Chuck Mangione	**Main Squeeze**	A&M SP 4612
Chuck Mangione	**Nadia's Theme**	A&M SP 3412
Chuck Mangione	**Feels So Good**	A&M SP 4658

AS PRODUCER:		
Gap Mangione	**She and I**	A&M SP 3407
Gap Mangione	**Gap Mangione!**	A&M SP 4621
Esther Satterfield	**Once I Loved**	A&M SP 3408
Esther Satterfield	**The Need to Be**	A&M SP 3411

PAT MARTINO

AS LEADER:	TITLE	LABEL & NO.
Pat Martino	**Exit**	Muse MR 5075
Pat Martino	**Starbright**	Warner Bros. BS 2921
Pat Martino	**Joyous Lake**	Warner Bros. BS 2977
Pat Martino	**Strings**	Prestige 7547
Pat Martino	**East**	Prestige 7562
Pat Martino	**El Hombre**	Prestige 7513
Pat Martino	**Desperado**	Prestige 7795
Pat Martino	**The Visit (re-release as Footprints)**	Cobblestone 9015
Pat Martino	**Live**	Muse 5026
Pat Martino	**Consciousness**	Muse 5039
Pat Martino	**Baiyina**	Prestige 7589

AS SIDEMAN WITH:		
Eric Kloss	**Consciousness**	Prestige PR 7793
Eric Kloss	**1 2 3**	Muse 5019
Eric Kloss	**Introducing Eric Kloss**	Prestige 7442
Stanley Clarke	**Children of Forever**	Polydor PD 5531
Barry Miles	**White Heat**	Mainstream MRL 353
John Handy	**New View**	Columbia CS 9497
Woody Herman	**The Raven Speaks**	Fantasy 9416
Sonny Stitt	**The Night Letter**	Prestige 7759
John Patterson	**These Are the Soulful Days**	Muse 5032

ALPHONSE MOUZON

AS LEADER:	TITLE	LABEL & NO.
Alphonse Mouzon	**The Drums**	Impulse 9272
Alphonse Mouzon	**Essence of Mystery**	Blue Note BN LA 059-6
Alphonse Mouzon	**Funky Snakefoot**	Blue Note BN LA 222-G
Alphonse Mouzon	**The Man Incognito**	Blue Note LA 584-6
Alphonse Mouzon	**Mind Transplant**	Blue Note LA 398-6
Alphonse Mouzon/ Larry Coryell	**Back Together Again**	Atlantic SD 18220
Alphonse Mouzon	**Virtue**	MPS 15498
Alphonse Mouzon	**Blue Note Live at the Roxy**	Blue Note LA 663-J2
Alphonse Mouzon	**In Search of a Dream**	MPS (1978)
Joachim Kuhn/ Alphonse Mouzon	**Hip Elegy**	MPS/BASF G 22794

AS SIDEMAN WITH:

Weather Report	**Weather Report**	Columbia KC 30661
Eleventh House	**Introducing The Eleventh House**	Vanguard VSD 79342
Eleventh House	**Level One**	Arista AL 4052
McCoy Tyner	**Sahara**	Milestone 9039
McCoy Tyner	**Song for My Lady**	Milestone 9044
McCoy Tyner	**Song of the New World**	Milestone 9049
McCoy Tyner	**Enlightenment**	Milestone 5501
Roberta Flack	**Feel Like Makin' Love**	Columbia KC 33297
Patrick Moraz	**I**	Atlantic 18175
Al DiMeola	**Land of the Midnight Sun**	Columbia 34074
Danny Tone	**First Serve**	Embryo 535

JACO PASTORIUS

AS LEADER:	TITLE	LABEL & NO.
Jaco Pastorius	**Jaco Pastorius**	Epic PE 33949

AS SIDEMAN WITH:

Weather Report	**Heavy Weather**	Columbia PC 34418
Weather Report	**Black Market**	Columbia PC 34099
Joni Mitchell	**Hejira**	Asylum 7E 1087
Joni Mitchell	**Don Juan's Reckless Daughter**	Asylum BB 701
Pat Metheny	**Bright Size Life**	ECM 1073
Ira Sullivan	**Ira Sullivan**	Horizon SP 706
Ira Hunter	**All American Alien Boy**	Columbia PC 34142
Pastorius/Metheny/Ditmas/Bley	**Pastorius/Metheny/Ditmas/Bley**	Improvising Artists 373846
Little Beaver	**Party Down**	Cat Records
Albert Mangellsdorff	**Trilogue Live at the Berlin Jazz Days**	MPS 00 68.175
Airto (Moreira)	**I'm Fine, How Are You**	Warner Bros. B 3084

JEAN-LUC PONTY

AS LEADER:	TITLE	LABEL & NO.
Jean-Luc Ponty	**Jean-Luc Ponty Jazz Long Playing**	Phillips 77810 L
Jean-Luc Ponty	**Sunday Walk**	MPS/BASF
Jean-Luc Ponty	**More Than Meets the Ear**	World Pacific Jazz ST 20134
Jean-Luc Ponty	**Electric Connection**	World Pacific Jazz ST 20156
Jean-Luc Ponty	**The Jean-Luc Ponty Experience**	World Pacific Jazz ST 20168
Jean-Luc Ponty	**King Kong**	World Pacific Jazz ST 20172
Jean-Luc Ponty	**Open Strings**	MPS/BASF 2121288-2
Jean-Luc Ponty	**Upon the Wings of Music**	Atlantic SD 18138
Jean-Luc Ponty	**Aurora**	Atlantic SD 18163
Jean-Luc Ponty	**Imaginary Voyage**	Atlantic SD 18195
Jean-Luc Ponty	**Enigmatic Ocean**	Atlantic SD 19110
Jean-Luc Ponty/Stephane Grapelli	**Jean-Luc Ponty—Stephane Grappelli**	American Inner City IC 1005

AS SIDEMAN WITH:

Various Artists	**Violin Summit/Wolfgang Dauner and George Gruntz**	MPS/BASF Saba 15099 ST
Various Artists	**New Violin Summit**	MPS/BASF
Elton John	**Honky Chateau**	MCA 2017
Frank Zappa	**Overnight Sensation**	DiscReet MS 2149
Mahavishnu Orchestra	**Apocalypse**	CBS KC 32957
Mahavishnu Orchestra	**Visions of the Emerald Beyond**	CBS PC 33411

FLORA PURIM

AS LEADER:	TITLE	LABEL & NO.
Flora Purim	**Butterfly Dreams**	Milestone M 9052
Flora Purim	**Stories to Tell**	Milestone M 9058
Flora Purim	**Open Your Eyes You Can Fly**	Milestone M 9065
Flora Purim	**500 Miles High in Montreux**	Milestone 9070
Flora Purim	**Nothing Will Be as It Was ...Tomorrow**	Warner Bros. 2985
Flora Purim	**Encounter**	Milestone 9077
Flora Purim	**That's What She Said**	Milestone M 9081/
Flora Purim	**Everyday, Everynight**	Warner Bros. BSK 3168

AS SIDEWOMAN WITH:

Airto	**Essential**	Buddha 5668
Airto	**Natural Feelings**	Sky/Buddha 21-SK (out of print)
Airto	**Seeds on the Ground**	Buddha 5085
Airto	**Promises of the Sun**	Arista 4116
Airto	**Identity**	Arista 4068
Airto	**Virgin Land**	CTI/Salvation SAL 701
Airto	**I'm Fine, How Are You**	Warner Bros. B 3084
Hermeto Pascoal	**Slave's Mass**	Warner Bros. 2980
Chick Corea	**Return to Forever**	ECM 1022
Return to Forever	**Light as a Feather**	Polydor PD 5525
George Duke	**Feel**	MPS/BASF MC 25355
Santana	**Welcome**	Columbia PC 32445

Santana	**Borboletta**	Columbia PC 33135
Duke Pearson	**How Insensitive**	United Artists (*out of print*)
Duke Pearson	**It Could Only Happen With You**	United Artists (*out of print*)

PATRICE RUSHEN

AS LEADER:	TITLE	LABEL & NO.
Patrice Rushen	**Before the Dawn**	Prestige 10098
Patrice Rushen	**Preclusion**	Prestige 10089
Patrice Rushen	**Shout It Out**	Prestige 10101

AS SIDEWOMAN WITH:		
Lee Ritenour	**Captain Fingers**	Epic PE 34426
Lee Ritenour	**First Course**	Epic PE 33947
Lisa Dal Bello	**Lisa Dal Bello**	MCA 2249
Flora Purim	**Nothing Will Be as It Was ...Tomorrow**	Warner Bros. 2985
Eddie Henderson	**Heritage**	Blue Note LA 636-G
Eddie Henderson	**Comin' on Through**	Capitol ST 11671
Harvey Mason	**Earth Mover**	Arista 4096
Bennie Maupin	**Slow Traffic to the Right**	Mercury SRM 1-1148
Donald Byrd	**Caricatures**	Blue Note LA 633-G
Sonny Rollins	**That's the Way I Feel**	Milestone 9074
John McLaughlin	**Johnny McLaughlin/ Electric Guitarist**	Columbia JC 35326

TOM SCOTT

AS LEADER:	TITLE	LABEL & NO.
Tom Scott	**Honeysuckle Breeze**	Impulse A 9163
Tom Scott	**Rural Still Life**	Impulse A 9171
Tom Scott Quartet	**"Hair" to Jazz**	Flying Dutchman
Tom Scott Quartet	**Paint Your Wagon**	Flying Dutchman
Tom Scott	**Great Scott**	A&M 4330
Tom Scott & the L.A. Express	**Tom Scott & the L.A. Express**	ODE PE 34952
Tom Scott & the L.A. Express	**Tom Cat**	ODE PE 34956
Tom Scott	**New York Connection**	Ode PE 34959
Tom Scott	**Blow It Out**	Ode PE 34966

AS SIDEMAN WITH:		
Airto (Moreira)	**I'm Fine, How Are You**	Warner Bros. B 3084
Norman Connors	**You Are My Starship**	Buddha 5655
Don Ellis Big Band	**Live at Monterey**	Pacific Jazz
Don Ellis Big Band	**Live in ? Time**	Pacific Jazz
Victor Feldman Quartet	**Your Smile**	Choice 1005
Herbie Hancock	**Death Wish (sound track)**	Columbia 33199
Quincy Jones	**I Heard That!!**	A&M 3705
Roger Kellaway Quartet	**Spirit Feel**	Pacific Jazz
Harvey Mason	**Funk in a Mason Jar**	Arist AB 4157
Earl Klugh	**Finger Paintings**	Blue Note BN LA 737-H
Thelonius Monk	**Monk's Blues**	Columbia CS 9806
Gerry Mulligan	**Age of Steam**	A&M 3036
Oliver Nelson Big Band	**Live from Los Angeles**	Impulse 9153
Howard Roberts Quintet	**Spinning Wheeel**	Capitol
Lee Ritenour	**First Course**	Epic PE 33947
Patrice Rushen	**Shout It Out**	Prestige 10101
Pat Williams	**Threshold**	Capitol ST 11242
Joan Baez	**Blowin' Away**	Portrait PR 34697
Eric Carmen	**Boats Against the Current**	Arista 4124
Carpenters	**Passage**	A&M 4703
Cecilio & Kapono	**Night Music**	Columbia PC 34300
Michel Colombier	**Wings**	A&M 3503
Neil Diamond	**I'm Glad You're Here with Me Tonite**	Columbia JC 34990
Les Dudek	**Les Dudek**	Columbia PC 33702
Arethra Franklin	**You**	Atlantic 18151
Grateful Dead	**Terrapin Station**	Arista 7001
Darryl Hall & John Oates	**Bigger than Both of Us**	RCA AFL 1-1467
George Harrison	**33 & 1/3**	Dark Horse 3005
Carole King	**Wrap Around Joy**	Ode 77024
Roger McGuinn	**Thunderbird**	Columbia PC 34656
Sergio Mendes	**Primal Roots**	A&M 4353
Joni Mitchell	**For the Roses**	Asylum 5057
Joni Mitchell	**Court and Spark**	Asylum 1001
Joni Mitchell & the L.A. Express	**Miles of Aisles**	Asylum AB 202
Randy Newman	**Randy Newman**	Reprise 6286
Billy Preston	**Music Is My Life**	A&M 3516
Johnny Rivers	**Outside Help**	Soul City 76004
Leo Sayer	**Endless Flight**	Warner Bros. K 3101
Boz Scaggs	**Silk Degrees**	Columbia JC 33920
Doc Severinsen	**Brand New Thying**	Epic PE 34925
Ringo Starr	**Ringo**	Capitol SWAL 3413

Steely Dan	**Aja**	ABC AB 1006
Barbra Streisand	**Butterfly**	Columbia PC 33005
Barbra Streisand	**A Star Is Born**	Columbia JS 34403
Paul Williams	**Just and Old-Fashioned Love Song**	A&M 4327
Paul McCartney & Wings	**At the Speed of Sound**	Capitol SMAS 11419
Nancy Wilson	**All in Love Is Fair**	Capitol ST 11317
Ravi Shankar	**Ravi Shankar Family & Friends**	Dark Horse 3001

COMPOSER (sound tracks):

Bernard Hermann	**Taxi Driver**	Arista 4079
Michel Polnareff	**Listick**	Atlantic 18178
Dave Grusin	**Three Days of the Condor**	Capitol SW 11469
Michel Legrand	**Thomas Crown Affair**	United Artists LA 295-G

WAYNE SHORTER

AS LEADER:	TITLE	LABEL & NO.
Wayne Shorter	**Adam's Apple**	Blue Note 84232
Wayne Shorter	**All Seeing Eye**	Blue Note BST 84219
Wayne Shorter	**Free Form**	Blue Note 84118
Wayne Shorter	**Juju**	Blue Note 84182
Wayne Shorter	**Motto Grosso Feio**	Blue Note LA 014-G
Wayne Shorter w/ Milton Nasciemento	**Native Dancer**	Columbia 33418
Wayne Shorter	**Night Dreamer**	Blue Note 84173
Wayne Shorter	**Odyssey of Iska**	Blue Note BST 84363
Wayne Shorter	**Schizophrenia**	Blue Note BST 84297
Wayne Shorter	**Search for the New Land**	Blue Note 84169
Wayne Shorter	**Shorter Moments**	Blue Note X 5009
Wayne Shorter	**Wayne Shorter**	Crescendo 2-2075
Wayne Shorter	**Some Other Stuff**	Blue Note 84177
Wayne Shorter	**Speak No Evil**	Blue Note BST 84194
Wayne Shorter	**Super Nova**	Blue Note 84332
Weather Report	**Weather Report**	Columbia KC 30661
Weather Report	**Sweetnighter**	Columbia PC 32210
Weather Report	**I Sing the Body Electric**	Columbia PC 31352
Weather Report	**Tale Spinnin'**	Columbia PC 33417
Weather Report	**Mysterious Traveler**	Columbia PC 32494
Weather Report	**Black Market**	Columbia PC 34099
Weather Report	**Heavy Weather**	Columbia PC 34418

Wayne Shorter, Weather Report, and others	**The Progressives**	Columbia CG 31574
V.S.O.P.	**V.S.O.P.**	Columbia PC 34688
V.S.O.P.	**The Quintet/V.S.O.P. Live**	Columbia C 2-34976

AS SIDEMAN WITH:

Miles Davis	**Nefertiti**	Columbia CS 9594
Miles Davis	**ESP**	Columbia PC 9150
Miles Davis	**Filles de Kilimanjaro**	Columbia PC 9750
Miles Davis	**Miles in the Sky**	Columbia PC 9628
Miles Davis	**Miles Smiles**	Columbia CS 9401
Miles Davis	**My Funny Valentine**	Columbia PC 9106
Miles Davis	**Sorcerer**	Columbia CS 9532
Miles Davis	**Water Babies**	Columbia PC 34396
Miles Davis	**In a Silent Way**	Columbia CS 9875
Miles Davis	**Bitches' Brew**	Columbia PG 26 (GQ 30997)
Steely Dan	**Aja**	ABC AB 1006
Joni Mitchell	**Don Juan's Reckless Daughter**	Asylum DB 701
Art Blakey and the Jazz Messengers	**Art Blakey & the Jazz Messengers**	Impulse A (5)(7)
Art Blakey and the Jazz Messengers	**Big Beat**	Blue Note BLP 4029
Art Blakey and the Jazz Messengers	**Night in Tunsia**	Blue Note 4049
Art Blakey and the Jazz Messengers	**Meet You at the Jazz Corner of the World**	Vol. I Blue Note 4054 / Vol. II Blue Note 4055
Art Blakey and the Jazz Messengers	**Freedom Rider**	Blue Note 4156
Art Blakey and the Jazz Messengers	**Mosaic**	Blue Note 4090
Art Blakey	**Buhaina's Delight**	Blue Note 4104
Art Blakey	**Free for All**	Blue Note BLP 4170-84170
Art Blakey and the Jazz Messengers	**Indestructible**	Blue Note 4193
Art Blakey	**Caravan**	Riverside 6074
Freddie Hubbard	**Here to Stay**	Blue Note BN LA 496-H2
Lee Morgan	**Best of Birdland**	Roulette RB 2
Wynton Kelly	**Kelly Great**	Vee Jay 3004
Benny Golson	**Pop + Swing = Jazz**	Audio Fidelity AFLD 1978
Bobby Timmons	**Soul Man**	Prestige 7465
Lee Morgan	**Search for the New Land**	Blue Note BST 84164
Lee Morgan	**Delightfulee**	Blue Note BST 84243
Lee Morgan	**The Gigolo**	Blue Note BST 84212

Freddie Hubbard	**Ready for Freddie**	Blue Note BST 84085
Freddie Hubbard	**Body and Soul**	Impulse S 38
McCoy Tyner	**Expansions**	Blue Note 84338
McCoy Tyner	**Extensions**	Blue Note LA 006-G
Gil Evans	**The Individualism of Gil Evans**	Verve V6-8555
Gil Evans	**Previously Unreleased Recordings**	Verve 68838
Anthony Williams	**Spring**	Blue Note BST 84216
Donald Byrd	**Free Form**	Blue Note BST 84118
Freddie Hubbard	**Here to Stay**	Blue Note BST 84135

RICHARD TEE

AS SIDEMAN WITH:

Ashford & Simpson	**So So Satisfied**	Warner Bros. WB 2992
Ashford & Simpson	**Come As You Are**	Warner Bros. BS 2858
Patti Austin	**End of a Rainbow**	CTI 5001
Patti Austin	**Havana Candy**	CTI 7-5006
Joe Cocker	**Joe Cocker Greatest Hits**	A&M SP 4670
Joe Cocker	**I Can Stand a Little Rain**	A&M 3663
Joe Cocker	**Jamaica Say You Will**	A&M SP 4529
Joe Cocker	**Stingray ***	A&M SP 4574
Hank Crawford	**It's a Funky Thing to Do**	Cotillion SD 18003
Hank Crawford	**We Got a Good Thing Going**	Kudu KU 08
Hank Crawford	**Wildflower**	Kudu KU 15
Hank Crawford	**Don't You Worry 'Bout a Thing**	Kudu KU 19 S1
Hank Crawford	**I Hear a Symphony**	Kudu KU 26-sl
Hank Crawford	**Hank Crawford's Back**	Kudu KU 33-sl
Blondie Chaplin	**Blondie Chaplin**	Asylum 7E-1095
Wayne Davis	**Wayne Davis**	Atlantic SD 7258
Cornell Dupree	**Teasin' ***	Atlantic SD 7311
Jackie DeShannon	**Your Baby is a Lady**	Atlantic SD 7303
Dynamic Superiors	**Dynamic Superiors ***	Motown D5 RS 7853
William Eaton	**Struggle Bunny**	Marlin 2211
Joe Farrell	**La Catedral y el Toro**	Warner Bros. BS 3121
Roberta Flack	**Quiet Fire**	Atlantic SD 1594
Roberta Flack	**Killing Me Softly**	Atlantic SD 7271
Arethra Franklin	**Young, Gifted & Black**	Atlantic SD 7213
Arethra Franklin	**With Everything I Feel in Me**	Atlantic SD 181116
Arethra Franklin	**Let Me in Your Life**	Atlantic SD 7292
Arethra Franklin	**Arethra's Greatest Hits**	Atlantic SD 8295
Eric Gale	**Ginseng Woman**	Columbia BL 34421
Eric Gale	**Multiplication**	Columbia UC 34938
George Harrison	**33 & 1/3**	Dark Horse DH 3005
Quincy Jones	**Walking in Space**	A&M SP 3023
Quincy Jones	**Body Heat**	A&M SP 3617
Quincy Jones	**I Heard That**	A&M SP 3705
Quincy Jones	**Roots**	A&M SP 4626
Margie Joseph	**Margie Joseph**	Atlantic (out of print)
Margie Joseph	**Sweet Surrender**	Atlantic (out of print)
Billy Joel	**The Stranger**	Columbia JC 34987
Robin Kenyatta	**Encourage the People**	Wolf (TK) 1201
Rahsaan Roland Kirk	**Kirkatron**	Warner Bros. BS 2982
Rahsaan Roland Kirk	**The Art of Rahsaan Roland Kirk**	Atlantic SD 2-303
Kenny Loggins	**Celebrate Me Home**	Columbia PC 34655
Lena Horne	**Lena & Gabor**	Skye SK 15 B
Lena Horne	**Nature's Baby ***	Buddha BDS 5084
Lena Horne	**Lena & Michel**	RCA Victory BGL 1-1026
Ralph MacDonald	**Sound of a Drum**	Marlin 2202
Ralph MacDonald	**The Path**	TK Marlin 2210
Van McCoy	**Van McCoy & His Magnificent Movie Machine**	H&L HL 6902-698
Van McCoy	**Disco Baby**	Avco AV 69006-698
Van McCoy	**The Real McCoy**	H&L HL 69012-698
Van McCoy	**Rhythms of the World**	H&L HL 69014-698
Herbie Mann	**Push Push**	Embryo SD 532 197
Les McCann	**Another Beginning**	Atlantic SD 1666
Odyssey	**Odyssey**	RCA APL 1-2204A
Houston Pearson	**Sweet Buns & Barbeque**	Prestige PRST 10055
Curtis Mayfield	**Original Motion Picture sound track Superfly written and performed by Curtis Mayfield**	Curtom CRS 8014-ST
Grant Green	**The Final Comedown**	United Artists BST 84415
Esther Phillips	**And I Love Him**	Atlantic SD 8102
Esther Phillips	**"Burnin' Live at Freddie Jett's Pied Piper L.A."**	Atlantic SD 1565
Esther Phillips	**Alone Again Naturally**	Kudu 09
Esther Phillips	**Esther Phillips Performance**	Kudu 18
Esther Phillips	**From a Whisper to a Scream**	Kudu 05 (out of print)
Esther Phillips	**You've Come a Long Way Baby**	Mercury SRM 1-1187
David Ruffin	**Everything' Coming Up Love**	Motown M6-866 S1
David Ruffin	**Who Am I**	Motown M6-849 S1

William Salter	**It Is So Beautiful to Me**	Marlin 2205
Tom Scott	**New York Connection**	Ode A&M SP 77033
Tom Scott	**Blow It Out**	Ode/Epic PE 34966
Paul Simon	**Paul Simon's Greatest Hits**	Columbia JC 34032
Paul Simon	**Still Crazy After All These Years**	Columbia PC 33540
Stuff	**Stuff ***	Warner Bros. BS 2968
Stuff	**More Stuff ***	Warner Bros. BS 3061
Phoebe Snow	**Second Childhood**	Columbia BL 33952
Phoebe Snow	**Never Letting Go**	Columbia BL 34875
Phoebe Snow	**Newport in New York '72**	Cobblestone CST 9028
Phillipe Wynne	**Starting All Over**	Cotillion SD 9920
Stanley Turrentine	**Don't Mess with Mr. T**	CTI 6030
Stanley Turrentine	**Salt Song**	CTI 6010
Grover Washington, Jr.	**All the King's Horses**	Kudu KU 07
Grover Washington, Jr.	**Soul Box, Vols. I & II**	2-Kudu KU 12/13
Grover Washington, Jr.	**Inner City Blues**	Kudu KU 03
Maggie Bell	**Queen of the Night**	Atlantic SD 7293
New York Community Choir	**The New York Community Choir**	RCA APL 1-2293
Ron Carter	**Anything Goes**	Kudu KU 25-S1
Ron Carter	**Blues Farm**	CTI 6027
Eugene McDaniels	**Natural Juices**	ODE SP 77028
Melba Moore	**Peach Melba**	Buddha BDS 5629
Melba Moore	**Melba**	Buddha BDS 5677
Robert Palmer	**Sneakin' Sally Through the Alley**	Island ILPS 9294
King Curtis	**Everybody's Talkin'**	Atco SD 33-385
King Curtis	**The Best of King Curtis**	Atco SD 33-266
Dusty Springfield	**It Begins Again**	United Artists UALA 791-H
Cissy Houston	**Cissy Houston**	Private Stock PS 2031
Chuck Mangione	**Main Squeeze**	A&M CSO 4612
Bob James	**Heads**	Tappan Zee/Columbia JC 34896
Chuck Rainey	**Chuck Rainey Coalition ***	Cobblestone CST 9008
Nikki Giovanni	**The Way I Feel**	Niktom NK 4201
Harry Belafonte	**Calypso**	RCA LSP 1248
Letta Mbula	**There's Music in the Air**	A&M 4609
The Sylvers	**Horizons**	Capitol ST 11705
Foster Sylvers	**Don't Be Cruel**	Capitol ST 11716

[* = *Arranger*]

RALPH TOWNER

AS LEADER:	TITLE	LABEL & NO.
Ralph Towner	**Trios/Solos**	ECM 1025
Ralph Towner	**Diary**	ECM 1032
Ralph Towner with Gary Burton	**Matchbook**	ECM 1056
Ralph Towner with John Abercrombie	**Sargasso Sea**	ECM 1-1080
Ralph Towner	**Solstice—Sound and Shadows**	ECM 1060
Oregon	**Music of Another Present Era**	Vanguard VSD 79326
Oregon	**Distant Hills**	Vanguard VSD 79341
Oregon	**Winter Light**	Vanguard VSD 79350
Oregon	**In Concert**	Vanguard VSD 79358
Oregon	**Oregon/Elvin Jones Together**	Vanguard VSD 79337
Oregon	**Friends**	Vanguard VSD 79370

AS SIDEMAN WITH:		
Larry Coryell	**The Restful Mind**	Vanguard 79359
Winter Consort	**Road**	A&M 4279
Winter Consort	**Icarus**	Epic KE 31643
Weather Report	**I Sing the Body Electric**	Columbia PC 31352
Horacee Arnold	**Tribe**	Columbia KC 32150
Horacee Arnold	**Tale of the Exonerated Flea**	Columbia KC 32869
Jan Garbarek	**Dis**	ECM 1-1093

MIROSLAV VITOUS

AS LEADER:	TITLE	LABEL & NO.
Miroslav Vitous	**Infinite Search**	Embryo SD 524
Miroslav Vitous	**Mountain in the Clouds**	Atlantic 1622
Miroslav Vitous	**Purple**	CBS Sony (*Japan*)
Miroslav Vitous	**Magical Shepherd**	Warner Bros. B 2925
Miroslav Vitous	**Majesty Music**	Arista 4099
Miroslav Vitous	**Miroslav**	Arista/Freedom AF 1040

AS SIDEMAN WITH:		
Chick Corea	**Now He Sings, Now He Sobs**	Solid State SS 18039
Roy Ayers	**Stoned Soul Picnic**	Atlantic SD 1415
Herbie Mann	**Windows Opened**	Atlantic S 1507 (*out of print*)
Herbie Mann	**Memphis Underground**	Atlantic 1522
Wayne Shorter	**Super Nova**	Blue Note 84332
Wayne Shorter	**Motto Grosso Feio**	Blue Note LA 014-G
Joe Zawinul	**Zawinul**	Atlantic 1579

Larry Coryell	**Spaces**	Vanguard 6558
Steve Marcus	**Green Line**	Victor World Group (*Japan*)
Sadao Watanabe	**Round Trip**	CBS Sony (*Japan*)
Weather Report	**Weather Report**	Columbia PC 30661
Weather Report	**I Sing the Body Electric**	Columbia PC 31352
Weather Report	**Sweetnighter**	Columbia PC 32210
Weather Report	**Mysterious Traveler**	Columbia PC 32494
Flora Purim	**Stories to Tell**	Milestone M 9058

NARADA MICHAEL WALDEN

AS LEADER:	TITLE	LABEL & NO.
Narada Michael Walden	**Garden of Love Light**	Atlantic SD 18199
Narada Michael Walden	**I Cry, I Smile**	Atlantic SD 19141

AS SIDEMAN WITH:

Mahavishnu Orchestra	**Apocalypse**	Columbia KC 32957
Mahavishnu Orchestra	**Visions of the Emerald Beyond**	Columbia PC 33411
Mahavishnu Orchestra	**Inner Worlds**	Columbia PC 33908
Jeff Beck	**Wired**	Epic PE 33849
Alphonso Johnson	**Moonshadows**	Epic PE 34118
Jaco Pastorius	**Jaco Pastorius**	Columbia PE 33949
Tommy Bolin	**Teaser**	Nemperor NE 436
Weather Report	**Black Market**	Columbia PC 34089
Alan Holdsworth	**Velvet Darkness**	CTI 6068
Roy Buchanan	**Loading Zone**	Atlantic SD 19138
Don Cherry	**Here & Now**	Atlantic SD 18217
Nova	**Wings of Love**	Arista AB 4110
John McLaughlin	**Johnny McLaughlin/ Electric Guitarist**	Columbia JC 35326

GROVER WASHINGTON, JR.

AS LEADER:	TITLE	LABEL & NO.
Grover Washington, Jr.	**Inner City Blues**	Kudu KU 03
Grover Washington, Jr.	**All the King's Horses**	Kudu KU 07
Grover Washington, Jr.	**Soul Box, Vols. I & II**	2-Kudu KU 12/13
Grover Washington, Jr.	**Mr. Magic**	Kudu 20
Grover Washington, Jr.	**A Secret Place**	Kudu 32
Grover Washington, Jr.	**Feels So Good**	Kudu KU 24-sl
Grover Washington, Jr.	**Live at the Bijou**	Kudu KU X 3637-M2
Grover Washington, Jr./ Various Artists	**CTI Hollywood Bowl Jazz, I & II**	CTI 7076
Grover Washington, Jr./ Various Artists	**Best Collection of CTI/Kudu**	CTI/Kudu GSW 3011-2

AS SIDEMAN WITH:

Randy Weston	**Blue Moses**	CTI 6016
Johnny Hammond	**Breakout**	Kudu KU 01
Idris Muhammad	**The Power of Soul**	Kudu KU 17
Eric Gale	**Ginseng Woman**	Columbia PC 34421
Eric Gale	**Multiplication**	Columbia JC 34938
Bob James	**Three**	CTI 6063
Bob James	**Heads**	Tappan Zee/Columbia JC 34896
Ralph MacDonald	**Sound of a Drum**	Marlin 2202
Alphonso Johnson	**Yesterday's Dreams**	Epic PE 34364
Don Sebesky	**Giant Box**	CTI X 6031-32
Lonnie Smith	**Mama Wailer**	Kudu 02
Charles Earland	**Living Black**	Prestige PR 10009
Leon Spencer	**Louisiana Slim**	Prestige PR 10033
Boogaloo Joe Jones	**No Way!**	Prestige PR 10004
Boogaloo Joe Jones	**What It Is**	Prestige PR 10035
Melvin Sparks	**Spark Plug**	Presige PR 10016
Johnny "Hammond" Smith	**What's Going On**	Prestige PR 10015
Johnny Hammond	**Wild Horses, Rock Steady**	Kudu 04
Bob James	**One**	CTI 6043

LENNY WHITE

AS LEADER:	TITLE	LABEL & NO.
Lenny White	**Venusian Summer**	Nemperor NE 435
Lenny White	**Big City**	Nemperor NE 441
Lenny White	**The Adventures of Astral Pirates**	Elektra/Asylum 6E 121

AS SIDEMAN WITH:

Miles Davis	**Bitches' Brew**	Columbia PG 26
Freddie Hubbard	**Red Clay**	CTI 6001
Freddie Hubbard	**Polar A C**	CTI 6056
Joe Henderson	**Live at the Lighthouse**	Milestone (*out of print*)
Joe Henderson	**In Pursuit of Blackness**	Milestone 9034
Woody Shaw	**Blackstone Legacy**	Contemporary S 7627/28
Eddie Henderson	**Realization**	Capricorn CP 0118
Gato Barbieri	**Fenix**	Flying Dutchman 10144
Gato Barbieri	**Caliente**	A&M 4597
Gato Barbieri	**Ruby Ruby**	A&M 4655

Luis Gasca	**For Those Who Chant**	Blue Thumb (*out of print*)
Santana	**Caravanserai**	Columbia PC 31610
Jaco Pastorius	**Jaco Pastorius**	Epic PE 33949
Brian Auger's Oblivion Express	**Happiness Heartaches**	Warner Bros. B 2981
Brecker Brothers	**Don't Stop the Music**	Arista AL 4122
Miroslav Vitous	**Majesty Music**	Arista 4099
Al DiMeola	**Land of the Midnight Sun**	Columbia 34074
Al DiMeola	**Elegant Gypsy**	Columbia 34461
Stanley Clarke	**Children of Forever**	Polydor PD 5531
Stanley Clarke	**Journey to Love**	Nemperor NE 433
Return to Forever	**Hymn of the Seventh Galaxy**	Polydor PD 5536
Return to Forever	**Where Have I Known You Before**	Polydor PD 6509
Return to Forever	**No Mystery**	Polydor PD 6512
Return to Forever	**Romantic Warrior**	Columbia 34076
Azteca	**Azteca**	Columbia (*out of print*)
Azteca	**Pyramid to the Moon**	Columbia (*out of print*)
Jimmy Smith	**Sit On It**	Mercury 1127
Joe Henderson	**If You're Not Part of the Solution, You're Part of the Problem**	Milestone 9028
Harold Alexander	**Raw Root**	Atlantic 1657
Weldon Irvine	**Time Capsule**	Nodlew 1002
Curtis Fuller	**Crankin'**	Mainstream 333
Buddy Terry	**Pure Dynamite**	Mainstream 356
Woody Shaw	**Blackstone Legacy**	Contemporary S 7627/28
Lenny Williams	**Lenny Williams**	Warner Bros. 2797
Pharoah Sanders	**Love Will Find a Way**	Arista 4161

TONY WILLIAMS (Compiled by Faybeth Diamond)

AS LEADER:	TITLE	LABEL & NO.
Anthony Williams	**Lifetime**	Blue Note 84180
Anthony Williams	**Spring**	Blue Note 84126
Tony Williams Lifetime	**Emergency I**	Polydor 25-3001
Tony Williams	**Emergency II**	Polydor 24-4017
Tony Williams Lifetime	**Turn It Over**	Polydor 24-4021
Tony Williams Lifetime	**Ego**	Polydor 24-4065
Tony Williams Lifetime	**The Old Bum's Rush**	Polydor PD 5040
New Tony Williams Lifetime	**Believe It!**	Columbia PC 33836
New Tony Williams Lifetime	**Million Dollar Legs**	Columbia PC 34263
V.S.O.P.	**V.S.O.P.**	Columbia PC 34688
V.S.O.P.	**The Quintet/V.S.O.P. Live**	Columbia C 2-34976

AS SIDEMAN WITH:

Miles Davis	**Seven Steps to Heaven**	Columbia CS 8851
Miles Davis	**Miles Davis In Europe**	Columbia CS 8983
Jackie McLean	**One Step Beyond**	Blue Note 84137
Kenny Dorham	**Una Mas**	Blue Note 84127
Herbie Hancock	**My Point of View**	Blue Note 84126
Grachan Moncur III	**Evolution**	Blue Note 84153
Eric Dolphy	**Out To Lunch**	Blue Note 84163
Sam Rivers	**Fuschia Swing Song**	Blue Note BST 84184
Herbie Hancock	**Empyrean Isles**	Blue Note 84175
Grachan Moncur III	**Some Other Stuff**	Blue Note 84177
Andrew Hill	**Point of Departure**	Blue Note 84167
Herbie Hancock	**Maiden Voyage**	Blue Note 84195
Miles Davis	**Four and More**	Columbia PC 9253
Miles Davis	**My Funny Valentine**	Columbia PC 9106
Miles Davis	**ESP**	Columbia KCS 9150
Miles Davis	**Miles Smiles**	Columbia CS 9401
Miles Davis	**Sorcerer**	Columbia CS 9532
Miles Davis	**Nefertiti**	Columbia CS 9594
Miles Davis	**Miles in the Sky**	Columbia PC 9628
Miles Davis	**Filles de Kilimanjaro**	Columbia PC 9750
Miles Davis	**In a Silent Way**	Columbia CS 9875
Miles Davis	**Water Babies**	Columbia PC 34396
Sam Rivers	**Contours**	Blue Note BST 84206
Charles Lloyd	**Nirvana**	Columbia CS 9609
Stan Getz	**Captain Marvel**	Columbia KC 32706
Gil Evans	**There Comes a Time**	RCA APL 1-1057
Chet Baker	**You Can't Go Home Again**	A&M SP 726
Sonny Rollins	**Easy Living**	Milestone M 9080
McCoy Tyner	**Super Trios**	Milestone M 55003
Michael Mantler	**Movies**	Watt 7
John McLaughlin	**Johnny McLaughlin/ Electric Guitarist**	Columbia JC 35326

FOREIGN RELEASES:

(1977) V.S.O.P.	**The Quintet**	CBS Sony (*Japan*)
(1977) Herbie Hancock	**The Herbie Hancock Trio**	CBS Sony (*Japan*)
(1977) Ron Carter	**The Ron Carter Trio**	Victor Records (*Japan*)
(1977) The Great Jazz Trio	**At the Village Vanguard, Vol. I**	East Wind EW 8053
(1977) The Great Jazz Trio	**At the Village Vanguard, Vol. II**	East Wind EW 8046
(1976) Sadao Watanabe	**I'm Old Fashioned**	East Wind EW 8037

(1977) The Great Jazz Trio	**Kindess, Joy, Love & Happiness**	East Wind EW 8056
(1977) Terumasa Hino	**May Dance**	Flying Disk VI J6002
(1977) Takehiro Honda	**Another Departure**	Flying Disk VI J6004

JOE ZAWINUL

AS LEADER:	TITLE	LABEL & NO.
Joe Zawinul	**Piano Giants**	Prestige 24052
Joe Zawinul	**Zawinul**	Atlantic 1579
Weather Report	**Black Market**	Columbia PC 34099
Weather Report	**Heavy Weather**	Columbia PC 34418
Weather Report	**I Sing the Body Electric**	Columbia PC 31352
Wayne Shorter, Weather Report, and others	**The Progressives**	Columbia CG 31574
Weather Report	**Mysterious Traveler**	Columbia PCQ 32494
Weather Report	**Sweetnighter**	Columbia PC 32210
Weather Report	**Tale Spinnin'**	Columbia PC 33417
Weather Report	**Weather Report**	Columbia PC 30661
Joe Zawinul	**Rise and Fall of the Third Stream**	Vortex 2002
Joe Zawinul	**Money in the Pocket**	Atlantic 3004

AS SIDEMAN WITH:		
Miles Davis	**In a Silent Way**	Columbia CS 9875
Miles Davis	**Bitches' Brew**	Columbia PG 26
Miles Davis	**Live-Evil**	Columbia G 30954
Miles Davis	**Big Fun**	Columbia PG 32866
Cannonball Adderley	**Planet Earth**	Riverside RLP 59404
Cannonball Adderley	**Jazz Workshop Revisited**	Riverside RM 444
Cannonball Adderley/ Nancy Wilson	**Nancy Wilson/ Cannonball Adderley**	Capitol T 1657
Cannonball Adderley	**Fiddler on the Roof**	Capitol T 2216
Cannonball Adderley	**Mercy Mercy**	Capitol T 2663
Cannonball Adderley	**74 Miles Away**	Capitol T 2828
Cannonball Adderley	**The Best of Cannonball Adderley**	Capitol SKAO 2939
Cannonball Adderley	**Price You Gotta Pay**	Capitol SWBB 636
Cannonball Adderley	**Walk Tall/Quiet Nights**	Capitol STBB 697
Cannonball Adderley	**Country Preacher**	Capitol CAO 464
Friedrich Gulda	**Gulda, His Euro-Jazz Orchestra**	Priser STR 3141 (*import*)
Dinah Washington	**What a Difference**	Mercury 60158
Dinah Washington	**Unforgettable**	Mercury 60232
Ben Webster	**Soul Mates**	Riverside 476

julie coryell

Julie Coryell was born and raised in New York City, where she attended the Professional Children's School, the Neighborhood Playhouse, the Herbert Berghof Studio, and The Actor's Studio. After graduating from high school, she attended The New School as a non-matriculating student and began a professional career in theater, appearing on Broadway. She soon moved to Europe where she collaborated with several musicians as a singer/songwriter. After a year and a half, she moved to Los Angeles, to pursue a career as a songwriter and actress. Her plans were changed, however, when she met and married jazz guitarist Larry Coryell.

The two moved to New York, where she collaborated musically with Larry for ten years. She assumed the role of manager for her husband, and co-produced three very successful benefit concerts in Manhattan. She also kept busy raising her two sons, Murali and Julian.

Since those days, Julie has focused on writing, producing, and directing plays. She has also worked as a professional astrologer/therapist, counseling thousands of clients. Murali and Julian, now both grown, are talented guitarist/singer/songwriters who have released several CDs and performed around the world. Julie can be contacted at 14 Broadview Road, #5, Woodstock, NY 12498 or at jewelcore@aol.com

laura
friedman

Laura Friedman was raised in Larchmont, New York. She studied painting and print-making at The Philadelphia College of Art (The University of the Arts) where she received her B.F.A. While in college, Laura began to listen to jazz, her first album purchase being Miles Davis's *In a Silent Way*. Out of her growing interest in jazz, she developed close and lasting friendships with John Lee, Stanley Clarke, and Gerry Brown, who were attending some of her classes.

Laura spent her junior year in London at St. Martin's School of Art. After graduation, she moved to Holland, continued her studies in art, and eventually sold one of her works, "La Contrabasse" to the Gemeenteelijke Commissie Voor Beeldende Kunsten (The Hague Museum of Art). At this time, Laura began to couple her talents as a photographer with her love of jazz. Her photographs have been used on the covers of several albums and in promotional materials for various jazz musicians.

Two decades after the original publication of *Jazz-Rock Fusion*, Laura is still producing prize-winning work in painting and photography. In 1997, the Pen and Brush Gallery in New York presented her with the Elizabeth Morse Genius Award for her work in watercolors. Other paintings by her have been exhibited at The National Arts Club in New York, and in competitions judged by Lisa Dennison, Curator of The Solomon R. Guggenheim Museum, and Ivan Karp, owner of New York's O.K. Harris Gallery. Her photographs have appeared in the book *Jazz: The Great American Art* (Grolier, 1995), and in many magazines. In 1984 Laura produced one of her finest achievements yet: her son, Alex, now a high school student in Manhattan.

bibliography

Apel, Willi. *Harvard Dictionary of Music*. 2d ed. Cambridge, Mass.: The Belknap Press of Harvard University Press, 1972.

Cole, Bill. *Miles Davis: A Musical Biography*. New York: William Morrow & Company, Inc., 1974.

Feather, Leonard. *From Satchmo to Miles*. New York: Stein and Day Publishers, 1972.

————, and Gilter, Ira. *The Encyclopedia of Jazz in the Seventies*. New York: Horizon Press, 1976.

Goldberg, Joe. *Jazz Masters of the 50's*. New York: The Macmillan Company, 1965.

Hammond, John, with Townsend, Irving. *John Hammond on Record*. New York: The Ridge Press, Summit Books, 1977.

Hentoff, Nat. *Jazz Is*. New York: The Ridge Press, Random House, 1976.

————. *The Jazz Life*. New York: The Dial Press, 1961.

Logan, Nick, and Wolffinden, Bob. *The Illustrated Encyclopedia of Rock*. New York: Harmony Books, a division of Crown Publishers, Inc., 1977.

Walton, Oritz. *Music: Black, White & Blue*. New York: William Morrow & Company, Inc., 1972.